WOMAN TO WOMAN

Anne Roper, was born in the USA and moved to Dublin in 1974. She holds a BA., from Memphis State University and a MA., from University College Dublin. She has been active in the women's movement since 1979, working with both the Dublin Rape Crisis and Well Woman Centres. She is a member of the Women's Studies Association and is a regular reviewer of feminist writing for *The Irish Times*.

First published in 1986 by
Attic Press,
44 East Essex Street,
Dublin 2.

Roper, Anne
    Woman to woman; a health care handbook and directory for women.
    1. Women — Health hygiene
    I. Title
    613'.04244   RA778
    ISBN 0-946211-24-8
    ISBN 0-946211-23-XPbk

Cover design: Keggie Carew
Typesetting: Phototype-Set Ltd., Dublin
Printing: Mount Salus Press Ltd., Dublin
Illustrations: Fenella Humphreys, Catherine McConville

The publishers gratefully acknowledge the following for permission to reproduce illustrations which first appeared in their publications; Faber and Faber, *Everywoman: A Gynaecological Guide for Life*, Derek Llewellyn-Jones; The Boston Women's Health Book Collective, *Our Bodies Ourselves*.

ACKNOWLEDGEMENTS

The idea for this book was gestating for some time. To all those who prodded me to do it, my sincerest appreciation. Individually, I would like to thank Brian Fallon, of *The Irish Times*, who encouraged my fledgling talents and published my first attempts at writing. I am also grateful to Lizzie Mellon and Aisling O'Reilly, whose friendship over the years fueled both my confidence and energy. Equally, I am indebted to Mary Paul Keane, Attic Press, and Roisin Conroy, Irish Feminist Information, for granting me this opportunity to appear in print.

During the writing, I depended a great deal on the help of Denis Cahalane. I want to thank him for his patience, objectivity and good humour. At the same time, I am deeply obliged to the staff and clients of the Dublin Well Woman Centre, but most especially to Emer Flynn, Felice Cohen, Terri Canavan, Margaret Whelan — and Joan MacNeaney, who gave me 'a room of my own'. The bottle of champagne goes to Bonnie Maher for naming *Woman to Woman*, and my gratitude to Marguerite Woods for refreshing my (sometimes) flagging feminism with youthful insights.

From an editorial point of view, I must extend appreciation to Siobhan Parkinson, to all the nurses and doctors who lent their expertise, particularly Dr Moira Woods, Anne Conway and Pat Rees. And finally, to Margaret Martin, whose encouragement and loyalty made the whole process worthwhile.
                                                                                    Anne Roper
                                                                                    March 1986

DEDICATION
*For **Estelle, Margaret** and **Erin** with love.*

ILLUSTRATIONS

CONTENTS

1. INTRODUCTION

This is a health guide written for women living in Ireland. Within its pages I include what I hope are health issues of common concern: sexuality, mental health, pregnancy, contraception and menopause. I have chosen the subjects which I feel are central to our mental, emotional and physical well-being. This choice was made bearing in mind my conversations with women over the last six years. During this time, I have worked in the field of self-help with the Dublin Well Woman Centre and the Dublin Rape Crisis Centre.

Neither self-help nor women's health issues are new. Women have always relied on one another for natural remedies, advice on fertility control and information on health worries. The public health services in Ireland have been sorely lacking. This book makes an attempt to extend the network of information to as many women as possible. Ultimately self-help is a political issue — a feminist issue. I believe that serious health problems (including mental illness and bad nutrition) have hindered women's full participation in society, that ill health has kept us 'in our place' as second-class citizens. Things have not changed radically with the new technologies. As recently as the 1950s women still died earlier than men in Ireland because of dietary deficiencies. And in some cases, this type of physical oppression exists today, only we excuse it in the name of drug therapy and medical technology. This book hopes to encourage women to have the confidence to take back control over our own bodies, our own health.

When two women meet, the conversation nearly always touches on personal concerns. When health is discussed, we often ask questions, compare facts and respond to each other's anxieties. We use the question and answer format routinely. For this reason, I have organised the book following that model. Other health guides are written like textbooks, with technical language or unfamiliar subject headings.

Say, for example, we have an itch. We look in the current edition of *Everybody* under the word 'itch' and find no such listing. We try 'irritation', but again, no luck. If we think to look up 'infection', we are confronted with fifteen pages of Latin names all with itchy symptoms. So we make an appointment with the doctor fearing serious disease. One consultation and £10 later, we find the diagnosis is a sort of sophisticated nappy rash. The cause: nylon underpants and tight trousers. 'Hygiene' was the code word employed by our health guide.

It is important that women living in Ireland have a book which speaks to us in our own language. Equally, a health guide published in Ireland must have at its foundation an awareness of the differences in this culture — a realisation that discussing issues of health and sexuality are acutely embarrassing to many women and a source of real anxiety.

Many of us lack information on sexual health. Our worry and fear may be rooted in this lack of knowledge, on not knowing exactly how our body works. Women often preface their questions with 'I feel so stupid . . .' or 'I know I should know this . . .'. I want to reassure them with this book that the same questions are echoed daily by countless other women, of all ages, who share the same concerns. Unless we extend our experience of health and sexuality, the meaning of specific symptoms or feelings will remain shrouded in mystery. By offering my version of health information to the reader, I hope to broaden the network of self-help health making it accessible to women living in Ireland.

The second section of the book is a directory. There are umpteen books in Irish shops which deal with women's health care. They are published in New York, London or Sydney. We read them, find just the help we need, and discover we must travel to an Oxford counselling centre, or a Boston advisory service for the solution to our worry. Where do we turn in Ireland? There are Irish directories on the market published in conjunction with government bodies or religious groups. They often ignore pregnancy counselling, lesbianism, sexuality, sexually transmitted disease and sex education — subjects central to women's health. Since sexuality and fertility control are at the foundation of women's health care, any attempt to disregard them only reinforces old values and stereotypes — perpetuating taboos that endanger our welfare.

For most topics discussed in this handbook there is a corresponding group, organisation or individual to whom the reader can turn for further help or information. I realise the book is not comprehensive. The limits of time and space have dictated the number of issues included. My hope is to point women in the direction of aid, and to alleviate some common anxieties which might ordinarily stop us from seeking support. As long as we know there is help, and that we have strength to help ourselves, our worries become manageable and in the end surmountable. This is the first step in gaining control over our lives.

2. THE POLITICS OF HEALTH CARE

I had been suffering from a nagging pain in my right side for nearly a year when my GP finally referred me to a gynaecologist. After waiting to see the specialist for nearly two hours (I had made my appointment a month in advance), I was shown to a cubicle by a nurse and told to take off my underpants. I waited a further ten minutes before the doctor arrived. By this time I was extremely nervous. The doctor did not introduce himself or ask me any questions (he did read the referral letter I brought). He told me to lie down and open my legs. The force of his hand entering my vagina for the internal examination nearly sent me out the window and into the carpark. When I opened my eyes in relief after the examination ended, the doctor was gone – I never saw him again.

I asked the nurse what they thought was wrong with me. She smiled and said, "Don't worry, Dr. X will be getting in touch with your GP."

The experience detailed above is not unusual. It is typical of the treatment many of us receive through the public health care system. The doctor/patient relationship is one of imbalance: the doctor as "professional" acquires training and information while the client needs her/his skill. The client feels vulnerable, frightened in case she is seriously ill; the doctor assumes the role of healer — our salvation from pain.

It hasn't always been like this in Ireland. Prior to the 18th century, women nursed and healed other women. Handywomen and midwives lived in the community and shared their knowledge. Medicines were found in the plants and herbs of the countryside. But this gradually began to change. As healers gained the respect of the community, their position won prestige. Increasingly, men saw this as one avenue to power. In 1692, the control of women's health was officially assumed by men. This was the year the Royal College of Surgeons began licensing midwives, with only four certificates being granted to women. This was the same period in history when women who offered "cures" were suspected of witchcraft.

By 1753, the medical profession refused to extend certification outside their male domain. In 1785, the first chair of midwifery was established in their teaching college, signalling the monopolisation of women's health in Ireland by the professional male.

Nowaday, doctors are viewed as experts in many areas affecting the health of women: while the Dublin Rape Crisis Centre suffered for years from inadequate funding and little recognition of their pioneering work, in 1985, a male master of the Rotunda hospital was able to set up a sexual assault treatment unit with government support and finance. The help of physicians is enlisted in the sexual problems of the disabled, as if sexuality was a medical condition. Home births are discouraged because they ignore the need for expensive and impersonal technology. Television and radio journalists interview anonymous doctors on subjects as varied as sex, sexuality, and mental health, often ignoring the input of countless lay people working in the area.

And medical technology invades our everyday life: drugs take the place of counselling, hysterectomies take the place of sterilisation, caesarean sections are performed instead of breech deliveries, symphysiotomies (a procedure which separated a woman's pelvic bone on a central line roughly where the pubic hair grows and made birthing easier but left the woman permanently disfigured and prone to arthritis) were offered (even as late as the 1960s) instead of free and comprehensive contraceptive choice.

If we are to find the best possible health-care treatment, and assert our needs, it is essential we recognise the power doctors have had in our lives. If we examine their training, we may even be surprised that so few have escaped the prejudices of sex and social class. Textbooks indoctrinate young students into seeing women as weak, hysterical and/or liars:

> *1. Many allegations of rape are false, possibly as many as eleven out of twelve. Such allegations may be from spite, jealousy, in order to*

precipitate marriage etc.
And in the same breath:
> 2. *Doctors must endeavour to show whether or not sexual intercourse has taken place, and note any injuries. He cannot say whether rape has occurred . . .*
>
> *The **man's** story may accord better with the facts than the **girl's**.*
> (emphasis mine)
>> (extract from *Lecture notes on Forensic Medicine*, D.J. Gee London: Blackwell Publications 1979.)

To date in Ireland, the majority of practising doctors and particularly consultants, (including gynaecologists) are men, the faculties of medicine are dominated by men and the government departments which cater for our health needs are legislated for by men. For the most part, these 'experts' come from the middle classes.

> *I work in a private clinic where one doctor suggested we use Depo-Provera [an injectable hormone] on a travelling woman who only came to us once or twice a year. When I pointed out that a six-month supply of the pill would give the woman more control over her fertility, (and an opportunity to discontinue use at any time), I was told 'These women can't be expected to remember to take a pill.'*

Age and stereotyping colour their treatment of us:

> *I had intercourse for the first time in twenty years. A week or so afterwards, I noticed a green, smelly discharge coming from my vagina. I asked my doctor to examine me and test for infections. I don't think he believed I could possibly have had sexual contact, so he never even looked. When I queried this, he said I had nothing to worry about.*
>
> *The next day, I went to a women's clinic where they found I had*

> *trichomoniasis. I can't believe I had*
> *the courage to get a second opinion. (a*
> *70-year-old woman)*
>
> *After a recent gynaecological*
> *operation my doctor warned me*
> *against 'having sex'. I got terribly*
> *confused. Did this mean all sexual*
> *contact or simply intercourse? I didn't*
> *feel comfortable discussing my*
> *sexuality with this person, so I*
> *avoided all sexual relations for six*
> *weeks.*

And if this subtle power play of 'professional judgement' were not enough to intimidate us on a personal level, the medical world as a whole presumes to impose its code of ethics on the entire population. Sterilisation facilities are granted to men, but are only available on a limited basis for women. Hospital boards decide whether the woman or the foetus has a health-care priority. Post-coital contraception (taken after sexual intercourse) may be prescribed as 'ovulation inhibitors' in pill form in rape cases, but post-coital intra-uterine devices are denied lest the ethical committee be affronted. Hysterectomies and mastectomies are performed in preference to more minor surgery because they are easier for the surgeon. The Medical Council refuses to allow a list of sympathetic practitioners of women's health to be circularised or published. GPs turn away women looking for contraception because they are unmarried. Home births are discouraged because money for back-up teams is not made available.

Health insurance companies refuse to reimburse us for contraception, sterilisation and mental health care (unless we see a psychiatrist). Drug companies and drug testing institutions experiment with our health under a camouflage of preventative concern. There is no independent body to which we can turn to voice our complaints about private medicine.

If we are to fight against the medical hierarchy and take control of our own health, we must educate ourselves in self-help and work together for change.

This is not as difficult as it seems. Women's groups all over the country from Donegal to Wexford have gathered together to talk, to share knowledge, to lobby for improvements. The Rape Crisis service networks began with meetings of committed feminists. The Association for the Improvement of the Maternity Services and the Home Birth Centre were organised by women who were unwilling to accept the *status quo*. Other groups began with one or two women defining a common interest and inviting others to their home to discuss the issues. Many of us start with ourselves, by reading and sharing information. We study self-help and talk to our neighbours about our fears of institutionalised health care.

If you know of no such group in your area, try contacting a local women's club or community information centre. Better yet, put up a notice in the local shop or community centre expressing your desire to form such a group. Contact existing groups for advice and support. Invite speakers to talk to your meetings. Begin to build a network of women helping women. Armed with new confidence and information, you will be able to take control over your health and over your life.

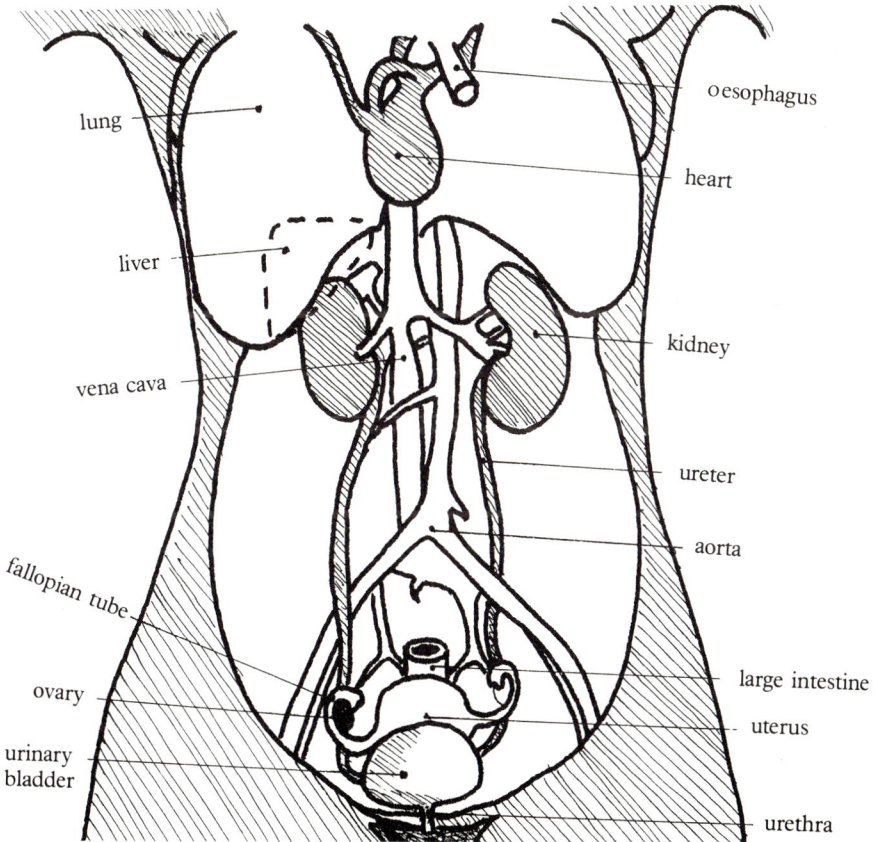

1. Internal Organs

3. A WOMAN'S BODY

Our body is a unique and special creation. There are so many complementary parts which mark each woman's individuality as a woman. When we mature, we notice rounded breasts and curved hips. We grow hair under our arms, on our legs, breasts, and between our legs. Each body is different and even the least suspected places, like the hidden area near our vagina, has its own distinct colour and form. Isn't it amazing, then, what we do to make our bodies conform to some standard view of womankind? We shave, pluck, dye and tan; we wear shoes that pinch and clothes which chafe. We take tablets or smoke cigarettes to control our weight, and starve ourselves into thinness. We even force vomiting or take laxatives in an effort to become that elusive woman we see on the television or in magazines. And if we fail to meet such exacting standards, we turn to drink or drugs to relieve the anxiety that we are less than perfect.

We have all allowed these niggling worries to affect us at some time or another. Equally, we share concerns about our health and emotional welfare. As women living in Ireland, we may share an additional burden of religious and social conditioning. We may feel our body should not be explored and appreciated for its individuality. Sexuality may have been a forbidden topic. Indeed, many of us haven't a clue how other ordinary women look and our conditioned reluctance to discuss sexual worries may keep us ignorant of just how the body works. Much of our apprehension about health is based on a lack of information. The first step in confronting our fear is to learn to appreciate our own body.

To know our body, we need to have a good look at it and feel its texture. There is no one definitive womanly shape. We are the product of inheritance, diet, exercise, and general health care. Our figure is only the outline of a being with immense mental, emotional, and physical possibilities.

It's important to familiarise yourself with every aspect of your form. The easiest way to do this is to place yourself naked in front of a full-length mirror. Beforehand, make sure the room is warm, the curtains are drawn and you have enough privacy. Notice the bone structure and skin quality.

2. A woman examining her body

Feel how the flesh on the thighs differs from that on the breast. What about the way you hold yourself? Do you feel proud enough of your body to stand tall? Notice the hair and smell of the skin. Appreciate your rounded tummy as part of being a woman. So too, the extra layer of flesh on the hips and thighs.

BODY IMAGE

Why then do we sometimes baulk at what we see reflected in the mirror? Perhaps the varicose veins and stretch marks don't correspond to the image of the woman we see nightly on television. We can 'pinch more than an inch' and rarely smell like the body mist men buy flowers for.

Rather than accepting our bodies as normal for us (when fit), we are constantly bombarded by advertising which labels fat or disability as failure, and thinness the ticket to success. Why? Because to sell useless items like diet soft-drinks and 'feminine hygiene' deodorants, manufacturing companies hawk their wares by equating their products with success, sex appeal and beauty. Since few of us look like the models they employ to sell their goods, we have to keep buying in an attempt to reach the ideal. In the meantime, the companies collect huge profits.

Department stores do their bit as well. Try buying attractive clothing in any size over fourteen. If your feet are larger than a seven, your choices are limited. Access to buildings and services is restricted to the able-bodied, clothing is designed for fashion and not for comfort or durability. We are encouraged to diet and exercise, not for health reasons, but to look well in a leotard. 'Getting our figures back' seems to be the priority following childbirth, rather than real health concerns. With so many subliminal and overt messages, it is no wonder we are sometimes made uncomfortable by what we see in the mirror.

Many of us like to dress up every now and again, as a means of expressing facets of our personality, but it's essential that we start viewing ourselves with health and fitness in mind rather than with some contrived notion of beauty sold to us by the commercial world. Large or small, fat or thin simply illustrate a system of measurement: no single attribute can define us as a woman.

PUBERTY

Just how did our body come to look like this? As girls we were often fat or thin, but any womanly curves seemed minor. The rapid changes which signal *puberty* (the early teenage years when we turn from girls into women) can be pretty startling. Sometimes there are aches and pains in the vulval region (see p. 18) which result from growth and development. Unless we know this, twinges or tenderness may be alarming. We may feel shy about budding nipples, or the appearance of hair beneath our knickers and under our arms. Sometimes it's difficult to adjust quickly enough to the metamorphosis we experience during adolescence. Our development may differ from other girls our age: a best friend's periods may have started while ours have not. We may begin to notice new secretions coming from our vagina (see p. 31, 33). Odours from under the arms can alter as hair grows and sweat glands mature. Most new smells are normal; they are a sign of hormone activity which marks our development as young women. Each of us goes through the process of puberty at a different rate. The feelings we experience during this time may frighten or please us. It sometimes helps to know that these reactions are shared by other women.

THE BODY PHYSICAL

The hormonal messages which change us from girls to women come from a gland at the base of the skull called the pituitary (PIT-YOO-E-TARY).

Glands are cell systems which secrete substances like sweat to various parts of the body. The pituitary sends communications to the sexual organs. Inside the body, below the surface of the tummy, are two *ovaries* where eggs are stored. The ovaries are situated on either side of the *uterus* (womb), and are connected to the uterus by the *fallopian tubes*. In a healthy woman, eggs are released on a regular basis from the ovaries into the uterus as part of the *menstrual cycle*. When the egg is discharged from the uterus at the end of the cycle, *menstruation* (a period) occurs. Blood and mucous are expelled at the same time and come out of the body through the *vagina*. The vagina is connected to the uterus by the *cervical canal*. The *cervix* (neck of the womb) has an opening called the *os*. All these internal sexual organs are held in position by the *pelvic floor muscle*.

Externally, the pituitary is relaying messages about breasts, hair and other sexual development. The surge of hormones which come into play at this time may alter our skin condition, producing spots and pimples, or may keep menstrual activity erratic.

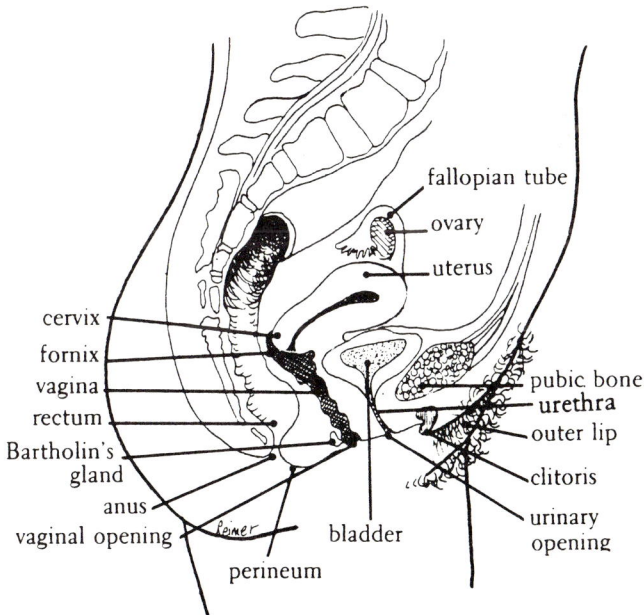

3. Female pelvic organs (side view)

THE BREAST

Many of us notice that our breasts vary in size from right to left. This is completely normal. The breast is made up of fat, connective tissue and the *mammary gland* which produces milk. The *ducts* carry milk from the glands to the *nipple* during breast feeding. The ability to produce milk is called *lactation*. The nipple and the *areola* make the dark centre point of the breast. During pregnancy, the areola may grow darker in colour. Most women's nipples tend to stick out when cold or aroused, but inturning *(inverted)* nipples are also normal.

Believe it or not, all women have about the same amount of glandular tissue in the breast and therefore size does not affect ability to breast feed or our sexual stimulation. What does make the breast differ is the amount of fat and this is based largely on diet and inheritance. The menstrual cycle, because it prepares the body for pregnancy and therefore lactation, can affect the size of and sensations in the breast tissue.

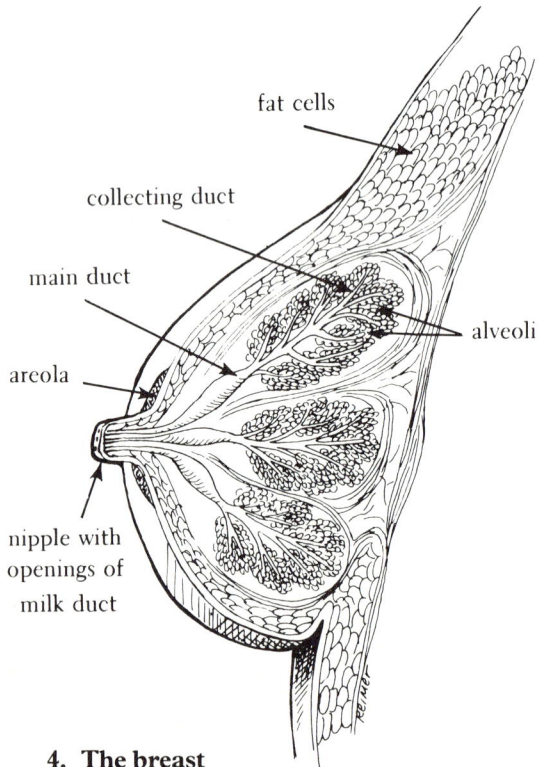

fat cells

collecting duct

main duct

alveoli

areola

nipple with openings of milk duct

4. The breast

THE VULVA

As we have seen, most of the hormonal messages transmitted to the sexual organs are in some way connected to menstruation. This regular cyclical discharge of blood and mucous signals *fertility* (the ability to become pregnant). The first sign of menstrual bleeding can come with little warning. It may occur when we are as young as ten or as old as sixteen. Often diet and heredity affect the onset of menstruation. The bleeding originates in the uterus and travels down the vagina to appear from the *vulval* area between the legs. This area is protected on the outside by pubic hair. If you open your legs, you will notice two large, outer lips, very like normal skin, called the *labia major*. By pulling them back, you will see that the underside is smoother and deeper in colour. You will also recognise a more fleshy pair of lips, smaller in size, called the *labia minor*. Both labial parts protect a pointy piece of flesh called the *clitoris*. This is covered by a light hood of tissue. The clitoris is a highly sensitive organ and, when massaged gently, can produce very pleasant sensations (see p. 57).

The size and form of the vulval lips may differ from woman to woman. With old age or pregnancy, they can change their appearance as a result of hormonal fluctuation.

If you investigate the area below the clitoris, but within the lips, you will see two openings. The first leads to the *urethra* and is the place *urine* (pee) comes out. Below that again is the entrance to the *vagina*. This is larger and moist to the touch. If you are lying down with your legs open or have one leg raised with a foot on a chair, you can easily put a finger deep into the vagina. It's quite elastic and can expand to take the head of a baby during childbirth. As you explore the vagina, you will notice the tight feeling of the surrounding muscles. In most cases, towards the roof of the vagina, you will feel the *cervix* which connects the vagina to the uterus. The cervix feels a bit like the tip of the nose. Since the uterus can vary in its position and size, don't worry if finding the cervix proves difficult: a friend or health-care worker will be able to assist you.

Outside the vaginal opening and below that again, is a smooth portion of flesh known as the *perineum*. Below that, and between the *buttocks* (bottom) is the *anus* (back passage) where we pass *bowel movements* (shit).

As we mature, our sexual parts share many functions. They are involved in both sexuality and fertility. The lovely sensation we get from tickling the clitoris can lead to an *orgasm*, a very strong feeling of physical pleasure. The vagina can encompass a *penis* (willie, micky) for *intercourse* (sex between woman and man) and possible pregnancy (see illustration).

In a healthy woman, the sexual parts, like the rest of the body, stay basically the same for the rest of her life. The exceptions occur in pregnancy, when hormones may lead to skin darkening and stretching, or when hips and breasts increase and varicose veins develop. After the menopause, the skin may lose some of its elasticity, becoming more porcelain and delicate. The texture may even alter so gradually that we hardly notice. Learning about these processes can be rewarding and reassuring. The knowledge we gain about our changing body will give us a feeling of control.

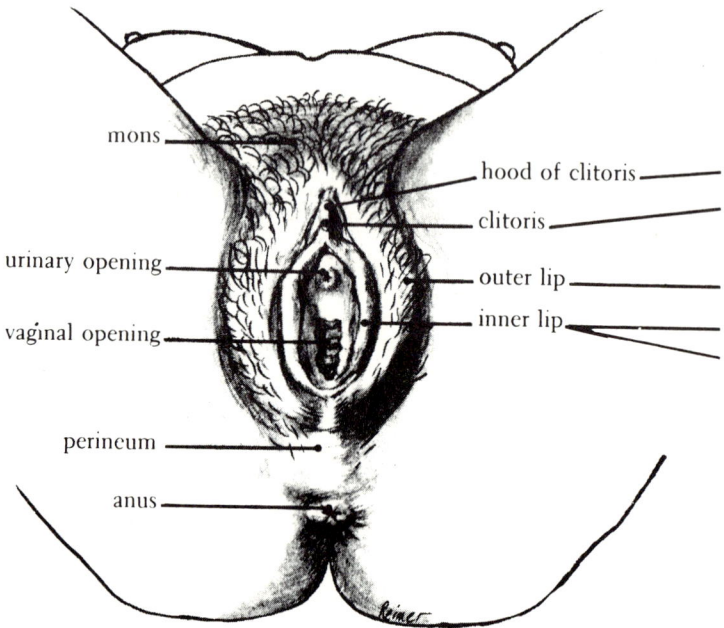

5. The vulva

4. MENSTRUATION

Menstruation, the regular pattern of cyclical bleeding coming from the uterus and vagina, is triggered by two hormones, *oestrogen* and *progesterone*. Hormones act like computer messages to the brain which give information for growth and development. The two hormones which come into play during the menstrual cycle direct the uterus to prepare for possible *fertilisation* of egg and sperm. *Endometrium*, composed of blood and mucous, coats the walls of the uterus to provide a cushion of nourishment for a potential *foetus* (a developing pregnancy). If no egg meets sperm, or if no pregnancy results from their fertilisation, the endometrium is expelled as *menstrual fluid* to begin the process over again. The pattern of ovulation and menstruation is called the *menstrual cycle*.

WHAT EXACTLY HAPPENS DURING THE MENSTRUAL CYCLE?

The menstrual cycle begins with the first day of bleeding. We call this *day one*. The bleeding may seem heavy or light, may coincide with uterine contractions and cramps, and may last anywhere from two or three days to over a week. How heavily we bleed varies from woman to woman. Recent studies suggest we all produce roughly the same amount of menstrual fluid, but it may be spread over a longer or shorter interval.

Once the bleeding stops, the old uterine lining has been expelled and the hormones instruct the ovaries to prepare for the release of a new egg *(ovum)*. In an 'average' 28 day cycle (see p. 183) this happens about fourteen days after a period begins and roughly fourteen days before the next period is due. The half-way point between periods is known as *mid-cycle*.

Each of us is born with a set number of eggs in both our ovaries. The oestrogen hormone activated in the first few weeks of our cycle gives the directions for egg release. This is called *ovulation* and some women can actually feel it happening. After ovulation, the egg travels down the fallopian tubes and into the uterus. It is swept along its way by hair-like helpers called the *cilia*.

If intercourse (see p. 58, 133) takes place and sperm is ejaculated (if the man comes) into the vagina, it is possible for fertilisation to occur. If a healthy environment has been prepared by the hormones, the fertilised ovum will travel into the uterus and attach itself to the lining. This is called *implantation.* If no fertilisation or implantation takes place, both oestrogen and progesterone signal the endometrium to begin shedding itself once more for menstruation. This takes about fourteen days from the time the egg has been released.

I DON'T HAVE A 28 DAY CYCLE. IS THIS NORMAL, OR AM I IRREGULAR?

Not every woman has a twenty-eight day cycle. Many of us have bleeding patterns which vary widely from this accepted 'norm'. The use of the expression 'average' is actually misleading. It does not mean that only this type of cycle is normal. Many of us have twenty-one day cycles, while others go five or six weeks between periods. No matter how many days elapse between periods, once regularity is present, there is no need to worry.

It is important to bear in mind, however, that since ovulation generally occurs fourteen days *before menstruation,* the most fertile time of the cycle is *not* always the middle of the cycle. In a twenty-one day cycle, fertility reaches its peak about seven days after a period begins, while in a 42 day cycle, the egg is released about twenty-eight days after menstruation commences.

ONCE I BEGIN MENSTRUATING, IS THERE ANYTHING SPECIAL I SHOULD KNOW ABOUT HYGIENE? WHAT ABOUT TAMPONS?

Once you begin menstruating, it may help to discuss general concerns with friends or family. In the beginning, it's probably a good idea to use a *sanitary towel* until you get to know your body more intimately. These can be bought in supermarkets and chemist shops and generally have a sticky back which holds them in place on your knickers. Some feel bulkier than others, so get advice or shop around. Manufacturers have yet to design one to fit all body types.

Some women decide to use *tampons* (cotton wool, finger-like inserts placed in the vagina for absorbing menstrual fluid). The easiest way to put a tampon in place is to squat down with a foot raised on a stool. Since you may feel nervous the first time, it's important to practise slow, relaxed breathing (see p. 45) to relax the vaginal and tummy muscles. Make sure you have privacy as this will help both concentration and relaxation. You

Menstrual Chart

Days of Cycle	Month					
	1	2	3	4	5	6
1						
2						
3						
4						
5						
6						
7						
8						
9						
10						
11						
12						
13						
14						
15						
16						
17						
18						
19						
20						
21						
22						
23						
24						
25						
26						
27						
28						
29						
30						
31						
32						
33						
34						
Total						

Day 1 on this chart is the first day of bleeding, continue down the column until you get your next period, then start the 2nd column etc.

For your annual menstrual chart see *The Irish Women's Guidebook and Diary.*

may need to lubricate the tip of the tampon with saliva or KY jelly (available in chemists and family planning clinics). Never use vaseline, as it promotes irritation.

As you slide the tampon into the vaginal opening, bear in mind that most vaginas slope backwards, at an upward angle, so you must aim the tampon in this direction. Gently ease the tampon in with the end of your finger or with the applicator. Since the vagina can expand to encompass a baby's head during labour, you needn't worry about the tampon fitting. As there are no actual sensations deep in the vagina, you may only feel the light pressure of the tampon going in. Keep the string hanging down outside the vagina for easy removal. This is done by gentle pulling.

Depending on menstrual flow, the tampon may need to be changed at hourly or longer intervals of time. If for some reason the tampon seems lost, don't panic. There really isn't anywhere for it to go — it can't sneak into the uterus. If it becomes difficult to remove alone, a friend or health-care worker can take it out. Seek help as soon as possible to minimise any risk of infection.

Tampons are marketed more vigorously these days and are aimed at the 'active' woman. Increasingly, women are questioning the use of tampons because there may be a link between them and vaginal irritations. Tampons come in different sizes and some are actually deodorised with chemicals (as if our natural odours somehow need freshening) which may cause allergic reactions. Sometimes the applicators pinch and the tampons become difficult to insert. It's important to bear these reservations in mind before choosing the tampon. Having said that, tampons do make some activities, like swimming, more accessible, and some women find them more comfortable than towels.

TOXIC SHOCK SYNDROME (TSS)

A word of caution: never wear tampons twenty-four hours a day. The vagina must be allowed to breathe. One suggestion is to wear tampons by day and towels by night.

There is an infection called toxic shock syndrome (TSS), which seems to be somehow related to the use of super-absorbent tampons by teenage girls. It is rare, but it is caused by the staphylococcus virus. Symptoms include a body rash, diarrhoea, fever, flu-like feelings and vomiting. Staph infections are not usually dangerous and often manifest themselves in boils or abcesses. The reason young women may be more susceptible to attack is that their vaginal mucosa (the tissue lining the vagina) is more sensitive to irritation. In rare cases TSS can be fatal, so if you suspect you have the disease, contact a doctor immediately.

It's perfectly all right to wash in either bath or shower during a period. A bath will allow the water to rinse out any bacteria which may have built up in the vagina. Don't believe stories which warn against washing your hair during a period. Even if you have a bath every other day, be sure to wash the vulva twice each day with a soft cloth or sponge of your own — and no soap. If you have no bath, fill a large basin with water and try to sit in it at least three times per week. Remove the tampon before washing, and don't worry about bleeding into the bath; this just doesn't happen.

Keep your wash cloth for personal use and sterilise it weekly in boiling water. Always clean your bottom from front to back — never let any *faeces* (shit) near the vagina as this can lead to infection. Cleaning the vagina with sprays of water, or by injecting liquid into the vagina *(douche)*, isn't necessary and can alter the natural balance of the tissue lining *(mucosa)* and cause irritation.

Avoid perfumes and soaps in the water you use, learn to accept the womanly smells as natural — they make up part of our sexuality and are attractive if you follow a simple cleaning routine.

WHAT ABOUT NATURAL SPONGES?

Some women use natural sponges as an alternative to tampons. A sponge is inserted in the same way as the tampon (see p. 26) but since it is not thrown away, it's essential to use special care when cleaning it. This is done simply by washing the sponge free of menstrual fluid and then boiling it in a saucepan of water — this will help prevent infection. Since you have to sterilise the sponges every time you use them, it's a good idea to keep a few clean ones in stock.

Another hint: tie a piece of string to one of the porous openings so the sponge can easily be removed from the vagina.

WHAT IS AN IRREGULAR CYCLE?

This is a menstrual cycle which shows no obvious pattern. It is a common feature of puberty and/or menopause. If menstruation fails to establish a routine outside puberty and menopause, there is not necessarily any need to worry unless the pattern is suddenly disrupted and *continues* to fluctuate wildly.

For example, if you have a period three days late one month, a week early the next, and seven days late the next — on a rhythmical basis — you are most likely healthy. If on the other hand, you begin to notice monthly gaps or intermittent/mid-cycle bleeding it's wise to have the situation investigated by a doctor.

MY PERIOD IS OVERDUE. IT'S NEVER BEEN LATE BEFORE. WHY NOW?

Any disruption in the normal pattern of menstruation can be alarming. Once pregnancy is ruled out as the cause, take a look at your current living habits: a change in diet, strenuous exercise, the contraceptive pill, menopause, stress, travel and illness can all suspend ovulation and menstruation temporarily. And then there are times when it is difficult to identify a direct cause.

If you continue for more than ten weeks without a period, and this is unusual for you, or if you suspect you are pregnant, a health-care worker will be able to help you.

CAN I 'BRING ON' A PERIOD?

First, we must define what is meant by 'bringing on'. To some of us this is an expression used in place of the word abortion. To others, it refers to the 'morning-after' pill or coil (see p. 167). Some women simply want vitamin supplements to rectify any natural deficiency which may have caused menstrual loss.

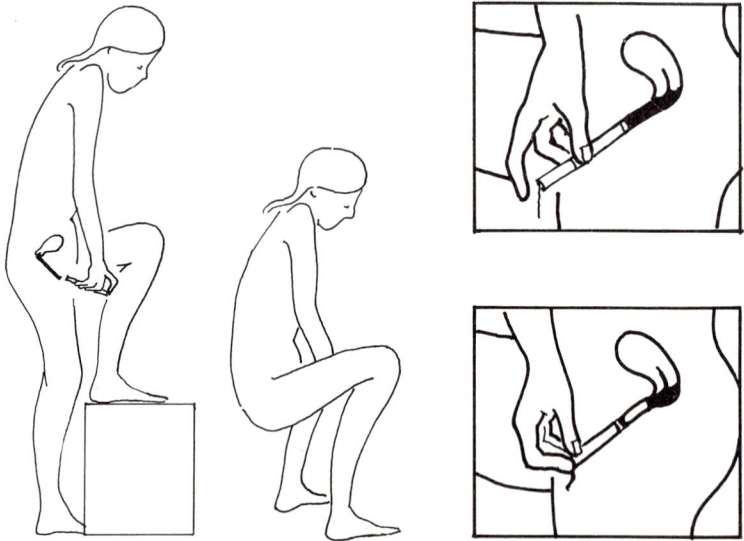

7. How to insert a tampon using two different positions

If you are already overdue a period, there is no legal way to 'bring on' a period in Ireland if pregnancy is the cause. Abortion is illegal in the twenty-six counties (see p. 186). 'Morning-after' contraception can prevent pregnancy if taken soon enough after one instance of unprotected intercourse, but it does not always cause a bleed (see p. 167). If you are worried about pregnancy, there is help available through pregnancy counselling agencies listed in the directory. *Never try to make yourself bleed.* It won't work and can damage your health permanently. Sharp instruments or large doses of laxatives and alcohol or tablets will simply make you feel dreadful and can cause real harm.

IS THERE ANY WAY I CAN DELAY MY PERIOD?

Some women use hormone tablets to alter the scheduling of their periods. The contraceptive pill can be used in this way, but a health-care worker will need to advise you. Be sure to give her/him plenty of notice, as you may need to be taking the hormones for a few weeks before this method can be used effectively.

IS THERE ANY WAY TO LESSEN THE FLOW OF A PERIOD?

Some women feel their periods are unnaturally heavy. Short term, there is lit le you can do except use sanitary products like the tampon or the contraceptive diaphragm (see p. 172).

If you want help over the long term, you will need to talk to a doctor or health-care worker. They will investigate the causes and discuss your options accordingly. Some women take the contraceptive pill to lighten their periods, others require a D&C (see p. 73). The remedy will very much depend on your needs.

MY DOCTOR USES WORDS LIKE AMENORRHOEA AND DYSMENORRHOEA. WHAT DO THEY MEAN?

If you fail to bleed at all, doctors will use the word amenorrhoea (A-MEN-O-REE-A). If periods are painful, the medical word is dysmenorrhoea (DIS-MEN-O-REE-A). If they are unusually heavy, the word is menorrhagia (MEN-O-RAJ-EE-A). Doctors use these words because they are taught them. Even if you never use the technical language, it's essential you know what health-care workers mean — this will make your relationship more equal. If doctors use words you don't understand, ask them to write it down and explain.

WHAT IS PRE-MENSTRUAL TENSION (SYNDROME)?

Pre-menstrual tension or pre-menstrual syndrome (PMS or PMT) is a set of symptoms which occur in our bodies after ovulation. They are the result of hormonal changes. The expression PMS has gained some notoriety in the last decade as a catch phrase for any emotional upset experienced by women (as if emotions were somehow abnormal). Since many of us notice varying symptoms 'pre-menstrually', it would seem more logical to view PMS as normal.

But some of us do have more severe symptoms. These include headaches, tiredness, moodiness, bloatedness, cramping, pain and lack of co-ordination. All the phrase 'pre-menstrual' means is that we experience certain physical and emotional characteristics prior to a period which are absent during the rest of our menstrual cycle.

Many of us feel frustrated by PMS because of our apparent lack of control over its manifestations. There are both natural and hormonal remedies which can alleviate some of the more uncomfortable aspects of PMS. In many cases, diet, proper nutrition, relaxation and vitamin supplements can help enormously.

To understand how PMS may affect you, keep a record of symptoms over a number of months. If you discover a pattern where PMS is to blame, you will be able to take preventative measures according the scheduling of symptoms. Family planning clinics, some health-food outlets, self-help groups and health care workers (including doctors) have information and assistance at hand.

HOW CAN I HELP MYSELF THROUGH DIETARY CHANGES AND SELF-HELP TECHNIQUES?

Since vitamin and mineral deficiencies can trigger PMS, eating a well-balanced diet is extremely important — and it doesn't have to be expensive. Good natural food sources include whole grain cereals, brown rice, marmite, liver, spinach, lentils, beans and fresh seafood. For more specific symptoms, particular foods are itemised below.

Sore breasts: Supplementing the diet with vitamin B6 has proved beneficial to many women. Taken in 50mg-tablet doses from the time of ovulation it seems to work well. Many women take the tablets every day as it is easier to remember it this way. Food sources of B6 include all those listed above. Because sore breasts are sometimes the result of fluid retention, cutting out salt and caffeine will help.

The oral contraceptive pill may deplete our body of natural B6, so supplements will certainly improve some side-effects.

Bloatedness: Many of us feel bloated in the breasts and tummy. By cutting down on our salt and caffeine intake, this may be alleviated. This means no tea, coffee or fizzy drinks, since they often contain caffeine, which contributes to the body's retaining water. Vitamin B6 will also help, but if you decide to try a diuretic (medication which helps you to pee), natural remedies are safest: try celery, cucumber and parsley. These can be made into juices.

Irritability: Many of us feel weepy or more easily angered in the two weeks before a period. This can be the result of stress and fatigue as well as the depletion of some nutrients. Both the B-complex vitamins and vitamin C have benefited many women. Anaemia (a deficiency of quantity or quality of red corpuscles in the blood) may also be a cause. Symptoms include fatigue, fluid retention and headaches. If you suspect anaemia is contributing to your PMS symptoms, have a blood count done to find out if you are in fact anaemic. Iron supplements will build up the blood.

In the meantime, natural sources of B and C vitamins (especially fruits, liver and eggs), will improve your condition.

WHAT ABOUT PACKAGED REMEDIES?

There are many products on the shelves of our local supermarket, health-food shop, family planning clinic and chemist which claim to help with PMS. Some are simply diuretics which can damage the kidneys if used long term. Check the labels and try to use more natural remedies. These would include oil of evening primrose and vitamin E or B6.

Other hints include getting plenty of sleep and exercise and avoiding tobacco, alcohol and other drugs which may interfere with the normal processing of nutrients.

I HAVE TRIED THE NATURAL REMEDIES WITHOUT SUCCESS

For some of us, the only help for severe symptoms of PMS may be hormone therapy. This can be in tablet or vaginal pessary (a pellet which is inserted) form. Some of us find that taking the oral contraceptive pill alleviates PMS (although for some women it may make matters worse) while others of us take progestogen therapy. There are health drawbacks to the use of hormone therapy (see p. 153) and these should be considered carefully before opting for them. Much of this treatment is expensive and not all of it is reimbursable on the medical card or through voluntary health insurance.

MY PMS APPEARS IN THE FORM OF PAINFUL CRAMPING

Cramps are one of the most uncomfortable side-effects of PMS. These may be treatable through relaxation and exercise. There are tablets which act to relax the uterine muscles (brand name: Synflex). These are not addictive and only one or two taken when cramps begin will halt later discomfort.

Some of us find that regular use of the oral contraceptive pill prevents or minimises cramping, but this seems a lot of medication for a few days of pain.

It may help to try some relaxation techniques. If we are able to relax the uterine muscles, then cramping will be considerably reduced. A hot-water bottle or a hot bath can help too.

RELAXATION SUGGESTIONS
1. Lie flat on your back on the floor and practise relaxing all the muscles in the body (see p. 45). It may help if you close your eyes and have both warmth and privacy. Next, slowly pull your knees to your chest and hug them, breathing slowly to a count of five. Now release the legs and return them to their original position. Repeat this exercise five times or as often as necessary. It acts to loosen the spine and massage the tummy muscles.
2. Sit Indian-style, cross-legged on the floor. Breathing slowly and evenly, filling the lungs and diaphragm (tummy) with air, force your knees away from the body and towards the floor. Use the inner thigh muscles and not your hands to do this. Hold to a count of five, breathing evenly, then relax. Repeat this twenty times in a rhythmical pattern.
3. Masturbation or other sexual stimulation combined with orgasm can relax the uterine muscles so effectively that cramping disappears. There is no reason to abstain from sexual contact during menstruation on health grounds, but you are not necessarily protected from pregnancy.

I NEVER HAD PMS BEFORE, BUT SINCE MY LAST BABY, I HAVE REALLY NOTICED THE CHANGE EACH MONTH
Any hormonal change our body experiences, like taking the Pill, going through puberty, or having a baby, can produce symptoms of PMS. This is quite normal and may be treated as outlined above. On the other hand, some women are lucky enough to find that having a baby has the opposite effect and cures their PMS or menstrual cramping.

I HAVE HEARD THAT THE CONTRACEPTIVE PILL CAN HELP PMS. WHY?
Some of us find relief from symptoms of pre-menstrual syndrome on the Pill because the particular hormonal imbalance we experience might be rectified by the introduction of synthetic (manufactured) hormones. In a way, the ingredients in the Pill return our body to the way it felt before we noticed PMS. Equally, for some of us, the oral contraceptive can spark off symptoms of the syndrome and discontinuing the Pill may eliminate these.

IS IT TRUE THAT GYNAECOLOGICAL OPERATIONS, LIKE STERILISATION, CAN LEAD TO PMS?

The only type of operation that might activate a hormonal imbalance is the removal of the ovaries. This can be part of a complete *hysterectomy*, which also means removing the womb. Sterilisation is a simple blocking or tying of the fallopian tubes so that the egg never reaches the sperm for fertilisation. Since the reproductive/menstrual cycle still occurs normally, PMS symptoms will not suddenly take place in our body after sterilisation. This is true of most other *gynaecological* (having to do with our sexual parts) procedures.

I FEEL VIOLENT SEVERAL DAYS BEFORE I HAVE MY PERIOD. IS THIS NORMAL?

In severe cases of PMS, we can actually feel totally out of control of our emotions. This can be very frightening. It is important to seek outside help from friends, relations or health-care workers if we feel the symptoms of a hormone imbalance will harm us or others. PMS can be treated successfully, and there is no need to be embarrassed about seeking help.

I NOTICE THAT I BRUISE EASILY BEFORE A PERIOD. AM I ANAEMIC?

Probably not, as long as you are eating a well-balanced diet. *Anaemia* is a result of iron deficiency; you may feel tired and sluggish. Lack of co-ordination is one symptom of PMS. Bruising could be the result of the clumsiness many of us experience pre-menstrually. Knocking things over is common. Sometimes this manifests itself in a lack of concentration, or by a feeling of unbalance. Self-help techniques and vitamin supplements can offer great benefit. (See also Chapter 5, especially the section on diet).

5. POSITIVE HEALTH CARE

SELF-HELP HEALTH

To keep fit and healthy, it's wise to practise simple self-help techniques. These are easy to learn, teach us a lot about our body, and can prevent real disease by early detection. There are many tests we can do routinely for ourselves. Monthly breast examinations and the monitoring of cervical changes or secretions are basic skills we can all learn.

BREAST EXAMINATION

The breast examination is very easy and fundamental to positive health care. To give yourself this check, begin by lying down on a flat surface. Some women like to examine themselves in the bath. The best time to test the breasts is about five to seven days after a period begins.

Once you are lying down, join the fingers of one hand together. Now raise the opposite arm, so that the breast tissue is completely exposed, and use your joined fingers to feel for lumps in a circular motion, starting at the outer rim of the breast. You will be looking for any lumpiness or alteration of the skin tissue. Tenderness is common and normal. Work your hand gradually around the circle until you come to the nipple. Next, use the same motion to check for lumps or swelling in the armpit and nearby areas. Then do the other breast. Once standing, look at the breasts straight on. Note any change in appearance, any puckering, discoloration or discharge. It's normal for one breast to look slightly larger than the other, or for one nipple to be bigger. If you notice any marked change from one month to the next, it's wise to seek a second opinion.

Some women prefer their partner to examine them, but it's extremely important for you to know your own body. Don't wait until s/he decides it's time — you need to check your breasts regularly. Breast disease is easily treated if discovered in time.

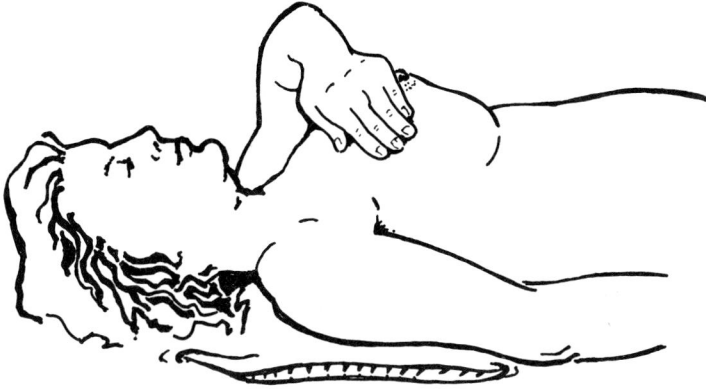

8. Breast self examination

VAGINAL SECRETIONS

When is a vaginal secretion a discharge? How do we know the healthy signs from the unhealthy? As we pass from puberty to womanhood, new secretions may prove baffling. Sometimes the secretion is clear, other times it is white or yellow. The texture can change from wet and slippery to sticky or tacky. This is quite normal. Hormonal activity alters these secretions as it prepares the sexual organs for ovulation and menstruation.

Diet, sexual activity and cleanliness play an important role in the smell, colour and quality of vaginal secretions. If we eat too much starch or sugar, or if we wash with a harsh soap, irritation may turn a discharge into infection. By monitoring these changes, and gaining familiarity with the pattern of secretions, we can alter our behaviour to clear the irritation ourselves.

SELF-EXAMINATION

Many of us are finding that the easiest way to check for vaginal and cervical changes is by self-examination. To do this, we need to invest in a speculum (average cost £2 for the plastic, disposable variety, available through medical suppliers), a mirror and a torch or lamp.

The speculum is a piece of medical machinery which is quite imposing until you learn how to use it. It works like this: hold your thumb and finger as if you were holding a glove-puppet, opening and closing. Now put your hand into your mouth with the jaw relaxed. Open and close your mouth with the puppet motion. The speculum creates this same activity in the vagina. By using a speculum, you will prop open the vaginal walls and be able to get a good look at the cervix.

To examine yourself with a speculum, you will need to sit up with your legs spread wide (having the knees bent helps). You can moisten the speculum with some saliva or KY jelly. Insert the device like you would a tampon, breathing slowly and relaxedly so there is no muscle tightness or pressure. The speculum should be closed while you are doing this. Once in place, you will be able to open the speculum and see inside. Be sure the handle is turned upwards. Aim the light from the torch into the mirror and

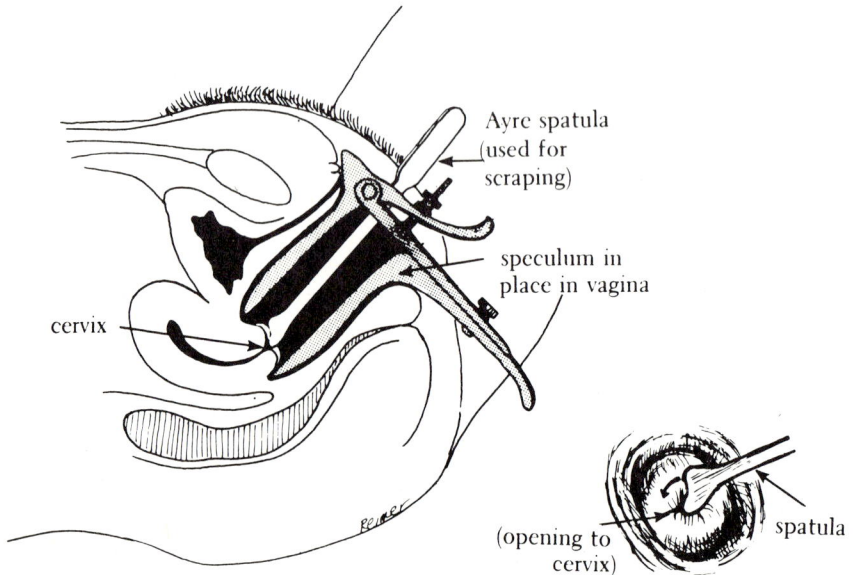

Ayre spatula (used for scraping)

speculum in place in vagina

cervix

(opening to cervix)

spatula

9. Pelvic self examination using a speculum

adjust it for a better view. The reflection will illuminate the vagina. Sometimes the speculum needs to be removed and replaced before it feels comfortable; occasionally it pops out. Be sure to leave it in the *open* position for removal, to avoid pinching your insides.

You will soon become familiar with the look and texture of the cervix and vaginal muscles at every stage of your cycle. When you need to visit a doctor for routine smear tests, you will know what to expect.

DIET

The American nutritionist, Adele Davis maintains that 'we are what we eat'. To many of us, however, diet is a concept about losing weight rather than about eating well for our health. We have been influenced by advertising which markets dieting as a means to an end; and the end advertisers have in mind is their image of what a woman should be.

If we extend the concept of diet a little further, we soon see that nutrition is also a political issue. Food items sold to us on television, radio and in the supermarkets are riddled with chemical concoctions and additives which do little to promote the healthy development of bones, muscle and human tissue. Such nutritional deficiencies may lead to a low resistance to infection or disease, hormone imbalance, stress and general feelings of ill-health.

Diet is crucially important because it affects the way we feel physically, emotionally and mentally. When we start eating the foods which are good for us — foods which contain vitamins, minerals and fibre — we will be setting the foundation for positive health care.

Adjusting our diet needn't be expensive or painful. Above all, it doesn't have to be boring or difficult. Foods like dried beans and fruits, root vegetables, nuts, lentils, cheese, eggs and wholemeal breads are actually less expensive in the long run than packaged or processed foods. And they don't spoil so easily, despite the fact that they don't usually contain chemical preservatives.

There are a number of things we can do with our diet to avoid many of the health worries discussed in this book. A balanced diet, combined with exercise and conscious relaxation will contribute to our total welfare.

We all need specific vitamins, minerals, proteins, fats and carbohydrates if we hope to work and play effectively. All these nutrients combine to fuel our energy. If we neglect any of them we will begin to feel the effects over time.

On the next page is a chart of approximate requirements for an adult woman. Pregnant, nursing (breast-feeding) or convalescing women may

NUTRIENT	FOOD SOURCE	WHY WE NEED THEM
PROTEIN	Fish, meat, eggs, dried beans, cheese and nuts. Ideally we should consume three portions daily. One portion might mean two tablespoons of nuts or four tablespoons of beans. Tinned vegetables should be avoided as many of their nutritional properties are lost in the preserving process. They also contain salt and sugar which have no real nutritional value.	Protein helps to build skin tissue, muscle, hair, and encourages hormone balance.
VITAMINS	Vitamins are found in fruit, vegetables, dairy products, beans and meat. They are also derived from whole-grain cereals, wholemeal breads, cod liver oil, nuts, fish, poultry, molasses, potatoes, yeast and wheat-germ. Ideally, we need three portions each day.	Vitamins help to protect us from the effects of stress, fatigue, infection and work to promote the easy assimilation of other minerals. Some vitamins also act as antitoxidants.
CARBOHYDRATES	These are found in wholemeal breads and pasta, some vegetables, beans and fruits. Four items from this list can be consumed every day. One portion is equivalent to one slice of bread or a cup of pasta. Try to avoid packaged cereals and eat raw flakes or muesli instead. Wholemeal foods also provide needed fibre.	The consumption of carbohydrates ensures that vital proteins are utilised for energy and body building. They also provide glucose for the brain.
DAIRY PRODUCTS	Found in milk and milk by-products like	These help build bones,

	cottage cheese, yoghurt, skimmed milk and hard cheeses. Three portions daily.	teeth, muscles and nerves. They can also help us to ward off infection.
IRON	Black-strap molasses, turkey meat, dried fruit, lean meat, liver, eggs, yeast and wheat-germ.	Helps to build blood and fight anaemia.
FIBRE (not actually a nutrient)	Whole-grain breads, pasta and cereal or bran.	Fibre or roughage is essential for healthy digestion. It can alleviate wind, constipation, piles and diarrhoea.
WATER	Fruit juices, herbal teas and mineral or tap water.	Water will help cleanse the body of toxic wastes.
DAIRY PRODUCTS	Found in milk and milk by-products like cottage cheese, yoghurt, skimmed milk and hard cheeses. Three portions daily.	These help build bones, teeth, muscles and nerves. They can also help us to ward off infection.
IRON	Black-strap molasses, turkey meat, dried fruit, lean meat, liver, eggs, yeast and wheat-germ.	Helps to build blood and fight anaemia.
FIBRE (not actually a nutrient)	Whole-grain breads, pasta and cereal or bran.	Fibre or roughage is essential for healthy digestion. It can alleviate wind, constipation, piles and diarrhoea.
WATER	Fruit juices, herbal teas and mineral or tap water.	Water will help cleanse the body of toxic wastes.

need to slightly alter quantities. And remember, when we are young, our bodies don't always see the immediate effects of bad nutrition. But as we grow older, bad eating habits will begin to affect our health. It's a good idea to re-educate your taste buds when you are young — but it's never too late to start.

A WORD ABOUT ALLERGIES

The situation is common enough. You eat a bar of chocolate, feel a buzz of energy for an hour or so, and suddenly experience a terrific headache or sluggish feeling. If this is the case, you may be suffering from an allergic reaction. Other food culprits which trigger these symptoms include eggs, milk, seafood, nuts, seeds, tomatoes and oranges. Many of us notice swelling glands or irritability when we eat white bread or wheat products. Or we break out in a rash of hives, or notice a gradual depression.

Monosodium glutamate (a preservative especially common in Chinese take-aways — marked MSG on packets) and sodium nitrate have been isolated as contributing to migraine headaches. Also implicated are chocolate, cheese, sour cream, red wine, avocados, ripe banana and cured meats.

The fumes from cleaning agents, petrol and smog constitute modern pollutants which can exacerbate many of these ill feelings.

Have a good look at what you are eating which may trigger these side-effects, then start removing them from your diet.

DIETING

We are most of us familiar with the 'fad' diet. For years, such gimmicky eating regimes have been used to market women's magazines — as if losing weight was our one and only concern in life. Many of the foods which go to make up the current 'diet of the month' offer incomplete nutrition and may damage our health. Nor do they help to educate us in a healthy approach to eating. Fad diets are based on the 'get thin quick' theory, and there simply isn't any way to do this safely.

WHY DIET?

First we need to examine why we want to diet: is it to please ourselves, to improve our health, or is it an attempt to be somebody else, to emulate a fantasy image of woman? Do we imagine we will be happier/sexier/wittier/more successful/more desirable and better able to cope with life if we only had a slimmer figure? Or do we truly want to shed excess weight because we feel unfit and unwell?

The factors which motivate us to diet may need a rethink. Most women will never look like the models used to promote commercial products, and why should we? If we are aware of how advertising preys on our worries and anxieties to market goods, we can make a conscious choice about accepting or rejecting the stereotypical image of woman.

OBESITY

Of course there are cases when obesity (being severely overweight) poses a health threat. Carrying excess weight on our frame daily can lead to physical strain. Some side-effects are heart disease, high blood pressure (hypertension), diabetes and arthritis. New research suggests, however, that the yo-yo effect of stopping and starting new diets may contribute to many of these illnesses.

At the same time, we must investigate *what* we eat, since many processed foods have little nutritional value. Neglecting essential nutrients may pose greater health threats.

I WANT TO LOSE WEIGHT BECAUSE I FEEL UNHEALTHY. WHAT IS THE BEST WAY TO GO ABOUT IT?
1. Look at what you eat and when. Note what situations trigger compulsive eating. Some women find that by keeping a diary they are able to pinpoint such factors. Others find this makes them concentrate too much on the idea of food.
2. Make sure the food you eat contains proper nutrients. If you neglect nutrition, you may actually feel hungrier. Some cravings occur when we deny our body vital sustenance.
3. Try to eat only when you are hungry and only weigh yourself once a week. Do not weigh yourself at meal times since this will only reinforce the old associations of food and weight.
4. Make the changes in your diet gradually. If you lose more than two pounds a week, it will be more difficult for your body to adjust. Remember that you are trying to train yourself out of bad habits — not into worse ones.
5. Talk to other women about what stresses and situations lead you to eat when you are not hungry. Discuss the whole area of body image and what effect it has on your desire to diet.
6. Get plenty of exercise. This will not only tone up loose muscles and

make you fit, but will help you to deal with some of the stresses which make you eat when not hungry. Many women find it actually curbs their appetite.

7. Involve yourself in some activity which takes your mind off the notion of dieting as a way of life.

TEETH AND GUMS

Many of the nutrients we consume are taken from food utilising the chewing process. For this activity to be efficient, we need to look after our teeth and gums. Poor nutrition may lead to gum and dental disease and lower our resistance to decay.

WHAT CAUSES TOOTH DECAY?
Dental decay is the result of bacteria. All of us have bacteria living in our mouths, but if the bacteria meets with sugar, it forms a substance called *plaque*. This clings to the teeth and takes on acid-like properties and corrodes our teeth.

HOW DO I PREVENT TOOTH DECAY?
1. Brush your teeth and use dental floss (available from a chemist) daily. This will act to remove the plaque on the surface and between the teeth.
2. Eat foods which contain calcium, vitamins A and D, phosphorus and fluoride (tap water contains the latter).
3. If you must eat sweets, confine their consumption to mealtimes, or drink water or eat other foods to counteract the build-up of sugar with bacteria.
4. Keep away from sweets that stick to the teeth.
5. Eat foods which help to rub off excess plaque. This list would include carrot sticks (raw), celery, apples and whole grains.

EATING PROBLEMS

The summer I turned fifteen, my parents separated. I had always thought myself fat and decided now was the time to diet. I started out sensibly enough by eating 1200 calories a day. Then I knocked it down to 600, and finally I was eating only three hard boiled eggs a day. I became very ill, lost three stone and still felt fat.

I wanted to 'keep my figure', but also felt this tremendous compulsion to eat. I found that by making myself vomit and by using laxatives, I could combine the two. The feeling of guilt was incredible until one day my sister confronted me. With her help I began looking at my behaviour.

Anorexia nervosa (AN-O-REX-EE-A) and *Bulimia nervosa* (BOO-LEE-MEE-A) are two types of eating disorders which predominantly affect women. Anorexia manifests itself in self-starvation, while bulimia involves eating normally or binging followed by forced vomiting or a laxative purge to control weight.

For many of us, food is associated with ideas of comfort and relief from stress. We may eat because we are lonely, bored, sad or under pressure. With anorexia and bulimia, however, food becomes the focus of these pressures. In many ways, those of us suffering from eating problems seem to be fulfilling society's view of what women should be: child-like, thin, disciplined, vulnerable and docile.

Long term, both illnesses are serious. The teeth, gums and throat are affected by repeated vomiting, while starvation can cause other health problems and even death.

There is help available, and self-help groups seem to be very successful. These are formed by women who share the problem and are able to talk openly about their fears and frustrations. The directory will guide you. There are also some organisations which offer family support.

MY DOCTOR SAYS I HAVE IRRITABLE BOWEL. SOMETIMES I HAVE DIARRHOEA, SOMETIMES CONSTIPATION AND TUMMY CRAMPS. WHAT TYPE OF SELF-HELP CAN I TRY?
Adding fibre to the diet seems to be one of the greatest helps in fighting bowel problems. The fibre helps to absorb waste material and scoot it along until it is emptied in a bowel movement. But fibre has to be eaten regularly. If we are not getting enough in our normal diet, we can add a spoonful of bran to our breakfast cereal.

OTHER TIPS

1. Drink a warm glass of water before breakfast every morning.
2. Try not to eat too quickly, as gulping food can mean taking in a lot of air. Using a straw may help when we consume liquids.
3. Avoid fizzy drinks as the air promotes flatulence (wind).
4. If beans make you windy, rinse them in cold water after an initial boil, or add carraway or fennel seeds to the cooking water.
5. Eat plenty of fruits and vegetables.
6. Try these exercises before breakfast: If you have any major tummy or bowel problems (like hernia) get the advice of a health care worker before commencing.

Exercise one
Before you get up in the morning, lie on your back and pull both your knees to your chest in the bed. Hug them while you breathe naturally in and out. Not only will this massage the internal organs but it will also loosen out the spine. Some women find this soothes uterine cramping too.

Exercise two
Think this exercise through before you do it and avoid it if you have any serious bowel disorder or have had recent lower abdominal surgery.

The purpose of this exercise is to massage the bowel gently. If done three times and always on an empty stomach (before breakfast is a good time), bowel movements will be easier to pass.

Standing up, bend your waist so you are leaning over like you are going to touch your toes. Now bend your knees slightly. For the next step, hold your nose with the two fingers of your right hand so that no air can be inhaled. Now exhale all the air in your lungs and diaphragm (tummy). Once you have done this, gently suck in the tummy using only your diaphragm muscles. Keep your mouth closed and do not inhale. Gradually release the muscles and take a breath. Repeat twice more in your own time.

IS THERE ANY WAY TO HELP THE DISCOMFORT OF PILES WITHOUT SURGERY?
Piles are prolapsed (saggy) bowel tissue, which, when irritated by bacteria or a hard stool, become itchy, sore and may even bleed.

Short term, to relieve the itch, you can try soaking in a warm bath with a cup of salt thrown in. If you have no bath, sit your bottom in a large basin of warm salty water or repeatedly sponge the rectal area with the same solution. Press the pile back into the anus gently with a finger. Inside, it will be less prone to irritation. Make sure you thoroughly dry the area afterwards.

Long term, you must have a look at what is causing the piles. Diet is the first thing to consider: are you getting enough fibre? Pregnancy can cause piles because of the pressure put on the bowel by the enlarged uterus. Finally, hygiene is essential. The following tips may help.

1. Always thoroughly cleanse the rectal area (area around the back passage) after a bowel movement. If you are currently irritated by piles, wash the area after each movement and pat thoroughly dry.
2. Avoid irritating your bottom with soap or a rough flannel. Some women find J-cloths ideal because they are soft, easy to boil clean, and can be disposed of if they are badly soiled. Their disposability also makes them a good choice for taking on holidays: far better than allowing a damp cloth harbouring infection to be put away in a suitcase.
3. Avoid tight trousers or tights which keep air from circulating around the area.
4. Try not to use hard paper when you wipe your bottom. Medicated baby wipes are useful when you are away from home.
5. Keep the area dry by dabbing it periodically during the day — especially in hot weather.
6. Avoid talcum powder as the perfume may irritate.
7. Try not to use ointments and creams unless specifically prescribed. These may cause allergic reactions and it is best to keep the area as dry as possible.
8. Never hold your breath while doing a bowel motion. Breathe regularly and evenly so that oxygen is being circulated to the muscles excreting the faeces (shit). This will limit the strain to the bowels. Never sit too long and strain. Allow the bowels to expel the faeces in their own time.
9. Regular exercise will promote regular bowel action.

DOES ANAL INTERCOURSE CAUSE PILES? IS IT DANGEROUS?

No, but it may cause bleeding and many women find it painful. If you do have anal intercourse, KY jelly will provide lubrication. Remember to clean the penis or vibrator afterwards before using it near the vagina or an infection may result.

Anal intercourse has been linked to the spread of the AIDS virus. This may be because both semen and blood are thought to be carriers of the disease. As with any other sexually transmitted diseases, you would have to have intercourse with an AIDS carrier before you have cause to worry.

STRESS AND RELAXATION

The word 'stress' conjures up all sorts of associations. To some of us, it suggests an inability to cope, coupled with feelings of anxiety or depression. More often, though, we feel its effects in physical symptoms first, and simply fail to recognise the danger signals: recurring headaches, fatigue, blemished skin or rashes, a missed period or sleepless nights. Rather than seeing stress as a sign of weakness, we need to recognise it as our body's defence against tension. Our physical symptoms occur *because* our body is dealing with the effects of strain. When we notice such symptoms, we can begin to deal with them as they happen or, in many cases, before they arise.

Stress and tension are the result of many factors, many of which are outlined in greater detail in Chapter 8. Relationships, or lack of relationships, poverty, overcrowding, city living, illness, drug use, isolation, overwork, understimulation, chemicals, noise, pollution and dealing with bureaucracy are contributory causes.

As women, we are particularly vulnerable because, in many ways, we feel powerless in a male-dominated society. Our role as wife and mother may put us on call twenty-four hours a day, with few opportunities for rest. As single women, we may be expected to care for ageing relations, or conform to an image of woman that jars with our perception of who we are.

WHY DO WE FEEL STRESS PHYSICALLY?
Stress and nervous tension make great demands on our bodies. To cope with these demands, we utilise tremendous amounts of energy and expend vast quantities of nutrients. Once these nutrients are sufficiently exhausted, our resistance to stress is reduced and physical symptoms result.

Eventually, these side effects wear us down. Vitamin and mineral supplements (especially B, C, zinc, calcium, magnesium and phosphorous) may help us to stave off stressful responses brought about by nutritional deficiencies.

HOW CAN I DEAL WITH STRESS IN A POSITIVE WAY?
Throughout this handbook, relaxation is suggested as one avenue to positive health care. This is especially true in the case of stress. Research is proving that a few minutes spent on conscious relaxation daily will defuse some of life's pressures and so reduce the risk of serious illness.

WHAT IS CONSCIOUS RELAXATION?
Some of us relax by watching television or reading a book. Or we may go

for a walk, get involved in sport, join a club or chat with friends. All of us need some sort of outlet. Conscious relaxation is just one more way to do this. The conscious relaxation technique illustrated here is based loosely on yoga asanas (positions) and meditation. It can be done lying on the floor or sitting in a chair. Ideally, you should spend ten to twenty minutes each day practising. Find a place where you won't be disturbed. It may be necessary to make the children take a nap or rest break — in a separate room. Don't feel guilty about this. You will be teaching them relaxation habits that will stand to them in their adult life.

It may take a few weeks before the full benefits of relaxation are felt. Allow your body and mind to gradually get used to the idea and it will come much easier.

CONSCIOUS RELAXATION

1. Sit or lie down in a comfortable position. Kick off your shoes and remove any restricting clothing. Loosen your waist band. The idea of this exercise is to concentrate on breathing so that the oxygen circulates throughout the entire body. Banish any worrying thoughts from your mind. As you breathe out, think of a word (like 'relax') which suggests relaxation. This will have a hypnotic effect. Sometimes if you slowly take in a deep breath, hold to a count of three and slowly exhale, you will actually feel the tension leaving the body on the exhalation. This deep breath can be done once or twice at the beginning of the relaxation session and will help to focus your mind on the task at hand.
2. Some women find that concentrating on pleasant or peaceful scenes helps to relax them. Others like to initially tense individual muscles and then relax them one by one, noticing the difference as they go along. Relax the fingers, arms, legs, tummy, shoulder, forehead, eyes, throat and so on.
3. After relaxing all the body parts, with continuous rhythmic breathing, slowly open your eyes, feeling refreshed and more energetic. If you find the process too difficult on your own, a session of yoga classes will teach you the basic skills. There are also tapes on sale which talk you through the stages of relaxation, or you can ask a friend to talk. You might even try taping your own voice going through the routine.

OTHER FORMS OF RELAXATION
Other forms of relations include *meditation,* which is designed to clear the mind of tension and, by relaxed breathing, cleanse our body; *massage,* which soothes tight muscles and helps us to relax through physical contact; *Tai chi,* which works by redistributing body energy; *Acupuncture and*

Acupressure, which involve inserting needles or applying pressure to key points so that energy is released and redistributed; *Chiropractic,* which helps alleviate bone misalignment; and *the Alexander technique,* a self-help method for obtaining similar results. Books are available on all these therapies, and you can generally find out about them in health-food shops.

HERBAL TEAS AND NATURAL REMEDIES

There are several herbal teas which sooth away tensions. Camomile is one. It can also help alleviate menstrual cramping, PMS and tummy cramps. Lavender and passion flower help reduce insomnia. Valerian is a herbal sedative and muscle relaxant. Scullcap is helpful for emotional stress.

Aromatic oils massaged into the skin can alleviate tension. Pine oil stimulates energy. Wintergreen soothes injured muscles and rosemary can ease tension headaches if massaged at the temples.

WHAT FOODS SHOULD I AVOID IF I WANT TO KEEP STRESS AT A MINIMUM?

Anything that contains caffeine should be eliminated. This chemical irritates the nervous system and interferes with the proper work of some vitamins. This means no tea, coffee, chocolate or soft drinks. Sugar should also be avoided. It may give temporary energy by increasing the blood sugar level, but the resultant fall of blood sugar makes us feel worse.

I CAN'T SLEEP AT NIGHT. CAN YOU SUGGEST SELF-HELP?

There are several things you can do to curb insomnia.
1. Eat well and get plenty of exercise during the day. This will help you burn up excess adrenalin caused by daily stresses and will aid relaxation. It's not a good idea to take vigorous exercise immediately before bed as this may make you feel more wakeful.
2. Avoid alcohol and any products containing caffeine after tea-time. These will only further stimulate you and make sleep difficult. Keep the bedroom free of cigarette smoke and try not to smoke before bed: this will only pollute the air you are breathing.
3. Only try to sleep when you are sleepy. If you can't sleep tonight, then busy yourself in some relaxing activity. Going without sleep will not seriously damage your health in the short term and your body will sleep when you teach it to relax.
4. Practise relaxation (see p. 45) so that sleep comes more easily.
5. Try some natural sleeping aids like warm milk, massage and teas made

especially for this purpose. Camomile and peppermint teas are particularly good.

6. Create a night-time pattern which suggests sleep to your mind. This may be reading or relaxation, bathing or meditation (see p. 45). Make this a routine.

7. Get up early in the morning and get out in the fresh air: take the children if you have to, but don't linger on in bed sleeping to compensate for lack of sleep at night.

8. Fill the bath waist-high with luke-warm water and sit in it for five minutes. Make sure you are covered warmly from the waist up. Alternatively, stand in *cold* water for five minutes. This will lower the body temperature and make sleep come more readily.

OCCUPATIONAL STRESS

Women have always worked, but now more than ever, we are taking up extra employment outside the home. Many of the occupations we choose (or are made to choose) involve chemical and industrial hazards. Others create stress because as women in a male-dominated business world we are often given the more boring and repetitious jobs. Rarely are we involved in the decision making nor do we experience promotion as rapidly.

Secretarial and computer staff are affected by fluorescent lighting, photocopying chemical fumes, and exposure to visual display units (VDUs). These have been held responsible for migraine headaches, nausea, eye complaints and irritability. VDUs are not recommended for use by pregnant women.

Hairdressers are at risk from the chemicals in sprays and dyes which can irritate the skin and damage the eyes. Standing up all day on hard floors may cause vein problems.

Dry-cleaning staff may be affected by the solvents used regularly. Noxious fumes can annoy the eyes, throat and nose. Laundry and hospital workers risk exposure to infection from garments, surgical linen, and other 'protective' clothing. Technicians are in danger from radiation and infectious diseases. Factory workers complain of back and circulatory problems resulting from standing all day in uncomfortable positions. Boring, routine jobs place stress on many women in the workplace.

Ideally, your trade union should be able to advise you on health guidelines, pay and work conditions. If your employer does not take your health seriously by providing protective clothing and a safe environment, it is important to have help in fighting the issue.

EXERCISE

Physical activity is an essential component of healthy living. It keeps the body supple, the muscles and joints flexible, and helps us to stay fit mentally. Regular exercise — activity which keeps the body on the move for at least a half an hour three to four times each week — gives the heart and lungs a workout and relieves tension and stress. A brisk walk is perfect. Many women like jogging, running, cycling or an aerobics class. Swimming seems to be the best overall exercise, but as long as the activity is regular, the form is irrelevant. The emphasis should be on enjoyment.

Some of us are a little embarrassed to take up physical exercise after a time of inactivity. We may feel foolish jogging in a track suit along with sleek athletic bodies, or we may be frightened of the strain and initial discomfort. Many of us were taught that vigorous physical activity is unfeminine. Or we may think we have to be dressed in the latest gear to do the whole thing properly.

And where do we find the time? It's difficult enough fitting in all the household chores and the baby-minding, or the job and shopping. We may feel frightened to go out alone for a run in the dark after work. Is it really worth the effort?

The answer is a resounding yes. For some reason, once you incorporate regular physical activity into your daily plan, many of these reservations disappear simply because the rewards are so great. Exercise makes us more alert and more energetic. It gives us confidence and strength. It clarifies the mind and banishes anxieties. And there are solutions to most of the drawbacks surrounding 'taking time for ourselves'.

Running clubs and women's groups organise teams of women from beginners' level to the more advanced. Group sessions are a regular feature. This makes exercise more fun and takes away the fear of being alone. Gyms and aerobics classes are now set up in many communities for all levels of physical ability. Getting family members or friends to share in the household chores and baby-minding will give you time for yourself. And if you think that nobody can do some of the home tasks as well as you, then let the tasks suffer, or retrain someone to do them better.

Exercise does not have to be expensive. Dancing to music on the radio for forty minutes three days a week is cheap enough. While running does require supportive shoes, the rest is free. Borrow a book on aerobic exercises or a record or tape from the library. Aerobics classes can be expensive, but setting one up among friends needn't cost a penny — and you can share the baby-sitting. Afterwards is the perfect time to talk about your health or other issues that affect your lives as women. Put a notice up in a shop window or the community hall asking for other eager beginners to get in touch. Together you can organise a fitness plan and a network of friends.

I HAVEN'T EXERCISED FOR YEARS. HOW DO I START BACK?

Any type of physical activity should be undertaken gradually. The first step is to learn warm-up and stretching exercises. Over a period of a few weeks, your body will be ready to take on more rigorous activity. If your goal is running, start by walking and build your stamina slowly. This will reduce the risk of injury. Running for set periods of time (say five to ten minutes) interspersed with brisk walking will soon follow, and you can build up the amount of time you are able to spend at the exercise. Within a few weeks, you'll be counting the miles.

The same rules apply for swimming, cycling or aerobics. Don't throw yourself in without warming up first. If you ignore this step, the soreness or injury which results may leave you disappointed and incapacitated.

It's important to dress appropriately and comfortably for any sport. This doesn't mean spending money. A touch of vaseline will ease chafing clothes or potential blisters if you put it on sensitive areas before you begin. Good supportive shoes are essential for running.

If you opt for running, be sure to do your cool-down exercises afterwards. This means stretching the muscles and tendons gradually so they don't become sore. You should concentrate your efforts on the backs of the legs, thighs and tummy. This will lessen the risk of cramp. If possible, soak in a hot bath afterwards, or get a friend to give you a massage.

If you are very overweight, or have been ill recently, you may want the advice of a health-care worker about the type of exercise which would best suit you in the beginning.

SHOULD I WEAR A BRA FOR EXERCISE?

Constant hopping up and down can damage the tissue which supports the breast. Larger-breasted women usually find exercise more comfortable when they wear a bra (the exception being swimming). This is a matter of personal choice. There are special sports bras available that hold the breasts firmly to the chest. They cost anywhere from £5 to £10.

IS IT TRUE THAT ONCE A BREAST IS INJURED, BREAST DISEASE IS MORE LIKELY?

Any sport or activity can lead to injury. The breast can be banged or bruised like any other body part. Sometimes a bruise will turn to swelling and lumpiness. If this happens, you should see a doctor. But this is a rare occurrence and the idea shouldn't prevent you from participating in healthy activity. (See also the section on breast disease.)

I LOST MY PERIODS WHEN I BEGAN RUNNING. IS THIS NORMAL?

Any new activity can alter the menstrual cycle. Many athletes find that menstruation stops when they are training hardest. Normally, it is not something to worry about, but if it persists for more than three months, and it concerns you, check with a doctor.

MY NIPPLES BECOME VERY SORE WHEN I RUN. IS THIS DANGEROUS?

This is usually the result of the nipples rubbing against a coarse material — your bra or T-shirt. Vaseline will help prevent it, but you may want to change to more comfortable clothing. Occasionally, this type of irritation can lead to discharge and/or infection. This would need to be treated.

I WAS TERRIBLY BRUISED NEAR MY VAGINA AFTER HORSE RIDING. IS THIS DANGEROUS?

Falling hard against the cross-bar of a bicycle or on the saddle of a horse can cause bruising or pain, but there is rarely any serious damage. Young girls may break the thin layer of tissue inside their vagina *(hymen)* doing this. The hymen is naturally broken by intercourse and sometimes by the insertion of tampons. You may experience some bleeding which is only temporary. There is no need to worry.

PRE-MENSTRUAL SYNDROME SEEMS TO AFFECT MY PERFORMANCE IN SPORTS

PMS can affect co-ordination, cause fluid retention, contribute to breast tenderness and swelling, and interfere with concentration. For these reasons, it can affect competitive performance. Some women note similar reactions during pregnancy.

CAN I STILL EXERCISE DURING PREGNANCY?

Yes: it's important to keep fit during pregnancy. This keeps you and the foetus more healthy. If you have been jogging all along, there is no need to stop unless you feel uncomfortable or sense something is wrong. Women who are physically fit find childbirth a little easier simply because they are used to physical exertion. Some women find swimming the best exercise during pregnancy.

WHAT EXACTLY HAPPENS IN EXERCISE? WHY IS IT SO GOOD FOR US?

Because exercise gets the heart and lungs working, they grow stronger. This increases the blood supply to the rest of the body tissue, including the muscles. As the lungs develop, their increased capacity makes the circulation of oxygen to the bloodstream more efficient — less energy is expended for basic tasks and can be focussed on making us healthy. Strong supportive muscles relieve many of the aches and pains which send us to the doctor.

PELVIC FLOOR EXERCISES (KEGEL EXERCISES)

One very important muscle in a woman's body is the pelvic floor (see p. 17). This muscle holds the uterus, bowel and bladder in place like a hammock. As with any other muscle, the pelvic floor needs regular physical exercise to maintain fitness.

WHY EXERCISE THE PELVIC FLOOR?
There are several reason why it is so important.
1. It can increase our enjoyment of sexual contact. As the muscles become stronger, the vagina becomes tighter. As the pelvic floor becomes more fit, we become more aware of it. The increased awareness can lead to greater pleasure.
2. The physical stresses of pregnancy can be dealt with more comfortably with a stronger pelvic floor muscle. The uterus and bladder are given greater support. There is less strain on the back and other muscles. Healthy muscles heal more quickly after childbirth. If the exercises are not done, the muscle becomes more strained with carrying the weight of a pregnancy.
3. Urinary control can be improved if you suffer from stress incontinence (wetting yourself). This may happen when you laugh or cough if the muscles are loose. If after trying the exercise for a few weeks you notice no improvement, consult a health-care worker.

HOW DO I PERFORM KEGEL EXERCISES?
To understand which muscles we are trying to exercise, try this simple activity next time you go to the toilet. As you begin to urinate (pee), allow only some of the stream to be expelled. Now try to stop the flow. The muscles you use to do this are the pelvic floor muscles. If you find it difficult to do this, stop the test and empty your bladder naturally. When you have finished, you can begin practising the exercises.

Another way to feel the movements of the pelvic floor muscle is by inserting a finger into the vagina and grasping the finger with the muscles.

Some of us need to use two fingers to feel the effect. Or we can try the exercise during sexual activity.

In the beginning, it may be easier to do these exercises while lying on your back. If they prove difficult and you are unable to feel what you are doing, put a pillow under your bottom so that the muscles are lowered by gravity and there is no excess weight fighting against them.

1. Draw up or pull in the pelvic floor muscle and hold to a count of five, relax and repeat five more times. Gradually build up to ten groups of five over the day. In the beginning, it may be a little sore and your ability to contract the muscles may decrease after the first attempt. This is normal. The first contraction will be the strongest. Don't overdo it in the initial stages — you don't want to hurt yourself. It's better to stop for a day than to further aggravate a strain.

2. Pretend you are grabbing a piece of paper between the cheeks of your buttocks; relax and repeat to the same count as outlined above. Or pretend you are stopping the flow of urine, relax and repeat.

3. Pretend your pelvic muscle is climbing a stairway. Gradually contract the muscle one step at a time. Hold to a count of three and then gradually descend the staircase. Do this five times a day, with a rest in between.

4. Pretend you are sucking water into the vagina. If you insert a finger into the vagina, it will feel as though the finger is being drawn in. Repeat five times over the day.

Remember that pelvic floor exercises can be done anytime, and no one will realise you are doing them. As you get more adept, you will be able to do them standing in a shopping or bus queue or while sitting at a desk.

A WORD ABOUT EXERCISE AND DISABLEMENT

After the car accident, I withdrew for months. I even tried to kill myself. It wasn't like a sudden inspiration, but eventually I started getting out in the wheelchair. And then I saw people racing in chairs in the marathon and I was hooked. Mind you, it's difficult enough training. There are no proper facilities, but I began with weight training and the psychological benefits were enormous.

Whether we are permanently or temporarily disabled through illness or injury, it is vitally important to keep fit. Exercises can concentrate on the parts we are able to use. This can be as simple as the rhythmical flexing and unflexing of muscles. Courses of physiotherapy with a helper may offer great benefit. Exercise when we are ill or recovering from an illness helps to keep the heart and lungs healthy and can prevent bedsores.

Those of us who have been institutionalised, be it for detoxification or mental illness, in a nursing home or a prison, should make exercise a part of our daily plan. This can prove difficult because of the emphasis on locking us away. But the benefits will be worth the effort. Exercise can give us a feeling of control over our own bodies.

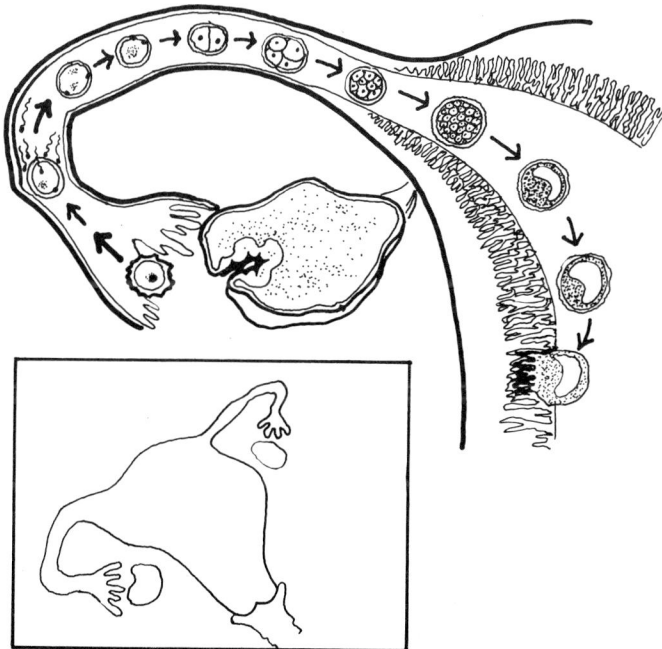

11. The beginning of pregnancy. The diagram shows fertilisation of the egg in the oviduct, and its development as it journeys through the oviduct to reach the uterus and implant

6. OUR SEXUALITY

What exactly does sexuality mean to us as women? Is it the way we feel about ourselves, or about others? Is it fancying the person beside you, or the sensuality of exploring your own body? Do we allow other people to define our sexual needs, or do we express our desires free from embarrassment and guilt?

There are both physical and emotional factors in the expression of our sexuality. For many of us, sensuality and sensitivity are tied up with loving kisses and cuddles we received as children. An awareness and a liking of physical sensation became a part of our childhood development:

> *I used to wake some mornings, rocking out of my sleep with a sense of delight running through my body. I never knew where it came from, or why, but I used to stop rocking in an effort to focus my attention more intensely on the enjoyment. Of course, the moment the rocking stopped, so did the pleasure. I must have been about two years old.*

Trying to duplicate such feelings during our waking hours was sometimes more difficult. It meant tracing that elusive ticklish spot, or remembering the images which triggered nice sensations. Exploration became exciting, nice fabrics and fur felt soothing to the skin. And if we weren't caught or scolded, wiggling in a chair or caressing between our legs made us feel happy and comforted.

> *I remember taking off all my clothes and running through the long grass. It would have been early on a summer morning, and the neighbour's wife*

saw me – I was in big trouble after
that.

I can still feel my body rolling in the
sand on a brilliantly hot day, and the
thrill of charging naked into the cold
sea – what a sense of freedom!

For some of us, the acts of touching, smelling and being naked were encouraged and nurtured; for others, these pleasures were forbidden. Our hands were slapped, our mouths 'washed out with soap', or we were sent to our rooms. Seeking parental approval, we often blocked sensual experiences from an early age, or tried to recapture some of the pleasure in private — always running the risk of being caught out, feeling anxious or guilty.

Perhaps brothers or sisters interrupted our privacy:

Why is Johnny's body so different?
That little thing between his legs looks
silly. Mummy says boys are fancy,
girls are plain. Mummy has big
muscles on her chest – Daddy has
them on his arms. Touching Johnny's
willy makes him giggle in the bath, but
Mummy says stop, that's nasty.

Where exactly did Johnny come from then? And as we asked questions we often met rebuffs: 'Ask your mother,' 'All in good time, pet,' 'Under a cabbage leaf,' 'now run along and play.' And as we grew older and started school, asking the same questions suggested voicing 'unclean thoughts'. The punishments were mighty, the ultimate being banishment to hell.

I was looking through an English
magazine my father had bought on
holidays. There were photographs of
models in underclothing. It suddenly
occurred to me at the ripe old age of
seven, that this might be considered a
sin. Since I knew from my catechism I
had reached the 'age of reason', I
worried anxiously in case I wasn't
suitable for my first communion.

We salved our conscience in the company of girl friends. We fell in love, walked hand in hand, and exchanged secrets.

> *Anne Marie says he puts his thing inside Mummy. It must hurt terribly. The baby comes from the back passage or the belly button. Mummy says she didn't want so many children, so he must do it the once, and then God decides every few years. I want to marry Anne Marie, but Mummy says that's silly.*

As we reached adolescence, we started noticing changes in our body. There were new smells, pointy nipples, hair sprouting everywhere and periods. We imagined we could do anything and felt hopelessly confused. We fought more with our mothers and worried about pimples. Why couldn't we be treated more like an adult? We were no longer babies but we needed reassurance. We talked about kissing and boyfriends.

> *Oh no . . . you mean you let him put his tongue in your mouth! He won't respect you. Show me how to do it . . . I could never let a boy do that, they're so dirty.*

And then came the pressure to like boys and have boyfriends. 'Tom-boys' were ridiculed, girls without fellows became social outcasts. For most of us, these pressures came too soon. We were more in love with some notion of romance, searching through a maze of muddled emotions, than ready for a sexual relationship.

> *Do you think he likes me? Will Mary be annoyed I'm not going with her? Can I trust him? He says everything will be all right, and that I won't get pregnant – you can't, he says, at least not the first time.*

For some of us, the very notion of intimacy with a boy, sexual or otherwise, seemed unattractive. We preferred the company of girls, but were signalled by our parents and peers that we musn't become too attached to Anne Marie or Mary; some day they would get married.

Physical and emotional sensations mingled again with so many rules governing our behaviour: Don't touch, Save yourself, Bad girl, Men won't respect you, Nice girl — what confusion! So many messages coming from the outside and as many mixed up feelings from within. Should I get married or become a 'spinster'? If I became a nun, would I regret it? What about having babies, and what exactly is a 'lezzer'? Did other girls feel the same way, or am I some kind of odd-ball, abnormal in some way? Is it possible to want sexual contact and not want a boyfriend? Is it okay to fancy the girl in science class? Where does this thing called sexuality begin and the rest of me fit in?

As women, we share a common bond of sexuality. For most of us, sexuality is an integral part of our being as a woman. It is the way we feel about ourselves *and* the way we respond to others. It is sometimes emotional, sometimes physical, and more often a combination of the two. There may be times when we want to be alone, and spells when we need companionship. Although our attitude to sexuality may vary according to upbringing and education, there is always room for growth and change.

But these thoughts are not always so clear. If we were raised to fear sexual contact, or were taught that physical sensations were wrong, then our sexuality may somehow seem blocked from free expression. We may feel overwhelmed or anxious about the powerful emotions we experience in sexual pleasure — or we may feel at a loss because we sense no pleasure at all. By fighting against the inherited stereotypes, prejudices and taboos, we may begin to perceive that sexuality is simply our unique perception of those emotional and physical sensations which bring us happiness and delight.

There are as many ways of expressing and receiving sexual pleasure as there are women to express and receive them. There are countless forms of sexual stimulation, and *orgasm* is only one of them.

There is no one specific type of orgasm. This feeling of pleasure has been described as a rush of warmth, a tingling, a surge of emotion, a wave of sensations, and something like a pleasant sneeze. Not every orgasm is the same and not every woman has one. We may experience orgasm by stimulating our nipples, or when someone kisses and licks our clitoris. We may feel intense pleasure during intercourse (when the vagina and penis meet), or when we masturbate with a vibrator. For some women, massage brings a feeling of contentment, but for most women, variations on all of these encounters heightens sexual awareness. Orgasm is not the goal.

Sometimes we find ourselves with a partner who seems ignorant of our needs. If our husband or boyfriend avoids hugging and kissing or caresses, it may be because he thinks sexuality is expressed through intercourse alone. We need to challenge the notion that the vagina is the source of all orgasm and hence all pleasure, and that penetration is the climax of love-making. If we decide to opt for intercourse, we must learn to express our needs and talk openly about what we enjoy.

Some of us may not like the idea of anything entering the vagina, but we may like to tickle or have our clitoris stimulated. We may enjoy kissing our partner's penis or vulva, or we may like using vibrators on our necks and backs.

There are a number of positions which may make sexual contact more pleasurable. Since every woman is different we must find our own way to communicate our individual sexuality. Physical disability, sexual orientation and relative inexperience do not define us as women, they simply open up infinite possibilities.

Some of us may want an emotional relationship with another person, while others may want or need no partner. There are many words used to define the sexual choices we make as women. But even within these categories, sexual expression is individual. The word *celibate* is used to refer to the state of wanting no sexual partner. Many of us choose celibacy because we wish to be independent of emotional ties.

For a growing number of women, celibacy means freedom to invest increasing energies into other areas of daily life: into work, friendship, emotional, physical and intellectual development.

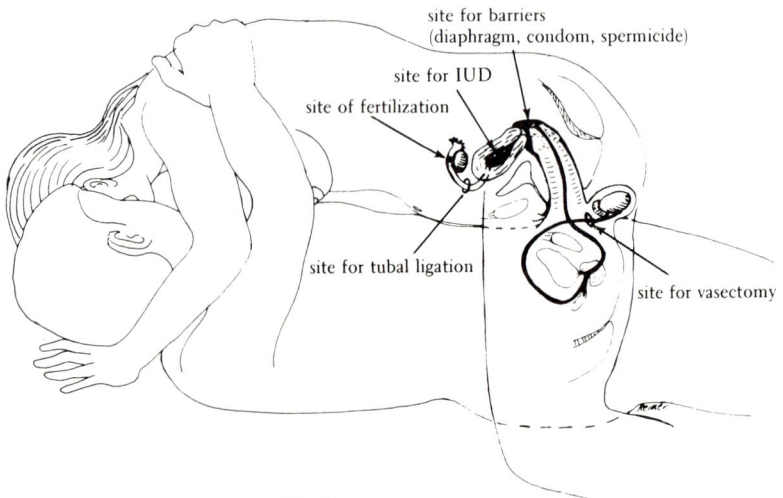

12. Intercourse

But how many of us truly choose to be free of sexual or emotional partners? Do we sometimes fear involvement with others? Do we have to accept solitary sexual expression because our choices are limited? Or because we simply need a rest between personal encounters? Do some of us choose to abstain from sexual relations because of a fear of pregnancy, or because we are afraid to confront our true sexual feelings? Are liaisons with men simply not worth the struggle to communicate our needs?

If we decide to express our sexuality with others, we may be labelled *lesbian* (if we choose the company of women), *heterosexual* (if we enjoy the partnership of men), and *bisexual* (when we have sexual relations with men and women).

Enjoying sexual pleasure differs from woman to woman. Kissing and touching sensitive areas of the body enhances arousal. Ears, neck, back, buttocks, thighs — all respond to caresses and massage. Skin comes alive with the lightest of pressure, the most delicate contact. Smell, taste and sight all contribute to the experience. The tummy, the vulva and the breasts respond to varying degrees of stimulation. Sexual excitement which builds up from prolonged stroking can lead to *orgasm*, but for many of us, the pleasure of intimate contact is equally important.

WHAT IS MASTURBATION? HOW DO I MASTURBATE TO ORGASM?

The easiest way to masturbate to orgasm, is by gently massaging the clitoris with your fingers or a vibrator. But first, it's a good idea to create a relaxed and comfortable atmosphere. Find a place where you won't be disturbed. Make sure you are warm. You may like to put on some music. Lying in a bed or bathtub may be just the ticket. Start to get to know your body, feeling for sensitive areas (ears, neck, tummy, legs). This may be difficult in the beginning. Remember you are fighting against years of conditioning which said 'Don't touch.' Practise over a period of time without rushing or forcing results. It isn't a competition.

Once you feel relaxed with your body, begin exploring the vulval area, the vagina and clitoris. Don't be afraid to put your fingers inside, nothing will bite you. Feel the clitoris. How does it respond? Much of the sexual pleasure we experience comes from exciting the clitoris, so you need to find what arouses yours. Your clitoris may like to be rubbed, or it may be stimulated by a light vibration or spray from the shower nozzle. Once you are able to give yourself pleasure, you will be able to show any partner what makes you happy.

13. Sexual contact between two women

SOME SPECIAL CONSIDERATIONS

Asthma In some cases, sexual arousal may bring on an attack. Antihistamines beforehand may help but can make us sleepy and interfere with the pill. We may feel breathless for some time afterwards. Asthma may improve during pregnancy.

Cerebral palsy Muscle spasms may increase with arousal and make masturbation more difficult (a vibrator may give more control). Genital stimulation is not usually impaired but spasms may make positioning a problem. This may be helped by pillows and non-genital stimulation. Vaginal irritation may improve with the use of KY jelly. Fertility, menstruation and pregnancy are not impaired.

Cerebral vascular attack (stroke) Paralysis may impair some functioning and can make positioning a problem. Menstruation and fertility are as before, but the contraceptive pill and pregnancy should be discussed with the doctor.

Diabetes Orgasm sometimes becomes more difficult and can vary in intensity. Vaginal irritation may be exacerbated by spermicides and use of the Pill (the latter should be discussed with doctor) with resulting thrush. KY jelly can help. Careful supervision during pregnancy is important and some fertility problems have been reported.

Epilepsy Some epilepsy medication can interfere with the hormone contraceptive pill but many women can take a higher dose pill successfully. Others find coil insertion brings on a convulsion. Some women also report a disimprovement in their physical condition following pregnancy.

Heart trouble In acute cases, doctor's supervision essential: get her/his advice. Gentle contact is more desirable as exertion may cause palpitations and chest pains. The Pill is generally ruled out as a contraceptive method.

Hypertension (high blood pressure) Over exertion is not advisable. The Pill is out and pregnancy should be avoided or strictly monitored.

Hysterectomy As with mastectomy, this operation may affect us more psychologically. Intercourse may not be possible for six to eight weeks afterwards. Some women notice a change in sensation during intercourse (not painful).

Kidney disease and dialysis As for high blood pressure. Sometimes menstruation becomes irregular or stops altogether. Pregnancy should be avoided.

Lupus erythematosus As for rheumatoid arthritis (see below). Also, vaginal dryness may need lubrication. Use KY jelly.

Mastectomy Positioning may need to be altered in the beginning to avoid discomfort, but this is temporary. Pregnancy should be avoided and hormonal contraception is dangerous. Get advice about alternative methods.

Multiple sclerosis Depending on the progress of the disease, spasms may make intercourse difficult. Arousal may increase spasms and in severe cases, genital sensitivity may be diminished. Muscle weakness may make some positions more difficult; there may be vaginal lubrication problems and sometimes incontinence. This can be alleviated by going to the toilet beforehand.

Opinions about pregnancy vary, but it certainly is possible. MS can improve during pregnancy, but the Pill should be avoided.

Ostomy Because ostomy victims are not obviously disabled, some women find it difficult to tell potential sexual partners about the bag they have to wear to collect faeces and worry about the smell or positioning of this equipment. Early disclosure seems to cause less anxiety. Fertility and pregnancy do not seem to be affected (if an all clear from cancer has been given). Some women notice pain during intercourse but this varies considerably. Many find that emptying the bag and having a wash before sexual contact relieves worry about hygiene.

Poliomyelitis Sexual arousal is unaffected, but pregnancy may be affected by abdominal muscle control. A corset may improve back support.

Respiratory disorders As for heart trouble and asthma.

Rheumatoid arthritis Pain, medication and tiredness may affect arousal. Some positions may prove uncomfortable. Menstruation, fertility and pregnancy are as before, but birthing may be difficult if the spine or pelvic bones are involved.

Spina Bifida Positioning and stimulation vary according to degree of disablement. There may be no clitoral stimulation. Pregnancy is possible but incontinence may be a side-effect.

Spinal cord injury As for spina bifida, this depends on where the injury occurs. Intercourse may be uncomfortable because of bladder irritation and lubrication problems. Wetting may be alleviated by going to the toilet before sexual contact. Pregnancy needs to be monitored and the Pill should only be used under supervision.

WHAT IS FOREPLAY?

This is a common expression used to describe a wide range of sexual activity which stops short of or leads up to intercourse. The term has been abused because it suggests that intercourse is the natural goal in sexual relations. Foreplay may mean masturbation, massage, kissing and fondling. 'Heavy petting' is another phrase for foreplay. Because each of us perceives sexual contact differently, we may not always mean the same things simply because we use similar expressions.

WHAT IS FRENCH KISSING?

This is a type of kissing which involves opening the mouth and touching tongues.

CAN I GET PREGNANT FROM 'HEAVY PETTING'?

If your partner is masturbated and he *ejaculates* (comes) near the opening of your vagina, there is some chance of pregnancy. If any of the *semen* (liquid containing sperm) enters the vagina from either of your hands, then you may not be contraceptively covered.

HOW DO I MASTURBATE A MAN?

Masturbating a penis is done by gently pulling up and down on the hard penis with your hand or mouth. The latter is called a 'blow job'. A man's orgasm usually ends with an ejaculation of white liquid called semen.

WHAT IS ORAL SEX?

Oral sex is when you kiss or lick your partner's vulva, clitoris or penis — or when they reciprocate. Many women like this form of stimulation because it is gentle and encourages orgasms. It is also a fun way to have sexual contact without intercourse and the resulting chance of pregnancy.

I HAVE A NUMBER OF PARTNERS OF BOTH SEXES. IS THERE ANYTHING I SHOULD BE CAREFUL ABOUT?

Your major worry would be infection, presuming, of course, your partners are as active as you. Sexual contact with diverse partners may increase your chances of sexually transmitted disease. See Chapter 12 for specific help.

MY DAUGHTER IS MENTALLY HANDICAPPED. I AM WORRIED IN CASE SHE IS HAVING SEX

She may be having sex. It is sometimes difficult for us as mothers to accept our daughters' sexuality, especially if she is handicapped. The most helpful thing you can do for your daughter is to prepare her for feelings of sexual interest. Sexuality is not based on intellectual or physical ability. A mentally disabled woman will have sexual desires similar to our own. There is a myth which suggests that the mentally disabled are promiscuous (easy). The truth is, they are often less inhibited about expressing sexual and emotional responses. Sex and contraceptive education are both important.

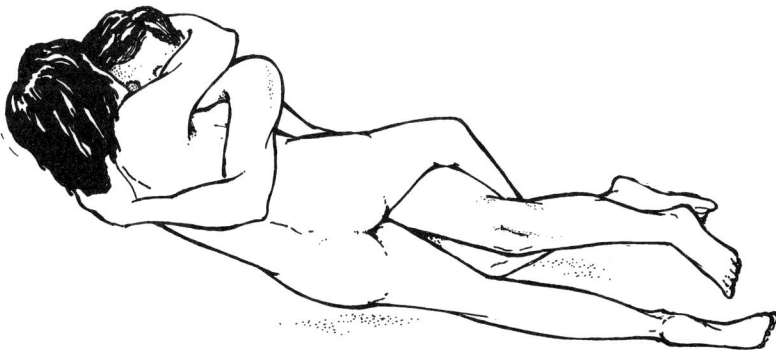

14. Sexual contact between a woman and a man

SINCE I HAD A MASTECTOMY, I HAVE LOST INTEREST IN SEX

If we undergo serious surgery like mastectomy (removal of the breast), it may take some time to work through the physical and emotional effects. Drugs and chemotherapy may inhibit our *libido* (level of sexual interest), or we may associate our breast with our sexuality as a woman. Major surgery performed under a general anaesthetic can leave us feeling exhausted, depressed and out of control. Our worry about possible disease can contribute to the debilitating effects of stress. And we may be angry about the way our surgery is undertaken. Is it any wonder, then, that sexual contact is low on our list of priorities?

An organisation called Reach to Recovery can help you cope with the mastectomy as your first priority. If your waning libido is then creating difficulties, they can put you in touch with further help.

I AM CONFUSED AS TO WHETHER OR NOT I AM A LESBIAN

Confusion about sexuality is normal. Sometimes it's made more difficult by social pressures which make one choice of sexual behaviour more acceptable than another. Lesbianism is a positive sexual, intellectual and/or emotional attachment to women. It can also be an expression of political beliefs about the way society is structured.

We have been conditioned to think that lesbianism is a form of mental illness; it is not. Talking to friends may alleviate some of our confusion. Try not to assume what their reaction will be. If you are met with rebuff, there are counselling lines set up specifically by lesbians to discuss your anxieties. These are listed in the directory.

CAN I BE ARRESTED FOR BEING A LESBIAN?

No, unlike the legal situation for male homosexuals, the law doesn't even recognise the existence of lesbians. However, public opinion may be very antagonistic, largely due to misinformation and fear. Women have been harassed and denied work opportunities because of their sexual orientation. Unfortunately, proving some of these forms of violence and discrimination may be difficult. (See also Chapter 9.)

CAN I BE FIRED FROM MY JOB FOR BEING A LESBIAN?

Women have been fired for reasons of sexuality, but employers usually concoct a bogus 'respectable' excuse. There is no reason why sexual preferences should interest colleagues, or affect your ability to do a good job at work. If you suspect you are being victimised for any reason of sex or sexuality, contact your trade union or the Equal Opportunities Agency.

MY SISTER GOT UPSET WHEN I TOLD HER I WAS A LESBIAN. NOW SHE SAYS I CAN'T BABYSIT ANYMORE

Family relations are often confused and hurt by our sexuality. The fact that you love someone of the same sex does not mean you are going to suddenly alter your personality and become a threat to children. There is a lot of education to be done in this whole area — for both sexes. The best place to start is in the home.

I AM DISABLED AND HAVE AN ABLE-BODIED PARTNER. I AM VERY NERVOUS ABOUT HAVING SEXUAL RELATIONS

Discussing these fears with your partner is the best way to overcome anxiety. This may mean letting her/him know you can or cannot enjoy intercourse and that other parts of the body can be aroused. There are so many ways to achieve sexual happiness, that some solution can be reached. An organisation called SPOD has experience here and can offer counselling if problems arise.

THE TWO OF US ARE DISABLED. WE WOULD LIKE TO LIE IN BED TOGETHER BUT GETTING THERE IS THE PROBLEM

An intimate friend or helper can assist you in this situation, if you can overcome the embarrassment of asking. This is a positive step and should be viewed as an effort to regain control over some aspects of your sexuality.

CAN I GET PREGNANT FROM ANAL INTERCOURSE?

Yes, but not if you're careful. Anal intercourse happens by introducing the penis into the anus (back passage). Pregnancy is possible if semen goes near the vagina. Anal intercourse is painful for some women and may cause bleeding, but it does not cause piles.

I FREEZE WHEN ANYTHING COMES NEAR MY VAGINA

This is quite common. The medical word for it is *vaginismus* (VAJ-I-NISS-MUSS). It is the result of the vaginal muscles contracting on reflex. Reasons for such involuntary reactions include a dislike or fear of intercourse or pregnancy, a dislike of our partner, fear of sexual abuse, sexual trauma, conditioning, anxiety and depression.

Alleviation of vaginismus involves identifying or discussing the causes, and gradually learning to relax. Once you feel confident and ready, you can try inserting small objects, like your finger, into the vagina until you feel comfortable. This is of course if you want to have intercourse or use a tampon. But only you can make this decision.

If you feel you need help with this problem you should contact a *psychosexual* counsellor. Your Health Board or family planning clinic can help.

I FIND INTERCOURSE PAINFUL

Painful intercourse is distressing. Sometimes it is the result of vaginismus, or simply a lack of stimulation and lubrication. It may also result from local irritations, or vaginal infections. Occasionally pelvic inflammatory disease (PID) or endometriosis (END-O-MEE-TREE-O-SIS), both gynaecological problems (see the section on gynaecological problems in Chapter 10) are the culprits. Any severe and unusual pain should be investigated by a doctor.

I'M NOT REALLY INTERESTED IN SEX AT ALL, BUT MY PARTNER IS WORRIED

Each of us goes through times when we lose interest in sex. We may be very busy, feel depressed or run down, or be worried about pregnancy. We may find our partner inconsiderate, or love-making a bore. All of these feelings are fine unless they create a problem for you and lead to unhappiness. Sometimes they sort themselves out — couples break up, hormone imbalances are rectified, contraception is found. At other times, we need outside help in examining and perhaps changing the existing relationship. If you find it difficult to talk things out with your partner, relationship counselling may help the situation.

I FANTASISE I AM WITH SOMEONE ELSE WHEN I AM HAVING SEX WITH MY REGULAR PARTNER

So do many of us. Everyone likes change and imaginative situations. What you think about is your own business. If you want to put any fantasy into action, however, it's best to make sure your partner likes the idea too.

MY PARTNER COMES BEFORE I DO AND SEX STOPS AFTERWARDS. WHAT SHOULD I DO?

It's important to tell your partner how you feel. Perhaps s/he sees orgasm as the goal of sexual contact. Sexual communication is a learned skill like many others. It doesn't happen naturally. Men who 'come' too early sometimes suffer from something called 'premature ejaculation' (see p. 68). It can be the result of tension, anxiety, depression or fear. Help is widely available from relationship counsellors, sexual therapists and family planning clinics.

ABOUT MEN

Men's sexual parts are similar to ours and develop from the same embryonic tissue. Their *scrotum* (the bag of wrinkled skin which holds the *testicles* or balls) corresponds to our outer vulval lips. The *glans* of their penis is like our clitoris. The *testes*, which make sperm, are similar to our ovaries.

When a man is sexually aroused, his penis begins to fill with blood and enlarge. It becomes hard and, in some cases, the foreskin (the hood which covers the uncircumcised penis) draws back. (If a penis has been circumcised the hood is surgically removed.)

If the penis is rubbed up and down, orgasm and an ejaculation of semen (usually containing sperm) result. Once a man ejaculates, he may need time to produce another erection.

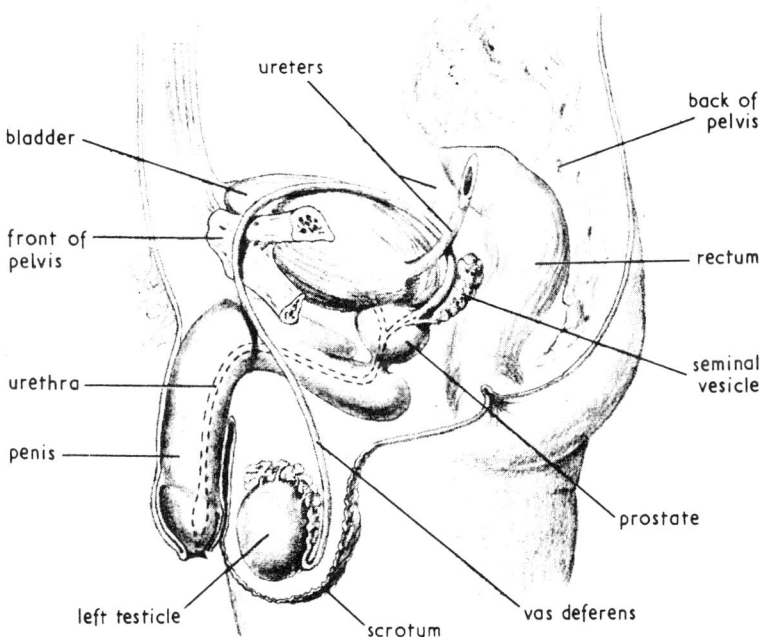

15. Male genital tract

SEXUAL PROBLEMS

Men can have sexual problems for many of the same reasons women do. These difficulties may affect us and cause distress. One such problem is *premature ejaculation*. This happens when a man cannot control his ability to 'come'. This is often the result of tension and stress. *Impotence* is another sexual problem. In this case, an erection is impossible. Men can also have painful sex due to infections, irritations and disease. Many of these problems can be worked out together or with the aid of a health-care worker.

7. GROWING OLDER

On my fiftieth birthday I sat down and took stock. I realised that all those years taking care of others had left me unsure of who I was. I felt depressed for a little while, and then I decided to get out and do something. I started adult education classes and now work three days a week in the community centre. I feel as young as ever.

I had never thought about my future much. I left money matters to my husband. When he died, I soon found that his pension wasn't enough to support us.

I met this lovely person and we started seeing one another. And then I was asked how old I was. My first reaction was to lie, in case they were put off.

Our attitude towards ageing has not always been positive. Again, we have been conditioned to associate energy, intelligence and sexuality with youthfulness. As women, we have been taught that much of our worth depends on the way we look and our ability to bear children. With such myths being perpetuated, it's no wonder confusion and depression often surround the process of growing older.

As older women, we are often treated as third-class citizens. More often than not, we are ignored or isolated through institutional care and segregated public housing. After a lifetime of unpaid work for others, we may be left in poverty and dependent on the state for aid. As a result we may feel vulnerable, frightened and angry.

For these reasons, it is essential we maintain a high level of health and fitness. Good health habits may improve our ability to cope with daily tensions and can slow down the ill-effects of ageing.

Just because we are older doesn't mean that daily pressures don't affect us. Nor does it mean we are better able to cope with stress. It's important to approach maturity taking positive health care into consideration. This may mean learning new skills, joining clubs, finding work or getting involved in women's or community groups. Preparing for retirement and taking extra care of ourselves will make our older years as rewarding as any that came before.

MENOPAUSE

Menopause means the end of menstruation. It is used widely to describe the time in our life when periods become irregular, though the true word for this phase is *climacteric* (CLIME-ACK-TER-ICK). When we have reached the menopause, and have gone a few years beyond, we are no longer able to conceive a pregnancy because ovulation ceases.

For most of us, the menopause occurs between the ages of 45 and 55. It can happen earlier or a bit later. This 'change of life' is the result of altered hormonal messages affecting our reproductive organs: our ovaries restrict their release of eggs and erratic bleeding may result. Some of us may go several weeks without any sign of ovulation followed by a series of periods in rapid succession. This fluctuation of hormonal activity can distress and confuse us. We may experience hot flushes, insomnia, heavy sweating and mood swings.

Most of these are normal physical reactions affecting ten per cent of women. We hear so much about these symptoms because they are the ones seen by doctors and subsequently written about in medical journals. For those of us who suffer discomfort during the climacteric, there is help available. It may be reassuring to know that we are not alone in experiencing these feelings and that they are completely natural. The menopause is one more phase in our growth as women. It is a time when our body learns to adjust to the end of reproductive activity.

For some of us, a future free from the worry of pregnancy seems quite exciting. But until our periods end completely, we still need to be careful about contraception. (See Chapter 11 for guidelines on fertility.)

WHAT HAPPENS AS WE APPROACH THE MENOPAUSE?

To understand the physical changes of menopause, we need to remember that hormones trigger the process. During the climacteric, they instruct the ovaries to limit some of its work so that egg release becomes sporadic. This disturbs the cycle of preparing the uterus for pregnancy. The withdrawal of hormones may take several years and be so gradual that we hardly notice any symptoms beyond the odd missed period — until suddenly our menstruation disappears altogether. For some of us, however, the change is so abrupt and strong that genuine feelings of illness and confusion result.

HOW DO I KNOW I AM GOING THROUGH THE CHANGE?

If the symptoms are minor, you may never realise you've entered the climacteric until you miss a number of periods. It is important to rule out pregnancy first. Other signs of the menopause include fatigue, overheating (hot flushes, sweats), irritability, sensitivity to stress, sleeplessness, headaches, weight changes, palpitations, dryness or irritation in the vagina, itchiness and a reduction in the amount of our pubic hair.

Although the menopause has occurred in women under forty this is rare, and any change in our pattern of menstruation not obviously connected to the climacteric should be investigated.

WILL I STILL BE ABLE TO GET PREGNANT DURING THE MENOPAUSE?

It is possible to conceive a pregnancy during the climacteric. As we grow older there are increased health risks attached to pregnancy and childbirth. Some birth defects, like Down's syndrome (mongolism) are more common in women over thirty-five. If you want to avoid pregnancy, you should investigate contraceptive choices. Some of your options are reduced as you approach the menopause. The condom, coil or cap are probably the most suitable methods. 'Natural' methods are unreliable in some instances because their success is based on observable hormonal changes which may be unpredictable during the 'change'.

HOW WILL I KNOW WHEN I AM NO LONGER FERTILE?

Fertility (our ability to conceive a pregnancy) is reduced, but not necessarily completely ruled out, once periods end completely. A simple guideline is: once you are of menopausal age and go through two years without a period, then you are safe to have unprotected sexual intercourse. (If you are over fifty, you need only wait about one year after the bleeding stops.) If in doubt, ask a health-care worker.

WILL I STILL FEEL SEXUAL DURING THE CHANGE?

As with any other stage of our growth and development, this varies from woman to woman. If we never enjoyed sexual relations before, we cannot suddenly expect to enjoy them now. For some of us, the freedom from pregnancy may actually fuel our sexual appetite. For others, side-effects like tiredness, sweating and irritability can put us temporarily off the idea of sexual contact.

We may experience some discomfort in the vulval area during the menopause. If you feel dry or sore, a water-soluble lubricant like KY jelly may ease the irritation. Pelvic floor exercises should be kept up as well: these may minimise the risk of stress incontinence.

I'VE BECOME VERY ANXIOUS/DEPRESSED SINCE I STARTED THE CHANGE

Many women notice emotional changes at this time of life. We may experience anxiety, panic attacks, mood swings and depression. Sometimes new and unexplained physical symptoms trigger these feelings. But other events may contribute to this response: children or partners leaving, the idea of growing old, being passed over for promotion, financial problems, unemployment, the death of friends and finding that we no longer know who we are.

If any of these emotions causes you distress, approach your friends for help or seek the advice of health-care workers. (See also Chapter 8.)

IS THERE ANY WAY TO AVOID SEVERE MENOPAUSAL SYMPTOMS?

For some of us, simply knowing our symptoms are normal can be greatly reassuring. Next, talk to friends of your own age who may have experienced similar feelings. Some women have banded together and broadened this network to self-help groups. Health boards and family planning clinics may be able to put you in touch with one of these (if not, set one up in your area).

The third step is to educate the people we live and work with. Don't allow them to make you the butt of their misunderstanding ('Don't mind *her*, she's going through the change' — nudge, nudge, wink, wink). Assert your health-care needs with health-care workers, and don't settle for anything less. And don't feel guilty or embarrassed for being a woman. (See also Chapter 5.)

Hormone replacement therapy (HRT) is another alternative to suffering the severe effects of the menopause. This involves taking regular doses of hormone tablets to replace those lost during the climacteric. This type of tablet does not prevent pregnancy and can only be prescribed by a doctor.

Unfortunately, many GPs are not trained to advise us on HRT, so enquire first before you waste your time with an appointment. Some hospitals (like the national maternity hospital in Holles Street, Dublin) have special clinics for menopausal treatment. HRT is designed to bring you through the change gradually and thereby relieve some discomfort. It is expensive, but is available on the medical card.

If a doctor offers you nerve tablets as a cure for menopausal symptoms, you would be wise to seek another opinion. Tranquillisers do not remedy these feelings.

IS HRT DANGEROUS?

Answers to this question vary. Perhaps it's time we considered why such a natural process should warrant continued use of synthetic hormones. We may ask if there are safer and more natural ways to ease some of the ill-effects of the climacteric? Any drug or hormone treatment needs to be monitored regularly. This holds true for fertility and contraceptive pills. For this reason we are urged to have routine cervical smears, breast exams, and in some cases of HRT, a D&C every two years to inspect the uterine lining (see below).

Long-term risks associated with HRT aren't fully researched. At the same time, oestrogen therapy has a potential for causing cancer. Make sure your doctor takes proper precautions to minimise any health hazards.

HOW IS THE WOMB'S LINING EXAMINED?

Normally this is done in a hospital by a procedure known as D&C (dilation and curettage). To do this, you will be put under a general anaesthetic. The next step is to widen (dilate) the opening of the cervix while the endometrium (lining of the womb) is cleaned out (curettage — 'curetting'). You may feel some cramping afterwards.

Once the uterine lining is removed, it is sent to a laboratory for testing. By doing this every two years, the doctor will be able to keep a close eye on any hormone build-up in the uterus which may lead to disease.

If you take HRT following a hysterectomy, a D&C is not necessary since the uterus has been removed.

CAN I BECOME ADDICTED TO HRT?

Hormones are not addictive. Many doctors even recommend the continued use of hormones following the menopause. In some cases it may reduce the deterioration of bone matter (osteoporosis) and can minimise some of the frailties associated with growing old. All the same, the decision to continue HRT should be made with as much information as possible. Read as much as you can on the subject (No Change by Wendy Cooper is excellent), and talk to other women about their experiences. Armed with this knowledge, you can make an informed choice.

CAN A HYSTERECTOMY CURE THE CHANGE?

Hysterectomy (HIS-TER-ECK-TOE-MEE) is an operation to remove the uterus. Since it is the ovaries which trigger hormonal changes connected to the 'change', this type of surgery will offer no relief. Indeed, if the type of hysterectomy performed includes the removal of the ovaries *(oophorectomy* — OO-FOR-ECK-TOE-MEE), you may actually experience menopausal symptoms earlier than normal. (See p. 124-128).

Doctors don't always explain why they have suggested specific treatment and sometimes they don't give us straight answers in case we worry. At the same time, some of their explanations confuse us. It may be easier for the surgeon to offer one solution over another because s/he is used to providing it. If you are in any doubt about suggested treatment, ask for more time and information, or get a second opinion.

HOW LONG DOES IT TAKE TO COMPLETE THE MENOPAUSE?

Normally, the whole process takes several years. But we all vary and you mustn't worry if a friend's 'change' seems smoother or worse sailing than your own. Discuss your feelings and actively pursue positive health care.

WHAT ABOUT DIET?

We may need to take extra care with our diet as we grow older. Sometimes our appetite diminishes and if we live alone cooking for one becomes less interesting. Eating regular, nutritional meals will entice lazy taste buds and give us energy. We should include foods rich in minerals, vitamins and fibre. Our finances don't have to affect the quality of our diet: beans and lentils can replace meats and are used easily in salads and stews. Liver is inexpensive and provides plenty of iron.

Fibre is even more important as our physical activity becomes restricted. Extra bran added to the diet will stimulate the bowel where previously vigorous exercise did the trick. (See also the section on diet in Chapter 5.)

HOW DO I PREPARE FINANCIALLY FOR RETIREMENT?

If you are looking after other people and not working outside the home, there are certain state benefits to which you are entitled. Chapter 13 will guide you. The Ministry of Women's Affairs has also compiled information for widowed and older women.

If you are planning to retire from paid employment, a talk with your union official or personnel officer may answer many of your questions.

Some companies now offer courses on retirement planning.

It's clear that many women are not eligible for work pensions because some jobs (like cleaning, and child-care) are not seen as work or PRSI/ social security contributions are not deducted from our wages. Much catering work is temporary or seasonal and pensions are not always provided. As long as you pay PRSI, you will be entitled to a state pension. It's important to examine company pensions carefully, as many discriminate against women. Work to have that changed before you retire.

I FIND SHOPPING MORE DIFFICULT. THE BAGS ARE SO HEAVY AND I'M AFRAID OF BEING ROBBED

If shopping is a problem, go some mid-week morning when shops are less crowded. Ask a friend to accompany you, to share the load. Invest in a little trolley for wheeling your parcels. Buy and cook foods which keep for several days so frequent trips out are unnecessary. Salads, coleslaw, potatoes, stews and spaghetti are ideal. Choose snack foods like cheese, wholemeal bread and eggs, which are easy to prepare and contain valuable protein.

Try to eat one hot meal each day. If this is difficult to manage on your own, there are 'meals on wheels' in the community available to anyone who asks for help. These are often arranged through the local church or community centre.

WHAT ABOUT EXERCISE? WON'T IT LEAD TO INJURY?

Some forms of exercise may appear more difficult as we grow older. Some of us never had time to spend on physical development. But the benefits of continued exercise are tremendous: heart and lungs which remain active cut down on our likelihood of heart disease, high blood pressure and hardening of the arteries. The risk of *emphysema* (a lung disease) and *osteoporosis* (brittle bones) is reduced. Increasingly evidence shows that exercise speeds vital nutrients to the skin and muscles, making them more elastic, consequently, they are less likely to suffer from damage.

It's best to start slowly if we have been inactive for some time. See Chapter 5 for more detail. Yoga, walking and swimming are good forms of exercise for older women, but running and other more vigorous activities are also possible.

MY DOCTOR TREATS ME LIKE A SILLY OLD WOMAN WHEN I GO TO HIM ABOUT MY MEDICAL WORRIES. IT'S NEARLY LIKE HE FEELS THEY ARE INEVITABLE. I WORRY ABOUT ALL THE MEDICATION I AM GIVEN

Older women often notice an increase in patronising attitudes from health-care workers. They appear to regard us as senile, vulnerable, asexual and inactive. How often have we heard someone say: 'Isn't she great for her age?' — as if years had anything to do with our ability to function as women? Some older women even find it difficult to get their doctors to listen to sexual worries or gynaecological problems.

It is up to us to make sure that we are treated properly by doctors and that our health is taken seriously. Some of the information detailed in Chapter 10 may help you to cope with the medical world. As far as medication is concerned, it is important to be aware of what we are being prescribed and why. We need to ask if there are any natural, homeopathic or dietary remedies for our problems. We must find out the possible side-effects of medicines and judge whether the benefits outweigh the disadvantages. We must check and recheck that one drug does not interfere with other medication, and we must not let health-care workers prescribe medication simply because they are too busy to discuss our real problems. We may find these issues easier to tackle if we confront our doctor with a friend.

WHAT ABOUT MENTAL HEALTH?
Sometimes keeping mentally fit seems more difficult as we mature. Unplanned retirement, redundancy, poverty, illness, the death of loved ones, separation from partners and confusion over our role as wife or mother, can create stress. To fight against the possible side-effects of these tensions, we need to set new goals, create new interests and engage in social activities which bring us out and broaden our outlook.

At the same time we need to be realistic. Travelling out at night may be more difficult and it may be easier to invite friends in. If you fear going about, take a friend for company. If memory loss proves frustrating and causes anxiety, keep a list of the things you have to do and tick them off as you go along. Set time aside for naps if you tire more easily. Many older women prefer brief cat-naps through the day and night and don't necessarily need eight hours of solid sleep.

Other ways to deal with daily stresses are to eat well and get plenty of exercise. But also, we may need to prepare for living alone. This may mean learning to drive, or teaching ourselves financial and household repair skills. We may need to anticipate the death of a loved one and the possibility of increased costs on less money. Medical and fuel bills may rise and we need to be aware of these possible changes.

We need to involve ourselves in the community, become politically aware, start adult education, or look for work in ordinary or voluntary jobs. We can travel (for free on public transport) and spend time in the library or in museums. There is plenty to do to keep mentally active — relaxation and positive health care will set the ground work.

WHAT ABOUT RELATIONSHIPS?

The greatest way to keep mentally and emotionally fit is to establish close and intimate relationships. This may seem harder as we mature because of ageist stereotypes and conditioning. A lifetime partner may decide to leave, we may separate, or s/he may die. If this happens, we must build new friendships with people we can trust. Sexual needs may be just as great and age should be no bar to enjoying our sexuality as women.

ARE THERE ANY OTHER HEALTH WORRIES I SHOULD BE AWARE OF?

As we grow older, and our bodies age, we may notice changes in our physical abilities. Hearing, sight and mobility may be affected. For some of us, mental confusion is a side-effect of ageing. As women, we may notice bladder and urinary tract problems like incontinence or infections. Kegel exercises (see p. 50) may improve muscle control, while changes in our diet may limit some irritations.

Being aware of our changing bodies can alleviate some of the anxiety which it prompts. Seeking the support of friends and health-care workers can make growing old a positive and rewarding experience.

8. MENTAL HEALTH

When I was eighteen, I visited the doctor because I thought I had leukemia. I tended to bruise a lot right before a period. I was studying for exams at the time and was anxious generally. I've always been a bit of a hypochondriac. The doctor (who had delivered me and knew my family situation well) noted my anxiety, reassured me, and gave me a prescription for valium. I carried that piece of paper around for six months, too scared to fill it in case I became addicted. Finally I tore it up. Ten years later, I attended a therapist for my recurring anxiety. That was four years ago, and with the self-help I've learned, I'm coping well.

'Mental health' is an expression used here to describe our ability to cope with emotional upsets resulting from daily stresses and social conditioning. Poverty, social class, colour, gender (our sex, as in 'male' or 'female'), sexuality, unemployment, illness and personal isolation can contribute to general feelings of tension. Each of us has experienced situations where emotions seem to dominate rational thought or activity. These periods of stress — when everything seems to be on top of us — may last a few days, weeks or years. All of us are able to handle different levels of tension at various stages of our lives. And we do this in our own unique way. Our general state of health, what we eat, how much we can afford to spend on food, how we exercise, physical ability, where we live, our self-esteem and what sort of relationships we form can be crucial factors in helping us to deal effectively with emotional distress.

Isn't it amazing what some women seem to cope with? A barking dog or scurrying mouse may frighten one woman witless, while a bomb-scare leaves her, at least superficially, untouched by 'nerves'. Each of us has been taught by our families and society generally to deal with life's pressures in an individual way. As we grow and develop, we learn that certain objects and circumstances spell danger and that others signify safety.

We find that some behaviour is acceptable and that other behaviour leads to punishment. We then store this information in our subconscious and, as time goes by, we call on memory to handle new stresses. We may use old coping methods based on stereotypes and taboos to deal with new problems, often without ever realising it.

Many of these borrowed coping mechanisms (like temper tantrums, bottling up anger, sulks or crying fits) may no longer be effective in adult situations. Often they mask our rage and mould us into agreeable 'ladies'. They may exhaust us emotionally, be ineffective for expressing our true needs or damage existing self-esteem and relationships. When we are tired or when attempts at communication or understanding fail, increasing tension may result. We may feel frustrated by our apparent inability to cope with life and this may magnify our original worry. Then too, we may question our power to handle adult problems. If our confidence is lowered sufficiently, we may find the difficulty seems insoluble without outside help.

For many of us, brainwashed by the idea that emotional distress is something to hide (in case we seem unsuitable for a particular job, or unable to care for ourselves and our children), we turn, not always to family or friends, but to the relative anonymity of 'professional' outsiders.

As women, we are particularly at risk. All our lives, we have been taught to nurture others. The competent, caring, 'well-balanced' mother figure has been our role model. If we are unable to share the burden of our many responsibilities, or decide to fight against the stereotypical image of woman, the resulting stress may overwhelm us.

Modern social pressures add to the tension: rising unemployment, cramped living conditions, temporary halting sites, lack of access to creche and health-care facilities, isolated and anonymous housing estates, sexual harassment, racism, discrimination at work, violence and sexual assault all contribute to the tension.

It's no wonder we sometimes feel we're going mad. How many of us were trained to deal with the pressures of modern life? So much of our education has been in the area of child-rearing, cookery, cleaning and looking after men in a community environment where we knew and relied on the assistance of neighbours. Rarely have we been taught to deal with the pressure of being a homemaker *and* breadwinner. How many of us learned how to feed a family where the dole money is spent on drink, gambling or drugs? How many of us have been conditioned to live in flats where families fight on all sides and the walls are paper thin? where we depend on the whims of social welfare officers for our next meal or the roof over our head?

How many of us get the support we need to cope with these pressures? How many of us, angered by the injustices of gender role, have been branded 'hysterical' when we look for change and speak out? Do we have role models to emulate for reassurance we are doing a good job?

And when we turn to outsiders for help, how many of us are offered drug therapy to keep us quiet or calm us down instead of counselling and a listening ear? Does social class and our gender as women affect the treatment we receive while experiencing emotional distress? The answer, of course, is yes.

The expression 'superwoman' is bandied about a lot these days. The portrayal of women on television and in advertising might lead us to believe that all women can do all tasks — from washing babies' nappies to working an off-shore oil rig — dressed, of course, in designer swimwear. If we don't match up to these 'accepted', male-imagined standards in our own minds, we may feel deficient in some way. We may be embarrassed to express our feelings or delay seeking help from colleagues, friends and health-care workers. We may be unaware of self-help methods for coping and we may fear the stigma attached to seeking psychotherapy.

It's important to know what we can do for ourselves to avoid some of the stresses that damage our mental health. Equally, we must examine the social/sexist forces which engender our depressive or anxious reactions. By taking a hard look at the way we live, and by accepting that some of the things we do (and some of the things that are done to us) may actually impair our ability to function positively, we may be able to alter self-destructive behaviour. On the other hand there are serious psychological problems (like schizophrenia and manic depression) which may need specialised care. But examining ways to help ourselves will give us the confidence to tackle most everyday psychological problems.

WHAT CAN I DO TO HELP MYSELF?

The best way to avoid emotional ill-health is to actively pursue positive health care. It's important not to allow others to define what are normal and abnormal responses to daily pressures. We must learn to accept feelings of sadness or happiness as part of an ordinary pattern of emotions. It's perfectly normal to be 'up' one day and 'down' the next, depending on events. These moods do not reflect an inability to cope. Equally, it's vital we learn to recognise daily stresses *as they happen* and deal with them accordingly. Eating well, getting enough rest and relaxation, avoiding drugs and chemicals, will keep us physically fit and better able to deal with daily tension.

Mental health is directly related to our physical condition. Quite often we express feelings of tension through bodily reactions, even though we think we are coping well. These symptoms may include headaches, rashes, aches and pains, irritations, spots, pimples, hair loss, nausea, vomiting, shaking limbs, diarrhoea, palpitations and irritability. By noting our reaction to strain, and by tracing what causes physical changes, we may be able to pinpoint and combat the manifestation of stress.

And to reiterate, it's essential we deal with stress as it occurs. If we are angered by our treatment from others, we must express our feelings rather than holding them in. Constructive ways of asserting our needs can be learned from other women. If we find communication impossible, we must learn new methods to express our frustrations or walk away from the stress. Relaxation and exercise are both useful aids in long-term mental health care.

As far as counselling is concerned, women are increasingly looking for alternatives to rigid psychotherapy. They are organising self-help groups or are learning counselling techniques which they can share with others (co-counselling). Examining the common social causes for mental ill-health in a group environment is one way to develop a support network and deal effectively with stress. (See also Chapter 5 for exercise and relaxation aids.)

I THINK I NEED OUTSIDE HELP, BUT I DON'T KNOW WHERE TO START

There are many ways to confront emotional problems and many types of therapy. Recognising stress and working to change the causes may limit our need for outside help. We may want to opt for peer counselling or co-counselling where we feel at an equal level with our counsellor, or we may seek the help of a psychologist or psychiatrist. An opportunity to examine and alter behaviour may appeal to some of us, while deep psychoanalysis is required by others. Modern psychotherapy combines many different helping methods and tailors the treatment to the individual. The more we know about therapies, the better able we are to demand the type we feel will suit us best.

As with all human interaction, not all therapists suit all women. And there are some 'professionals' operating with dubious credentials. Don't be afraid to go elsewhere if you feel the therapy is doing you no good. Ask friends and health-care workers for recommended counsellors. Let the therapist know what you want from the sessions and don't settle for anything less.

WHAT ARE THE DIFFERENCES BETWEEN THE VARIOUS TYPES OF THERAPISTS?

Counsellor This is a person who is trained to counsel but who may not have a university degree or medical qualification. Often, counsellors are trained to deal with specific areas of stress (relationships, sexual assault, violence, pregnancy). They usually try to limit the inequality of the doctor/patient relationship as a necessary part of building the client's self-esteem. Counsellors generally refer the client for specialist care if the need exists.

Clinical psychologist These people are university trained and often work in the area of testing for 'normal' and 'abnormal' behaviour. They do not necessarily have counselling skills. On the other hand, a psychologist may be as qualified in counselling as some psychiatrists — but their emphasis is away from drug therapy.

Psychiatrist This is a medical doctor who is trained in psychology, generally by working in mental hospitals as well as attending lectures. S/he can prescribe drugs and is often attached to the public health-care system. If consulted privately, they are quite expensive.

Social worker This is a person who has taken specific courses in social work at university level. They often work with the family unit and deal with problems by considering social forces at work. Because they are greatly overworked, they are often blamed for inefficiency.

Psychoanalyst Most psychoanalysts are also psychiatrists, although some psychologists have this training too. A psychoanalyst must undergo analysis themselves before they can treat you. Analysis involves examining your personality over a long period of time. It can take several years and is expensive.

How to choose a therapist will depend on your need, where you live, and in some cases, how much you can afford. The Health Boards offer a free service and although the venue may be a psychiatric hospital, and the waiting list long, it is possible to be seen as an out-patient. The service is confidential, and in most cases requires a referral letter from a doctor or health-care worker. In the case of private therapy, allowances are often made for the unwaged, but this is strictly by negotiation. (For example, the Marriage and Family Institute in Dublin has a scale of fees where you choose the category of payment.)

HOW DO I MAKE AN APPOINTMENT WITH THE HEALTH BOARDS? IT'S ALL SUCH A MAZE OF BUREAUCRACY

Knowing who to ring, and where to go with the Health Board system is confusing, causes great stress, and actually puts many of us off seeking help. You may have to ring several hospitals or health clinics before you find someone suitable within your Health Board area. Discussing our worries over the telephone with a faceless voice can be intimidating. It will help if you write down what you want to say before you ring, and have pen and paper handy for jotting addresses and phone numbers down. To avoid some of the anxiety, here are several steps you can follow for better results.

1. Get the name of a therapist, counselling service or local hospital from friends, the mental health association, social workers, teachers, GPs, family planning clinic or women's group. Find out if a referral letter is necessary and who should sign this.

2. Look in the telephone book for your Health Board and ring, asking for the chief psychiatric or medical officer's number.

3. Next, ring the number and ask to speak to her/his secretary. Ask the secretary who is offering the type of service you require in your area. Ask if a referral letter is strictly necessary. If so, have the letter addressed to the counsellor whose name s/he suggests. You may have to briefly explain the type of problem you need help with (anxiety, depression, sexual difficulties, child-guidance, etc.). If you prefer a woman therapist, find out if any are operating in your region.

4. Once you have the name and number of the counsellor, ask around about her/his reputation. If you like what you hear, ring and make an appointment.

It may seem difficult to assert your needs when feeling anxious or depressed. It's important to try in the case of psychotherapy. If you are unhappy with the counsellor, or dislike the treatment, you have the right to see someone else. Don't be afraid of your own judgement. Your feeling of unhappiness is a valid enough reason for change.

IF I GO PRIVATELY, HOW MUCH WILL IT COST?

Private therapy varies in price from about £15 per hour to as much as £45. The average fee is £25 per session. If you see a medical doctor or psychiatrist, the cost is redeemable through voluntary health insurance (VHI or BUPA). At the moment, most medical insurance companies will not accept receipts from counsellors or psychologists. This seems ludicrous, since many of these health-care workers offer drug-free, preventive therapy, which keeps many potential 'patients' out of psychiatric hospitals — in fact reducing insurance costs in the long run.

HOW LONG DOES THERAPY LAST?

This depends on what sort of agreement you make with the counsellor and the type of therapy. For minor degrees of depression or anxiety, as few as five one-hour sessions may leave you feeling able to cope alone. Appointments can be made at weekly, fortnightly, or monthly intervals depending on the problem and the amount of work which needs to be done. You can always return for refresher sessions with the counsellor, even after you decide the therapy has come to an end.

HOW WILL I KNOW WHEN I NEED HELP? I DON'T WANT TO WASTE ANYBODY'S TIME BUT I FEEL THINGS ARE GETTING ON TOP OF ME

The whole purpose of this book is to share self-help and preventive health care. This applies to the broad area of mental health as well. We hear messages coming from all sides which seem to tell us we must be able to cope with every upset on our own if we wish to be seen as an adult. There are those who lead us to believe that emotional distress is something to be ashamed of. Of course this is not the case.

It is important to seek the help of friends, family and health-care workers, *before* things get on top of you. For one thing, it is easier to see a way out of the distress if we are not in the midst of high anxiety or deep depression. Secondly, this will help build our confidence to handle any setbacks.

You are not wasting anybody's time. Indeed, that's what the health-care worker is being paid for, whether by private means or by the state. And most health-care workers find that helping a distressed client is easier when the client comes along *before* she feels snowed under.

CAN I BE COMMITTED TO A MENTAL INSTITUTION BY FORCE?

It is possible for us to be admitted against our will by two medical doctors. You may first be asked to go in voluntarily. This is usually the best option, because you then have the power to release yourself after seventy-two hours.

Don't let the fear of hospitalisation keep you from seeking help. This is not common procedure nowadays, and you generally have a say in whether or not you are placed in hospital care.

WHAT WILL HAPPEN WHEN I FIRST VISIT A COUNSELLOR?

The first session usually takes about an hour and involves identifying the symptoms which led to your seeking help. The counsellor will want to hear what you expect to gain from the therapy. S/he will probably get a general idea of your background by asking questions about your family and personal relationships or any medication you may be taking. Once both of you decide that your needs can be met, further appointments are arranged. In some cases, you may opt for group therapy. This is always done with your approval and is supervised by trained health-care workers.

Modern therapy can help us recognise and alter behaviour that leads to stress. In the sessions, we learn to examine what motivates feelings of anxiety or depression and how to cope with or change the causes. The counsellor can only act as a guide in the best of therapies: the rest is up to you.

WHAT IS DEPRESSION?

Depression is a state of physical, mental and emotional fatigue. Tiredness, sadness, feelings of grief and boredom can leave us more than simply 'down in the dumps'. Depression may manifest itself in tearful outbursts, a desire to stay in bed all day, in difficulties concentrating or with feelings of hopelessness and regret. In extreme cases we may even feel suicidal.

Depression can strike at any time, but is usually the result of a build-up of stress. It may appear after childbirth, or in the first year of marriage or on separation. It may be the result of starting a new job, or losing an old one. We may become depressed through family violence, incest or the death of friends. Repeated work or family pressures, the onset of a disability, serious operations and treatment for cancer, or drug dependency can also contribute to feelings of despair.

We may go through brief periods of depression without the need for outside help, or we may opt for guidance. We must remember that seeking support is a normal, healthy response to depression. Mental distress does not mean we are 'crazy'. There are always reasons for our feelings. Sometimes we need an objective opinion to point them out. Looking for guidance is one step further on the road to recovery.

WHAT IS ANXIETY? WHAT CAUSES IT?

Anxiety is a feeling of fear or dread. It may manifest itself in reactions of panic, tenseness, crying, sweaty palms, a jumpy knotted tummy or palpitations and chest pain. Many of us experience anxiety as the fear of fear itself — a sense of intense foreboding, in the convinced belief that something bad will happen to us if we undertake a particular action. We may be constantly worried about ourselves and about others.

Some of the situations which trigger depression in some of us signal anxious feelings in others. If we focus our anxiety on a particular object or situation, we may develop a phobia: one woman may be frightened to leave the house *(agoraphobia)* or to be in the same room with a dog or cat.

Another woman may fear flying or dislike the idea of confined places (*claustrophobia*).

We can live with some of these fears, and some of them are both healthy and rational. But if panic causes distress, or interferes with our ability to undertake desirable activities, then seeking help may provide relief.

WHAT CAUSES PANIC ATTACKS AND HOW CAN I STOP THEM?

When we are frightened, a chemical called *adrenalin* is produced by a gland in our body. This chemical signals us to either face the dangerous situation or run away. Adrenalin gives us the energy to take life-saving action, like running away from a charging bull or jumping out of the way of a bus. It gives us the courage to challenge an intruder or run to safety.

In modern society, adrenalin is often used daily in stressful situations: attending interviews, talking with social welfare officers, returning damaged purchases, walking down dark streets, queueing for transportation, contending with traffic and noise and fending off attacks of violence. We get used to some of these pressures, but others heighten our sensitivity to stress. If adrenalin builds up over time and isn't discharged, we may end up expending it by screaming at the kids, kicking the dog, having a good cry, or (worse still) bottling it up. Eventually, these combined stresses can lead to anxiety and panic attacks.

As a preventive measure, exercise and relaxation will help you stave off panicky reactions. By releasing adrenalin through physical activity and relaxed, conscious breathing, you will be able to control feelings of anxiety. When you feel an attack coming on, concentrate on relaxation and let the panic come. Remember that panic cannot kill you and that you are in control.

IS THERE ANY WAY TO STOP HYPERVENTILATION?

Hyperventilation means over-breathing. Sometimes in a panic attack, we feel our breath coming so fast and furiously, we are sure a heart attack will follow. There is no danger of this happening, but to control the breathing, try this exercise.

Lie down with your back on the floor. Keep your feet on the floor, but draw your heels up against your buttocks. Now cross your right hand over to your left shoulder and your left hand to your right shoulder. In this position, concentrate on breathing normally. You will find that hyperventilation becomes impossible and that you are forced to take deep breaths from the diaphragm. Knowing you can control this aspect of a panic attack will give you greater confidence.

I FEEL MY PROBLEMS ARE CAUSED BY OUTSIDE EVENTS – YET I KEEP HEARING THAT I SHOULD BE ABLE TO DEAL WITH IT

In many cases, the structure of society and the people we live with lead to distress in our personal lives. Poor housing, inadequate child-care facilities, erratic public transportation, political violence, little or no access to technical or higher education and job opportunities, and literacy difficulties are huge issues often outside our control.

In the home, overcrowding, violence, incest, rape, alcohol and drug addiction cause rational anxiety and depression. We may feel angry and aggressive towards family members because of financial worries, boredom or the unequal assumption of family jobs and responsibilities. We may see our marriage or relationship as a major cause of our distress. We can feel tied down, or disappointed with failed expectations and a mundane job.

Identifying the cause can be done alone, or you may require the help of friends or a local women's group. Communities of women have worked for change in their area by setting up groups to cope with drug addiction, alcoholism, depression and crisis intervention (for violence in the home). Individually you can seek out the aid of established organisations like the Rape Crisis Centre, or Women's Refuge (Family Aid) for temporary relief from the problems. As long as we work together as women and lobby to change these injustices, there is reason to believe we may be getting to the root of much of our problems. (See the directory for relationship counselling, adult literacy programmes, drug addiction therapy, etc.)

MY DOCTOR GAVE ME TRANQUILLISERS FOR POST-NATAL DEPRESSION. IS THERE ANY OTHER HELP AVAILABLE?

Post-natal depression can be caused by hormonal changes following childbirth, or by the new and exhausting responsibilities of motherhood. Mention your feelings to the visiting nurse if they haven't cleared once you get home. If the depression persists, it's important to discuss the matter further. 'Nerve tablets' do not cure post-natal depression on their own, but talking to friends, or health-care workers will help.

Distress following an abortion may also lead to depression. Reasons for this include feelings of isolation, of having no one to confide in. There may be confusion over the choice, relationship problems or religious worries. Pregnancy counsellors offer a comprehensive service.

I NEVER WANTED SO MANY CHILDREN. SOMETIMES I GET SO ANGRY, I BEAT THEM. IT FRIGHTENS ME

It's very hard sometimes to find non-destructive ways to vent our anger. Lack of money, rows, anxiety and the constant pressure of daily living can lead us to strike out against the people we are closest to. Because we have been taught that a loving mother is the 'norm', we become confused by the force of anger and hurt being trapped with children generates. Often we feel little love for a screaming child and our patience is pushed to breaking. Once we hit out, it may seem difficult to gather courage and seek help unless we are prepared to break the stereotypical image of motherhood. Feelings of guilt often hold us back — how could we have done this to our own flesh and blood?

If you feel the urge to batter your child, or live with someone who does, there are crisis services and refuges which offer help. They will be able to see you through the immediate difficulty and help you find ways to change the things which provoke a violent reaction.

It's also important to remember that you are not necessarily a violent person, but that circumstances have provoked your response to stress. Situations can create anger and frustration. We need to learn positive ways to deal with these feelings.

DRUGS AND MENTAL HEALTH

> *I tried smack (heroin) when I was thirteen. Everyone in the flats were doin' it. I tried glue before but it made me sick.*

> *My doctor told me I had a chemical depression following my last baby. I took tranquillisers for three years until I wasn't myself any more. I joined a group to come off them . . . it was bloody hard, but I did it. Some of the other women gave up.*

Too many of us are offered drug therapy instead of counselling or guides to self-help. Many of us become addicted to the chemicals we ingest. 'Nerve' tablets (tranquillisers) are widely prescribed by doctors. We dose ourselves with alcohol, nicotine and 'over the counter' medication for relaxation. Our first use of addictive substances may come through social activity, or as temporary medical treatment until the doctor feels we are ready to discuss the problem 'rationally'.

Many doctors feel cases of schizophrenia and manic depression, can only be successfully 'controlled' with drug therapy. Alternative health-care workers question who it makes the control easy for, the doctor or the patient? The arguments for and against are heated. It is important that we educate ourselves about drugs: their use and their side-effects, so we can make a conscious decision about using them or not.

Many of us are beginning to see that the use of mind-altering drugs, like tranquillisers, alcohol, marijuana, nicotine, glue and heroin either quietens us down when we express anger about injustices, or helps us to turn that anger inwards. Addiction to chemicals is not a conscious act. It happens over time through habit. The tablets or liquids help us quench the pain of modern living, but they offer no cures.

I fell into the trap quite by accident. I worked in a so-called 'high-powered' job and was constantly in demand at home and in the office. I began skipping lunch breaks and working late because I wanted a promotion within the firm. A friend of mine gave me diet pills when I told her I needed to be alert for a meeting. I then made the rounds of doctors feigning a weight problem. Before I knew it, I was hooked to the damn things.

I used to light up a cigarette every time I had to confront some uncomfortable situation. Eventually, I grew used to them as soothers and even the thought of giving them up filled me with anxiety.

My parents fought all the time and my father spent most of his money on drink. As a teenager, I would sneak some of the whisky and water down the remainder of the bottle so he wouldn't know. It meant I fell asleep happy and ignorant of the rows – that

*is until I couldn't do without the bottle
myself.*

WHAT ARE TRANQUILLISERS?

These are chemical medicines, usually in tablet form, which are meant to induce a feeling of tranquillity and peace when taken during times of stress. Those of us who attend the doctor to discuss health worries are often prescribed tranquillisers as a temporary measure — to see us through a 'bad patch'. Sometimes this helps by giving us a few days of rest. In more cases than not, the causes of our stress remain unchanged, but we accept them, feeling dopey, less worried and unable to deal effectively with the real problems.

Sometimes, ignoring our worries through a haze of tranquillity is easier. We may renew our prescription until the body can no longer function without the drugs. If we try to withdraw from the medication, we may experience a backlog of acute anxiety or depression

Chemical names to be wary of are: diazapem (valium), chlordiazepoxide (librium), lorazepam (ativan), nitrazepam (mogodon), flurazepam (dalmane), bromazepam and clorazepate.

I FIND IT DIFFICULT COMMUNICATING WITH MY DOCTOR AND AM SOMETIMES AFRAID TO ASK ABOUT WHAT IS BEING PRESCRIBED

Our feelings of vulnerability when we seek the help of a health-care worker often colour the way we receive information. It's a good idea to take a friend along to sit through the first session with you. This way any confusion can be cleared up with someone you trust.

When you go to make an appointment, be sure to tell the receptionist that you will require a longer than usual appointment — that you want to *talk* to the doctor. Tell the doctor you are *not* interested in drug therapy if this is the case. If s/he still feels it's necessary, and you agree, find out what you are being prescribed, its side-effects, and its addictive properties. Ask the doctor to write down the name of the drug for you. Here are some of the most commonly prescribed types of medication.

Tranquillisers Often called 'nerve tablets' these may be prescribed (quite wrongly) for menopause and pre-menstrual syndrome (see p. 27 & 70). The most commonly prescribed tablet is *Valium.* It can be addictive. Women who take tranquillisers over a long period note a decrease in sexual interest, skin rashes, fatigue, nausea, constipation and irregular periods.

Self-help methods for withdrawing are currently based on vitamin supplements and group work. Get help if you need to come off — you are not alone.

Sleeping tablets These are often barbiturates and are extremely addictive. Because users may acquire an immunity to lower doses, and consequently up their intake to curb insomnia, these tablets have a greater incidence of overdose connected to their use.

Other, non-barbiturate sleeping tablets can lead to physical dependency, headaches and feelings of being hungover. This type of medication may be dangerous when mixed with alcohol.

Anti-depressants Often given in 'chemical' depression, these tablets can take several weeks to show results. Side-effects include constipation, fluid retention, weight gain and blurred vision. Valium is not an anti-depressant.

Diet pills Can be addictive and have numerous side-effects including, dry mouth, gastro-intestinal (stomach) and skin problems, anxiety, insomnia, dizziness, aggression and sweating.

MY DOCTOR GAVE ME NERVE TABLETS. THEY HELPED FOR A WHILE, BUT NOW I WANT TO COME OFF AND AM FINDING IT DIFFICULT

Some GPs are too busy to listen to our problems within surgery hours. If you are offered tranquillisers, which you don't want, or if you are referred to someone who offers only drug therapy, it is essential you make your needs clear. If the doctor ignores you, it's time to go elsewhere.

Some of the Health Boards are working on inadequate funds and the staff are overstretched for time. They may suggest drug treatment as a 'band-aid service' until they have time to talk to you. This really isn't good enough. Drugs may only mask the problem and can be addictive. Delays in counselling will only undermine your attempts at self-help. Speak up and speak out if this happens to you. Tranquillisers will keep you quiet, when what you need to do is talk.

IS THERE ANY HELP FOR WITHDRAWING FROM NERVE TABLETS?

Most of the large country hospitals will help you to come off any drug through detoxification. 'Detox', as it is called, means that your body is cleansed of poisonous (toxic) chemicals. Increasingly, there are self-help support groups organised to help sever dependency on drugs without going into hospital. Ultimately, the decision to withdraw is yours. Going through detoxification means waiting until the drugs have time to flush completely out of your system. The procedure is generally painful and unpleasant. Symptoms include fever, vomiting, diarrhoea, cramps and chills. The process doesn't cure an addiction, but does begin the practice of life without drugs. Remember, you don't have to do it alone.

Jervis Street Hospital in Dublin has a special unit for drug users. You can be referred or simply walk into casualty. If you feel group work, a community support service or individual therapy would suit you better, consult the directory for details of services.

WILL MY ADDICTION HURT MY BABY?

If you take *any* drugs within the first three months of pregnancy, the foetus (developing baby) may be damaged. This includes wine, beer, aspirin and hormone therapy. In the case of heroin use, the baby may be born with an addiction of its own.

WILL DIET PILLS HARM ME?

Diet pills obtained on prescription act like amphetamines or 'uppers' and can be addictive. They characteristically leave the mouth dry and erase the appetite. They can make you feel more energetic, but once they wear off, depression can result. They are not good for you and can damage your health.

WHAT OTHER DRUGS ARE HARMFUL?

Heroin addiction leads to digestive, bowel and kidney problems. Resistance to disease is considerably lowered and heroin can eventually kill you. Glue and cocaine-sniffing damage the nasal passages. Many drugs have potentially brain damaging properties.

I FEEL MY DEPRESSION IS LEADING ME TO DRINK

More women than ever before are turning to drink, tobacco and other drugs to numb the senses and keep anxiety or depression at bay. And is it any wonder? Advertising suggests that the sophisticated, successful 'superwoman' is glamorous simply because she drinks champagne and smokes long cigarettes.

Then too, we may not always recognise the danger signals: drinking to excess alone, missing work on a regular basis because of hangovers, hiding our drinking habits from friends, blackouts and spending too much of our time and money in pubs. Once we identify these factors, we have tackled a major barrier in effecting change.

Alcohol, when drunk in small quantities can be pleasant and relaxing. But it is important to remember that over the long term, if abused, alcohol can lead to brain damage, muscle disease, liver and heart problems, stroke and gastro-intestinal (stomach) disorders. Many women notice they break out with thrush (see p. 198) following a night of drinking. Bear in mind also that alcohol may affect the development of a foetus during pregnancy.

Groups and individual therapy to deal with the addiction may be found in the directory

I'M FINDING IT TOO HARD TO GIVE UP SMOKING

Tobacco, because it contains nicotine, is addictive. We all smoke for different reasons: boredom, reward, tension and to curb the appetite. Once you identify what triggers the desire to smoke, giving them up will be easier. Try to substitute another healthy activity for the smoking one. Conscious relaxation (see p. 45) or exercise can help. When the desire to smoke seems overwhelming, try running on the spot for a count of fifty, or practising relaxation.

There are products like nicotine chewing gum which are designed to aid the process of giving up, but they won't curb the need. Herbal cigarettes have helped many, but 'cold turkey' seems the most successful method.

This means you must stop smoking immediately and forever. It helps to prepare in advance by reading up on the subject and avoiding situations like pub meetings where you feel under temptation.

Some women try acupuncture and hypnotism, but unless a certain amount of will power exists, these methods have very little effect.

MY PARTNER SMOKES. WILL THIS AFFECT MY HEALTH?

Yes, smoking can affect non-smokers. This means partners, children and a developing foetus. Smoking can also affect fertility.

IS IT TRUE THAT COFFEE CONTAINS DRUGS?

Coffee contains caffeine, a chemical stimulant. If used too much, it can lead to health problems like nervousness, irritability, pre-menstrual syndrome, kidney disorders and fluid retention.

Some soft drinks also contain this ingredient and diet drinks include some chemical additives which remain relatively untested as far as long-term side-effects are concerned.

9. VIOLENCE AGAINST WOMEN

I had been out drinking with some girl friends. We always went to the same pub on a Saturday night and hung around with the same crowd. There was a fellow I had seen there several times, and when he asked me if I'd like a lift home I said yes. On the way to his car – I later found out he had none – he attacked me. I never had sex before. The trial was two years later, and of course he got off.

My parents had a farm down the country. There was this man who used to live in and help out with the chores. He used to make me touch him when my mother was out, and he said he'd kill me if I told. From the time I was nine, I lived in fear of the things he would do to me. I never told any one until I was twenty-six and had a sort of nervous breakdown.

My husband used to bring home a friend when they were drunk. Often he would beat me up in front of the children and then he and the friend would take turns raping me. Once he put a plastic bag over my head . . . I nearly suffocated.

Physical violence and the threat of physical violence constitute major health hazards for women. Violence against women is the natural extension of society's oppression of women. To 'keep us in our place', men exert control through physical abuse. How many of us have been intimidated by the building site jeers, the pub lecher, the group of lads who follow us home 'for the crack'? And when we arrive home, how many of us have to account for our whereabouts? Do we get a slap for talking back, or a kick for questioning male authority? How many of us submit to sexual contact not because we want to, but because we are afraid what will happen to us if we don't?

In the last ten years, women have begun to fight back singly and in groups. Rape crisis centres, hostels for battered women, and the Sanctuary Trust, for incest survivors, have been set up by committed women on the basis of self-help — in an effort to regain lost control. Women working together are examining what causes violence and are trying to re-educate a social attitude which views woman as helpless victim — a receptacle of men's rage and inadequacies.

THE EXCUSES AND THE MYTHS

Until the 1970s most crimes of violence against women were kept quiet in Ireland. Rape statistics were scant, wife-beating was a way of life, and incest or child abuse was thought impossible in a Catholic country. If rape did occur, society concurred that the women must have 'asked for it' by her lifestyle, her mode of dress and the company she kept. It was easy to regard the attacked women as a weak or submissive victim rather than a strong survivor of physical abuse. It suited society's vision of woman as property and chattel. But no more: the myths are being exploded, the excuses ignored. Women are challenging old assumptions. These include:

The abuser
• He must be mentally ill
• He was only gratifying a sexual urge
• He says she wanted it
• He's only acting the lad
• His wife provokes it: she's a frigid bitch

The survivor
• It's her duty as his wife
• She led him on; she really wanted it
• Look at the way she dresses — she's asking for trouble

- She got paid to pose, she must enjoy it
- She was giving off sexual vibrations
- She made the whole thing up

FIGHT BACK

In the past, we have learned that to avoid violence, we must alter *our* behaviour, that in some way, we were at fault. We have been warned NOT to wear certain clothing, NOT to venture out at particular times, NOT to travel alone, NOT to fight back. This suggests that women have provoked the violence done to them. This simply isn't true, but it is a useful social tool for keeping women out of the workplace, out of the pub and out of male-dominated society generally.

Violence acts by creating an atmosphere of fear. This fear manipulates our behaviour and helps to perpetuate the male hierarchy. Each individual act of violence contributes to the whole. We may hear of one woman's rape and avoid the area where it happened (forgetting that most attacks occur in the home by people we know). We avoid certain employment or entertainment because of the sexual harassment involved. We curtail our activities to keep a watch on our children. The violence succeeds because it 'keeps us in our place'.

We no longer have to accept these restrictions, difficult as they may seem to break. We *can* live alone, we *can* travel freely, we *can* fight back against oppression if we equip ourselves with confidence and a sense of personal autonomy. At the same time, there are things we can do to minimise the threat of violence, and angry as we may be at having to protect ourselves, they are options we may find useful.

1. If the violence comes from a partner, get legal advice (see AIM) before vacating the family home. A barring order, which may block your partner's access, will help your chances in securing a share in the property.

2. To keep abusers out of the house, keep windows locked and porch lights on at night. Put heavy locks on all doors. Use only your initial and last name on the letterbox and in the telephone book.

3. Organise a neighbourhood watch or a woman friend to whom you can turn in emergencies.

4. Buy a peephole for the door or a heavy chain and never let strangers into the house. Always check identification before letting ESB or gas men in. When in doubt, say no. Some of us call out 'I'll be right back Tom (or Bob, or Mick), I'm just answering the door,' before we open it.

5. When out and about, stay alert and aware of your surroundings. Walk confidently. Avoid isolated spots.

6. Dress for comfort of movement, so you can escape more easily.
7. Check that taxi drivers really are taxi drivers and never get into one where there is more than one man. Sit in the back seat and make sure you know how to open the door straight away.
8. Keep your own car doors locked when you are driving and don't pick up male hitch-hikers on your own.
9. Carry a whistle and blow it when under threat. Or scream FIRE when attacked. (If you shout RAPE it may just frighten people away)

SHOULD I FIGHT BACK PHYSICALLY?

This is a contentious issue among women. Some of us find that self-defence gives us confidence to ward off some types of physical abuse, but there are other women who feel it may further provoke a violent reaction.

If you decide quite spontaneously to resist an attack, the element of surprise may be your best defence. A scream, or some other distraction may give you time to run away or call for help. If you decide to hit out, concentrate on sensitive spots, like the shins, genitals and eyes.

RAPE

The legal definition of rape is severely limited: it is 'unlawful sexual intercourse without a woman's consent'. This narrow interpretation excludes vaginal penetration by bottles, broom-handles, fists as well as buggery (anal intercourse) and forced oral sex. And of course, as viewed by men, this definition of rape makes sense: for what could possibly hold more power than the male penis?

In practice, rape has been difficult to prove. The jury must be convinced 'beyond all reasonable doubt' that the woman's version of the story is true and the man's is false. Often as not, defence lawyers choose a predominantly male jury to ensure a verdict in favour of the man. And since rape is one of the few crimes which may warrant a lengthy sentence, few (predominantly male) judges can see their way to recommending a guilty verdict. Time and time again, therefore, rape pleas are reduced to the more acceptable and less contentious charge of 'sexual assault'. Furthermore, because rape laws were developed primarily to protect woman, not for her own sake, but as man's property, rape within marriage is not recognised as rape in Irish law.

WHAT SHOULD I DO IF I HAVE BEEN RAPED?
1. Go to a safe place and look for help. Don't be afraid or ashamed. You are not at fault and you may need medical attention. If you are injured and

unable to get out of the house, ring or send a friend.

2. If you live near Dublin, the Sexual Assault Unit in the Rotunda Hospital, Parnell Square (tel. 748111) can see you immediately. If you are in danger, ring 999 and ask for the police. Or ring one of the Rape Crisis services.

In the Sexual Assault Unit a woman doctor and nurse will be on call to meet your needs at any time of the day or night. If you decide to report the rape to the police, a ban garda will be called in to witness your examination and take your statement. This will include an internal check-up, a record of any scratches, bruises and broken bones, samples of hair, nail scrapings and saliva and the clothes you were wearing at the time of the attack. Therefore, *it is vital you do not wash yourself or your clothes before contacting the police.*

3. If you decide not to make a charge against your assailant, it is still important to have a medical screening for injury and sexually transmitted diseases. It may take up to three weeks following the attack for traces of the latter to be evident. A 'morning-after' pill can be given by your own doctor or in the Assault Unit and may prevent pregnancy. IT MUST BE TAKEN WITHIN SIXTY HOURS OF THE ATTACK. If you know of no-one to prescribe this medication locally, ring one of the larger family planning clinics for help immediately.

4. If you decide to make a charge, the police will ask you for a statement, 'in your own words'. You are entitled to have a friend or Rape Crisis Centre counsellor with you for this procedure. Sometimes they can help you decipher some of the legal jargon used by the police.

Once the attack is reported to the police, a file will be compiled for the Director of Public Prosecutions (DPP) before the case can come to trial. This can take as long as two years. Since you are only considered as the state's chief witness (women being viewed as property), you will have little say in the way the case proceeds. Talking this over with a Rape Crisis Centre counsellor will help you to understand all the implications.

Until recently, a woman was able to claim for criminal injuries in the case of rape. In 1986, the government announced the abolition of this provision, making rape a crime of little importance.

If the case goes to court, your past sexual history may be used in evidence with the judge's discretion. If you take the witness box, you will be forced to face the rapist and his friends. You will not always meet the legal people who are acting on your behalf.

IS IT POSSIBLE TO GET PREGNANT FROM A RAPE?

Yes. Somewhere along the line, a myth developed that pregnancy was impossible in cases of sexual assault. The Dublin Rape Crisis Centre's 1984 report recorded that ten per cent of their clients who were too late for 'morning-after' contraception were subsequently shown to have positive pregnancy test results.

If you find that you are pregnant following an attack and wish to discuss your options, the directory will guide you towards pregnancy counselling.

I FEEL SO CONFUSED AND JUMPY SINCE THE ATTACK.
MY FAMILY DON'T SEEM TO UNDERSTAND.
IS THIS NORMAL?
Common reactions to rape include anxiety, depression, panic attacks, bouts of 'seeing' the attacker, nightmares, feelings of distrust, lethargy, anger, aggression, irritability, crying, sexual difficulties, guilt, self-blame, humiliation, fear of being alone or with men and an alteration in our dress and activities.

Family and friends often do not understand the profound effect rape can have on your life. They may suggest you 'snap out of it' because they are finding it difficult to cope. It is important to bear in mind that our fears are rational and the stress we may feel can be alleviated with self- or outside help. It may be impossible to put a rape or assault out of your mind forever, but over time, your ability to cope can improve. This takes time and patience. It may help your friends to seek counselling too.

MY PARTNER FORCES ME TO HAVE SEX WHEN HE'S
DRINKING
If anyone forces you to have sex against your will, whether married or living together, then this is an act of rape, although this interpretation is not yet legally recognised. Remember, you don't have to put up with such abuse. And you don't have to accept drink or drugs as an excuse. There are agencies which can offer you refuge and help. Sometimes we depend financially and emotionally on our attacker, and severing ties may appear insurmountable. You can escape violence in the home by seeking the support of others.

CHILD SEXUAL ABUSE

The choice of 'child sexual abuse' in preference to the legal term 'incest' is used here deliberately. Although a feminist definition of incest would include any sexual violation of a minor by a person in a position of trust (usually an adult male), the law confines its interpretation of incest to sexual contact — generally intercourse — between blood relatives. This would exclude step-fathers, step-brothers, unmarried partners of the mother, school teachers, social workers, doctors, house-parents and priests.

Child sexual abuse is another extension of male power. In 1984, 152 cases of child sexual abuse were reported to the Dublin Rape Crisis Centre. The 1985 statistics will illustrate an unprecedented increase in reported cases (due in some instances to the Sexual Assault Unit and a publicity campaign highlighting the problem).

Child sexual abuse is more common than we would like to admit. Moreover, it illustrates quite clearly how sexual abuse is perpetuated using fear as the controlling mechanism. How many of us were warned 'Don't tell, or I'll get you'? How many of us have ever been taught that it is permissible to say no to an adult? How many of us have turned for help and had our pleas ignored? How many of us have approached a neighbour or friend to find that we weren't believed or they didn't want to interfere? How many of us have closed our minds to child sexual abuse, because we wrongly believed that a child is the property of her/his parent?

The answers are 'many' and for diverse reasons including education, conditioning and society's view of the nuclear family. The myths that colour our perception of child sexual abuse are untrue, but they help to prevent us from facing reality.

FACTS ABOUT CHILD SEXUAL ABUSE

The facts are:
- Child sexual abuse is a reality
- Children do not lie about sexual abuse
- Children do not ask for sex
- Children have their trust in adults abused
- Child sexual abuse and incest are criminal offences
- We do not own our children
- Mothers don't naturally collude with the abuser
- Child sexual abuse is not confined to one social class
- The overwhelming majority of child sexual abuse is perpetrated by men
- Child sexual abusers are not mentally ill
- Mothers of children who are sexually abused are not at fault

WHERE CAN I GO FOR HELP?
Both incest and child sexual abuse are currently being treated in the Sexual Assault Unit in the Rotunda Hospital (in the case of emergencies) and by Rape Crisis services or by other groups working with the survivors. A new organisation called the Sanctuary Trust plans to offer counselling and ongoing care for victims of abuse. For immediate accommodation, hostels and refuges are listed in the directory, or you may have a friend or

neighbour who will listen to your story and take action.

WHAT HAPPENS IF I SEEK THE HELP OF ONE OF THESE GROUPS?

Initially they will offer you a counselling service and/or accommodation. If you decide to press charges, they will follow the procedures outlined under the rape section. In the case of a pre-school child, much of the information is gathered over several sessions using dolls and games. Sometimes children are examined under anaesthetic so the trauma is lessened.

WILL THE FAMILY BE SEPARATED?

If the abuser lives in the family home, it is possible that he will be separated from the children. Counselling is vital if this happens, because the abused child often feels tremendously guilty, thinking that she caused the break-up. She must be reassured that it was the behaviour of the abuser which led to the separation.

I WAS RAPED WHEN I WAS TWELVE AND HAVEN'T WANTED A SEXUAL RELATIONSHIP SINCE

This is a normal reaction to a violent assault. Quite naturally, we may harbour feelings of anger and distrust concerning relationships with men. It can be difficult building any sort of contact when violence forms the basis of our sexual experience. No-one willingly chooses to remind themselves of past horrors, and the sexual act may spark off unpleasant or frightening memories. Sometimes we stop short of seeking help because we fear other people's reactions. Rape Crisis Centre counsellors are familiar with your feelings and are there to help.

I HAD SEX WITH MY FATHER FOR OVER A YEAR. I'M SO DISGUSTED WITH MYSELF

Many of us blame ourselves for sexual abuse. It is sometimes easier to cope with the idea that we are responsible for the violence inflicted on us. Otherwise, how could we continue to live in the same house with the abuser? Indeed, in some cases, sexual abuse is the only physical contact we receive from a parent whose affection we crave.

And as we grow older, we judge our childish needs and behaviour with adult eyes. We forget that to disobey Daddy or Uncle Pat was a punishable offence, that we were warned never to tell. We may feel frustrated anger because Mammy didn't know that our bed-wetting and running away were reactions of stress and anxiety. We blame ourselves because we are too angry and too afraid to blame the real culprit — a person we loved.

Crisis centres will be able to help you. It doesn't matter whether the assault took place yesterday or ten years ago.

I THINK MY DAUGHTER IS BEING ABUSED.
WHAT SHOULD I DO?
Ask her directly, but do so in a reassuring and safe way that lets her know she is not at fault. Use words that she understands and let her know she will not be punished. When you find out who is doing the abusing, seek help from the Rape Crisis Centre about how to deal with the situation. If intercourse has taken place, whether vaginally or anally, your daughter will need a medical examination for injuries and sexually transmitted disease. Counselling will also help you to cope with the situation.

As a preventive measure, we must start teaching our children that they can say no to adults and that their bodies are for themselves alone unless, as adults, they decide to share them. We must listen to what children say and try to build an atmosphere of trust where open communication is possible.

BATTERY

Physical violence which seeks to control us in our own home is called battery. Sometimes this violence extends to the use of weapons like brooms, pokers, glasses, bottles and even shotguns. Neighbours may be reluctant to interfere and barring orders may prove hard to enforce. Since women are viewed as men's property, society accepts woman abuse as a logical extension of male power. Violence becomes a learned response for many men: they see their own father beat their mother and assume this is 'normal' behaviour. The problem is made worse because we often depend on our partner or father for the food we eat and the roof over our head.

We may live in hope that their violent reactions might dissolve, but more often than not, this simply doesn't happen. And because their control over us has been so absolute (and our fear so great) we question our ability to escape, to face life without violence. How will we earn money? Will we lose the family home? Will the children suffer without a male role model? Sometimes our fear of coping alone is far greater than the fear of beating. How do we break the cycle of abuse?

Initially, we may feel escape is impossible. We get little help or reassurance from family and friends that separation is an acceptable alternative. Social pressures urge us to 'stick it out', to work on the relationship. But this is impossible if the abuser refuses to seek help. Once our demands in this area are ignored, we may have no option but to leave the situation if we want to protect our life and self-respect.

WHAT SHOULD I DO IF I AM BATTERED?
Try to protect yourself with your arms and legs. The most vulnerable areas are the tummy and head. If at all possible, leave the house or send one of the children for help. Don't fight back unless you feel you have a chance of success. Instead, focus your mind on escaping the abuse as soon as you can. Call the police or a crisis service for assistance if you are too badly injured to move.

Remember above all else that you do have other options beside sharing the house with a man of violence and there are many groups who can help you to find the way.

SEXUAL HARASSMENT

> *I worked as a waitress and every time I would go into the pantry, the manager would lock me in with him. He used to tease me and tickle me, thinking this was a great game, but I was frightened. I finally left, I couldn't bear him near me.*

> *In our local, the ladies' toilet is in the bar, not the lounge. Every time I walk through there, I get slagged and jeered. Some of these fellas I've known since school.*

Sexual harassment is a form of physical or verbal abuse designed to humiliate and embarrass women. Ultimately, it is yet another way men seek to impose their control over our behaviour. Harassment in the workplace is the most recently publicised occupational stress, but sexual intimidation and innuendo occurs in the street, the pub, at parties and on public transport. Its aim is to make us as uncomfortable as possible for involving ourselves in a 'man's world'. Its expression is often camouflaged beneath teasing and 'good humour'.

Harassment may come from your employer, a company client, a bus driver, a co-worker, a supervisor, a teacher or a clergyman. It may show itself in suggestions, intimate touching or direct sexual proposition and assault. We don't have to put up with sexual harassment. Being vocal about the reality of harassment will help other women and perhaps re-educate a few men.

HOW CAN I COPE WITH SEXUAL HARASSMENT AT WORK?
1. Keep a record of the harassment, noting time, date, the gist of the conversation and any physical contact. If witnesses are present, take down their name or ask them to help you.
2. Be aware of some of the warning signs which precede harassment: a locked door, someone taking the telephone off the hook, staff being sent out of the room on messages. These may be your cues to take action.
3. Build up a support network with women colleagues. Work together as a team, and make your complaint together. A band of women is less likely to be ignored.
4. Tell the harasser loudly and clearly in front of witnesses that his behaviour must stop.
5. Talk to your union official or personnel officer. If this doesn't work, get in touch with the Employment Equality Agency for advice or seek the help of a local women's group.
6. Talk about sexual harassment generally. This will act to educate your co-workers and create a climate where women who have been abused feel safe to speak out.
7. Remember that sexual harassment is illegal and you have recourse through the law.

WHAT ABOUT PUBLIC HARASSMENT?
The approach you take in dealing with public harassment may vary according to the particular situation. In a pub, bar staff will often assist you in warding off harassers. Public employees (busmen, road workers, etc.) can be reported to the appropriate personnel department. Building site labourers can be dealt with through their employers. Sometimes a group of women's names on a letter works better than a single signature. But be wary about tackling a group of men face to face.

Sometimes, however, explaining that the harasser's behaviour is offensive will make him think twice before doing it again. You will need to weigh up whether the stress of confrontation is worth the effort.

PORNOGRAPHY

Pornography, translated from the Greek, means 'the writing of whores'. Defined and perpetuated by men, it has become a thriving business which degrades our sensibilities with a wholly male view of sexuality. There can be no subtle distinctions between soft and hard core — all pornography is an abasement of women. Research verifies what we already know: that pornography provokes violence; that pornography *is* violence against women.

While the more brutal forms of pornography are as yet unavailable in the south of Ireland, the increase in video film traffic and sexist advertising gives enough cause for alarm. The aim of all pornography is the same: to control women by viewing them only in the context of their bodily parts. As propaganda, pornography is highly successful. How many of us used to think there was something perverted in the *women* who posed for money rather than the men who controlled the publicity machines? How many of us refuse to acknowledge that women pose for pornography because they have been taught that this is all they are suitable for — or because they are supporting a drug habit, or because they are forced to pose by pimps?

That Irish culture allows women to be promoted in a sexist and pornographic manner precisely reflects how women are viewed in Irish society today. Pornography acts as an accurate mirror of a culture where woman's role is seen only in terms of her use as a sexual commodity.

SOMEONE IN OUR OFFICE IS SENDING PORNOGRAPHY THROUGH THE POST TO THE WOMEN WORKERS. IS THERE ANYTHING WE CAN DO?

This is a very subtle form of sexual harassment and there are a few things you may want to know before you proceed against the offender:

1.   Unsolicited pornography sent through the post is a criminal offence. The definition of pornography may depend on the perceptions of the recipient.

2.   If you know who the culprit is, you may be able to take a legal case as well as one of sexual harrassment. Letting them know this may halt further activity.

3.   If you don't want to take a case, tell your union official or personnel officer of the problem. Keep the offensive material in case you decide later to charge the individual.

4.   Band together with your co-workers to stop this type of harassment.

5.   There is an organisation called CASE which is campaigning for reform in the area of pornography legislation. They may be able to offer further advice. They are listed in the directory.

10. SOME COMMON HEALTH WORRIES

THE DOCTOR

Every once in a while, if we are worried about our health, we may seek the help of a doctor. We may find a suspicious lump or vaginal discharge. Or we may be pregnant, suffer an injury or need contraceptive advice. Knowing what to expect when we visit a doctor's surgery will increase our confidence and give us control over what happens there. If we feel nervous, we can take a friend along. If we are confused by the doctor's language, we can ask her/him to write down medical terms, or speak to us in plain English. We can make a list of our concerns so we don't forget vital questions, and we can ask the doctor to write our her/his reply so we can review it calmly at home.

WHAT TO WEAR

If we plan a visit to the doctor, we may feel more confident if we dress for the occasion. This means wearing a skirt so we don't have to undress for gynaecological (internal and vaginal) examinations. We can simply pull up our clothes when the time comes. If we anticipate a breast exam, we can wear a button-down blouse so we don't have to undress completely.

During the check-up, we can ask for a blanket to cover exposed parts. Equally, we can request to see the procedure and remove any covering. We can ask for someone to be present in the same room with us during the examination and bring a friend into the surgery if the doctor is a man and doesn't have a woman assistant.

You can teach yourself many of the procedures the doctor uses by consulting the self-help section of this book. Simple techniques like breast examination and checking daily vaginal discharges will provide an accurate picture of your changing health and fertility.

HOW TO ORGANISE A DOCTOR

Part of the code of medical 'ethics' involves not allowing doctors to advertise their services. This is meant to protect the public at large from charlatans, but in fact keeps women ignorant of who can best serve us. So how do we organise ourselves with a doctor who understands our needs as women?

If we are medical card holders, our choice is limited. Each area Health Board circulates a list of doctors including a contact address and telephone number. This list tells us nothing about the doctor's services. We may find the doctor we attend refuses to prescribe contraception for 'moral' reasons, and for us this means the hassle of changing to one who will. It can be a long-drawn-out process of trial and error. One way around this is to contact family planning clinics and friends for names of sympathetic GPs. Alternatively, many family planning clinics will see you for a reduced fee (generally £4 or £5) if you present a medical card. They will absorb the cost themselves. In northern areas, family planning clinics offer a free service.

If you decide to go privately, ring first and check that the doctor you choose offers a wide range of services. This may include infection screening, ante-natal care, counselling and contraceptive advice.

FEES FOR PRIVATE HEALTH CARE

Doctors charge anywhere from £6 to £25 for a consultation depending on the service they are giving and any related lab tests. Below is an approximate scale of costs:

Consultation with a gynaecologist	£25
Check-up with GP (including smear, breast exam, blood pressure, rubella vaccination or screening)	£9
Pregnancy test (these are free in hospitals and in northern family planning clinics)	£5
Ante-natal visits with GP (if the doctor is involved in the joint scheme with the hospital services)	free
Infection screening	£10-£30

VHI will cover all except contraception.

SERVICES

All the tests and services detailed in this section are free and available with the medical card. Some are exempt from laboratory costs for hospital services card holders. Privately, you should not expect to pay any money outside the cost of the consultation for any of these services. The exceptions to this would be any extraordinary lab fees (*not* rubella or smears) and any medication or contraceptive device.

When you attend the doctor, make sure s/he knows what you are worried about and make sure they don't fob you off. If you suspect an infection, make sure they do all the swabs and blood tests. If you request contraception like the Pill, insist on regular smears, breast exams and blood pressure checks. Don't settle for anything less.

HOW TO MAKE AN APPOINTMENT

With the name and telephone number of a recommended doctor in your hand, ring the surgery and ask when consultations are scheduled. Next pick a time that suits you, informing the receptionist (or whoever answers the telephone) what you want to see the doctor about (pregnancy test, contraception, menopause, etc). If the surgery hours operate on a first come, first served basis, rather than by appointment, ask her/him to suggest an hour when the doctor will have time to discuss your health concerns at some length.

WHAT TO EXPECT WHEN YOU ARRIVE AT THE SURGERY

First of all, you may be asked to answer some questions or fill in a form about your general state of health. A nurse or receptionist may go through these details with you or the doctor may ask you her/himself. You may have to wait some time before the doctor can see you. This is not always the doctor's fault, but if you want to be out by a certain time, find out a rough estimate of how long you will be delayed.

Depending on your reason for seeking the doctor's advice, any of the following tests may be carried out while you are in the surgery.

BLOOD PRESSURE

Often, this is the first test we undergo. While your blood pressure is being taken, the doctor may chat with you about any worries and try to reassure you about the rest of your visit.

The procedure for taking blood pressure is simple and painless. Your arm will be wrapped in a piece of cloth which can blow up like a balloon. Once securely fastened, it is pumped full of air to apply pressure on blood vessels running through the arm. The health-care worker will listen to the force of pumping blood with a stethoscope (the equipment medics wear around their neck and put in their ears). An accurate blood pressure reading may pinpoint early signs of circulatory and heart problems.

WHAT IS A NORMAL BLOOD PRESSURE READING?
Anything from 110/60 to 120/70 or even as much as 140/90. Blood pressure readings can alter with age and activity and still be within healthy limits. The numbers indicate the amount of force exerted by the blood on the arteries as it passes through. High blood pressure is the result of excess pressure: blood may find it difficult to pass easily through old, diseased or hardened arteries where elasticity is reduced.

HOW DO I MAINTAIN A HEALTHY BLOOD PRESSURE READING?
By eating properly (cutting out excess salts, caffeine, smoking, alcohol and hormone treatment), exercising regularly, and practising conscious relaxation (see p. 45).

For some of us, serious high blood pressure turns to illness (hypertension) and we may actually need prescribed medication. Some of the symptoms of high blood pressure are over-heating, dizziness, headaches and an overall feeling of pressure.

URINE AND PREGNANCY TESTING

Routine urine testing (urinalysis) is a straightforward procedure. You will be asked to produce a small sample (three thimbles full should be sufficient) in a sterilised (boiled clean) container. Some of us find it easier to do the sample at home and bring it with us in a sealed jar.

Urine may contain properties which indicate signs of pregnancy or ill-health. Proteins in the sample may point to an infection; sugar may be a sign of diabetes; a hormone called *gonadotrophine* may signal a pregnancy.

Sometimes we are asked to give an MSU (mid-stream urine sample). This is done by peeing slightly, catching the next bit of urine in the container, and then emptying the rest of your bladder into the loo. This may prove difficult if your pelvic floor muscles are weak: it's a good idea to practise Kegel exercises (p. 50) if this is the case.

In urine tests other than for pregnancy, a piece of multi-coloured paper is dipped into the sample. Depending on how the chemicals on the paper react, a diagnosis may be suggested. For pregnancy tests, urine is mixed with a serum. Between two minutes and an hour later, the sample may alter its appearance enough to indicate a positive result.

HOW WILL I KNOW WHEN TO HAVE A PREGNANCY TEST?
Once you engage in intercourse (especially if you are not using contraception) and miss a period by over two weeks, you should have a pregnancy test. If you are irregular, count four to five weeks after the sexual act before going for a test. There is no point in having a test too soon, because the result will not be reliable.

CAN I FIND OUT IF I AM PREGNANT BEFORE MY PERIOD IS DUE?
There are some tests being developed which will give this information. They are not widely available in Ireland. For the time being, you will have to wait until you are overdue.

CAN THE DOCTOR TELL I'M PREGNANT WITH AN INTERNAL EXAMINATION?
Some women notice cervical changes at the early stages of pregnancy. The doctor may wait until you are nearly ten to twelve weeks pregnant before examining you internally. This is because s/he relies on feeling the enlarged uterus to gauge foetal development. This is called a *gestation* check.

I HAD SEX LAST NIGHT. HOW CAN I FIND OUT IF I GOT PREGNANT?
There isn't any way to find out at the moment. If the risk of pregnancy worries you, see the section on post-coital (morning-after) contraception.

ARE PREGNANCY TESTS 100 PER CENT ACCURATE?
Some hospitals claim to have tests that are foolproof. With other pregnancy kits, certain conditions, like menopause and drugs (marijuana), may alter the reading. In these cases you may note a false positive result. If you receive a negative result (no, not pregnant) when you are one week late and a positive (yes, pregnant) result a week later, the reason probably has to do with slower hormone development. In this case the positive result is probably correct. It can take some women up to three weeks after their period is due to show a positive test during pregnancy. But this is not the norm.

HOW LONG DOES A PREGNANCY TEST TAKE?
Some take two minutes, others an hour. Some GPs send their tests to a hospital and you may have to wait a day for the answer. Family planning clinics usually do an hour test or less. You may be asked to wait, call back or ring for the result.

CAN I HAVE A TEST IF I FEEL PREGNANT BUT AM NOT LATE ENOUGH FOR A TEST?
There would be no point in this. The test looks for hormonal signs. Even though you may feel pregnant, the hormones may not have had time to develop. You may be wasting money.

WHAT DO THE WORDS 'POSITIVE' AND 'NEGATIVE' MEAN?
'Positive' means yes, you are pregnant, while 'negative' means no. Occasionally an inconclusive result is given. This means that for some reason, the urine sample reacted oddly with the testing agents. You will probably be asked to repeat the test in a week's time.

BLOOD TESTS

Blood tests are usually only carried out at our request or if we relate symptoms to the doctor which suggest an illness which can be checked through a blood sample. Some hormonal disorders, sexually transmitted diseases and anaemia are examples of this. One routine blood test all sexually active women should have is the *rubella titre*, a test which checks whether we are immune to german measles. Although we may have been vaccinated against this illness in school, some of us lose our protection over time, or if the vaccine is not properly administered. See below for more information on german measles.

WHAT HAPPENS IN A BLOOD TEST?
The health-care worker will take blood from a vein in the crook of your arm. This is done with a needle and syringe (the plastic tube attached to the needle). We may feel squeamish about having blood taken, so it's a good idea to practise relaxed breathing during the procedure, focus our minds on something more pleasant and look away. Blood tests don't hurt, but they do create a peculiar sensation in the arm which may frighten us if unprepared and tense.

Blood samples are then injected into a sterile container (anywhere from 5ml to 10ml are taken on average: about ten thimbles full at maximum). These are then sent to the laboratory for testing. In the case of rubella, an immune result means both you, and any potential foetus you are carrying, are protected from german measles.

WHAT IS RUBELLA?
Rubella or german measles is a mild illness but with serious effects during pregnancy: it can lead to miscarriage and birth defects (blindness and

deafness being most common). It is preventable through inoculation. This is done free of charge for all women in public health clinics and maternity hospitals.

HOW LONG AFTER AN INOCULATION CAN I GET PREGNANT?

You will need to wait at least three months for the vaccine to take effect. It takes the body this long to build up immunities to the virus. Some doctors then check for resistance with a second blood test. You can request this.

HOW DO I GET GERMAN MEASLES AND WHAT IS IT LIKE?

You contract german measles by being in close contact with someone who is infected. The symptoms include a rash on the face and chest, a light fever and flu-like feelings. These may last no more than two days, but the virus remains in the system for two to three weeks afterwards. It is highly contagious in the week prior to symptoms and for a few days after they first appear.

HOW MUCH CONTACT DO I HAVE TO HAVE BEFORE I WORRY?

If your sister's best friend has a daughter with rubella, there is no need to panic, but have the test anyway. If your children have german measles, then you are at risk.

WHAT HAPPENS IF I AM NOT IMMUNE AND HAVE BEEN IN CONTACT WITH GERMAN MEASLES? I AM PREGNANT

Once you are pregnant, there is nothing the doctor can do. Inoculation against the virus would only introduce rubella to your system.

WHAT ARE MY OPTIONS?

There are no tests to reassure you about the health of the foetus. Discussing the risks with a counsellor or doctor may help clear some of the worry and confusion.

BREAST DISEASE

In the self-help section (see p. 32), we learned how to do a breast examination A doctor uses the same technique. You will be asked to lie down on the couch with your blouse open or off. It's important to dress for the occasion with something that opens easily at the front. This will make you feel less vulnerable.

Occasionally, the doctor may find an unusual lump and will send you to a specialist for a second opinion. This is done more commonly now and doesn't mean the doctor thinks you have cancer. There are many other breast diseases — most of them quite harmless — which need specialised care. If your doctor decides your symptoms are harmless and you are still worried — get a second opinion.

I FOUND A LUMP IN MY BREAST A FEW DAYS BEFORE MY PERIOD. SHOULD I WORRY?
Any new or unusual lump should be checked out. But a lot of us find that our breasts become quite lumpy as we near a period. The breast may feel grainy, or you may notice tiny pellets below the skin surface. This occurrence is connected to the hormone action in the breast in anticipation of pregnancy. They generally disappear with menstruation. Because the lumps are so common, it's best to have your check-up *after* your period when the doctor can make an accurate diagnosis.

I HAVE A LUMP ALL THE TIME. MY DOCTOR SAYS I'M FINE

Most lumps are harmless and your doctor is probably right. Many of us experience benign (non-cancerous) disease and lumps. This includes cysts which may cause discomfort. They can be treated by a doctor who will drain off the trapped fluid.

Dysplasia is another term doctors use. This refers to a lumpy breast condition prior to a period. *Fibroadenoma* refers to the single lump (sometimes called a 'mouse') which may feel mobile beneath the surface of the skin. Some nipple discharges are harmless, but all should be investigated.

IS THERE ANY CURE FOR BENIGN LUMPINESS?
Single lumps can be removed surgically. Overall lumpiness is somtimes helped by hormone treatment, like the pill. Natural remedies include those listed under the pre-menstrual syndrome heading on p. 27.

AREN'T THERE ADVANCE TESTS FOR CHECKING BREAST LUMPS?
Yes. There is a test called mammography which provides a sort of breast X-ray. It is only available in some of the larger hospitals and at the moment requires a doctor's letter of referral. Plans are afoot to provide an open clinic service in the near future at the Mater Hospital in Dublin.

For the moment, mammography is not done routinely because it is expensive and some doctors worry about too much exposure to the technique. If your anxiety is not relieved by a physical examination, ask the doctor to refer you for mammography.

I HAVE BEEN REFERRED TO A BREAST CLINIC AND CANNOT GET AN APPOINTMENT FOR TWO WEEKS. I'M WORRIED SICK

It's difficult to relax when we are faced with the unknown. Bear in mind that most lumps (eighty per cent) are harmless. Ask your doctor why you are being referred. Sometimes the answer will dispel any fears about cancer. Breast clinics treat all forms of breast disorders. Luckily, the most common ones are not cancer.

I HAVE FOUND A LUMP IN MY BREAST AND I AM TOO SCARED TO ASK THE DOCTOR WHAT IT IS

Many of us feel great anxiety or panic when we find a lump in the breast tissue. We may even put off seeking help, frightened that the doctor will tell us we have cancer. Only about ten to twenty per cent of lumps are cancerous; but the earlier it is checked out, the better your chances for eliminating the possibility of cancer, treating your breast condition and relieving your anxiety.

It is a good idea to keep a check of when the lump first appeared. We often notice them before a period and they disappear afterwards.

IS THERE ANYTHING I CAN DO TO PREVENT LUMPS ON A SELF-HELP BASIS?

Benign lumps can be eliminated in some women by vitamin supplements and dietary changes. It can take up to six months to notice the full effects of such treatment. Cutting out smoking, caffeine, tea, salt, fatty foods, fries and aspirin may help.

Vitamin B6 may also help to reduce the discomfort of lumps and Vitamin E (800iu's) is prescribed in America for fibrocystic disease of the breast. Finally, oil of evening primrose can be used to supplement the diet.

WHAT CAUSES BREAST CANCER?

Breast cancer seems to be the result of dietary, environmental and hormonal factors. Women whose diet contains high levels of fatty foods are more susceptible. Certain types of pollution and radiation may also make us more vulnerable.

Some hormones have been linked to cancer development. Oestrogen is potentially cancer causing and some women who have their ovaries removed seem to be at less risk from the disease.

WHO IS MOST LIKELY TO GET BREAST CANCER?

There seems to be some confusion over this question. Women who have a family history of breast cancer on the mother's side may be at risk; older women between the ages of forty and sixty equally may be more vulnerable. Women who have had breast cancer before may be less resistant to the disease, so if you are in this position, regular breast examination is essential. If you have cancer in one breast already, then you are more likely to have your remaining breast affected.

IS BREAST CANCER CONTAGIOUS?

No, nor is it the result of bumps and bruises or any injury.

HOW IS BREAST CANCER DETECTED?

Initially, a lump or discoloration, discharge from the nipple, or swelling can be detected by self-examination. Any suspicious symptoms should be checked out by a doctor who is up to date with modern detection techniques. GPs will generally refer you to a breast clinic (there is an excellent one in St Vincent's Hospital in Dublin) where a specialist will provide a thorough service. If you are in any doubt about your family doctor's diagnosis, it is vital you get a second opinion.

WHAT HAPPENS IF THE DOCTOR THINKS THE LUMP IS SUSPICIOUS?

First of all, they will suggest the lump be tested for disease. This may be done in the early stages by *needle aspiration*. In this procedure, a needle enters the lump and draws out any fluid for testing. This may be done even if the doctor suspects the lump is benign (not cancerous) — though you may have to request the procedure before a biopsy in some cases — and is not done routinely.

The next step may be a *biopsy*. This is the surgical removal of part of the breast tissue containing all or part of the lumps. It may be done under local or general anaesthetic. Sometimes biopsies are suggested as a preliminary procedure before a mastectomy (breast removal). The surgeon may ask you to sign a consent form which gives her/him permission to perform a mastectomy if the tissue proves cancerous. Signing this form will mean s/he doesn't have to wake you before removing the breast.

Not all of us are able to make clear decisions in this situation and you may want time to consider other options to mastectomy. The mastectomy can be postponed for a few days for you to decide.

DO I HAVE TO HAVE A MASTECTOMY IF I HAVE BREAST CANCER?

No, and not all doctors recommend it. To date, statistics indicate that lumpectomy plus radiation treatment (see below) may be as successful in treating breast cancer as mastectomy. Of course, your decision may depend on many factors and there are no hard and fast rules which apply to all women.

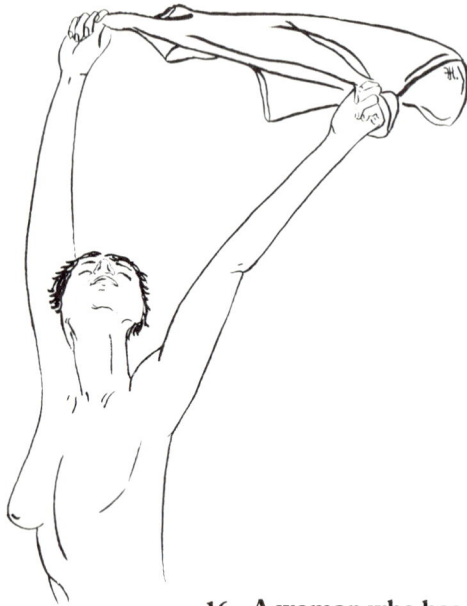

16. A woman who has had a mastectomy

ARE THERE ALTERNATIVES TO MASTECTOMY?

Yes. A *lumpectomy* involves removing the lump and some of the surrounding tissue in the breast. This may leave scar tissue and alter the shape of the breast. *Radiation therapy* is sometimes considered following a lumpectomy. This may be carried out for several days every week for several weeks and has side effects like skin problems and tiredness.

WHAT HAPPENS IN A MASTECTOMY?

The simplest form of mastectomy removes the breast but leaves the glands under the arm and chest cavity intact. The next type would be to remove these glands along with the breast. This is called a *Total mastectomy with auxiliary dissection*. A *modified radical mastectomy* removes the breast, glands and some muscle. In this final type of operation, the lungs and ribs remain unprotected by muscle tissue and are therefore more vulnerable to injury.

There is a great deal of pain attached to all of these operations and recovery may take several months. How we react to the loss of a breast may depend on our general state of health, our support from friends and family, and the amount of information we receive from health-care workers.

IS BREAST CANCER FATAL?

If diagnosed and treated early, breast cancer can be cured. Treatment may involve the partial or total removal of breast tissue. This depends on how far the cancer has spread. In severe cases, glands from under the arms may be removed. Radiation and drug treatment may be prescribed. These can make you depressed and ill.

If you are receiving cancer treatment, it is important to avoid pregnancy and some hormone treatments, as they may stimulate the growth of the cancer.

I HAD A BREAST REMOVED AND AM EXTREMELY DISTRESSED

Breast removal *(mastectomy)* is a frightening experience. Many of our feelings are linked to general ill-health, drugs, anxiety, grief and exhaustion. Other reactions are associated with our sexuality: now that my breast is gone, will I still be attractive? There are many agencies and individuals offering support for you.

CAN I HAVE PLASTIC SURGERY TO REPLACE THE BREAST?

Yes. When this is done may depend on other treatments being used. Another option is a *prosthesis*. This is a bra filling matched to your former size. Medical suppliers have trained professionals to help you, or your doctor may advise.

MY BREASTS ARE SORE. IS THIS A SIGN OF DISEASE?

It's more likely to be the result of fluid retention, directly related to hormonal changes. Doctors often use the term *mastalgia*. The self-help remedies on p. 28 may help. Some women find starting or stopping hormone tablets ends the discomfort. Vitamin B-6 helps.

WILL A BRA HELP THE TENDERNESS OR PREVENT DISEASE?

Wearing a bra can make the breast more comfortable. Some of us simply wouldn't be without one. Other women find bras a nuisance. As there is no actual muscle in the breast, a bra can give support to larger and heavier breasted women. It will not prevent disease, but can offer protection from sports injuries.

MY BREASTS ARE NOT THE RIGHT SIZE. CAN I DO ANYTHING ABOUT IT?
We can all find some portion of our body too small or too large. There are fashions in breasts just like in the clothes which decorate them. If you are unhappy about your body proportions, you may be unhappy about other things too. Have a good chat with a friend or counsellor. You may be far more influenced by social standards than you realise. Don't be afraid to be yourself: accept and enjoy your body.

Plastic surgery is available but is expensive. Get trustworthy advice first. Remember, though, altering one part of the body will not change your life.

I HAVE HAIR ON MY BREASTS AND NIPPLES. IS THIS NORMAL?
This is common. If we all stopped plucking and pulling, we would see just how many women have hair all over the body. It's important not to irritate the sensitive breast tissue by attacking it with bleaches, creams or tweezers.

Occasionally a hormone imbalance can cause a very hairy appearance called *hirsutism*. Adjusting the imbalance will clear matters up.

IS THERE ANY WAY TO AVOID SAGGING BREASTS?
The only help is exercise and good eating habits. Concentrate on activities which build up the muscles behind the breast, like swimming. Once the breasts start to sag, there is very little you can do. Good posture helps.

DOES BREAST SIZE AFFECT BREASTFEEDING ABILITY?
No.

CERVICAL SMEAR

The cervical smear test (also known simply as a smear or pap test) is a routine preventive check for cervical cancer. In Ireland, doctors recommend having a smear done every two years. This policy applies to any woman who has been heterosexually active and is still under menopausal age. For those who have completed the climacteric (menopause), cervical screening is made at five-yearly intervals and can be discontinued after the age of sixty-five (by this time the cervix has altered to a degree making cancer unlikely.)

WHO NEEDS A SMEAR?

Woman who are sexually active. There seems to be alink between cervical abnormalities and some properties in semen. Celibate and lesbian women are, for the most part, less prone to cervical abnormalities. There are of course exceptions: if you have ever had sexual intercourse or sexual relations with a man (including oral sex), or have been in contact with any sexually transmitted disease, (or if your partner has) then you should have a smear test done regularly.

WHAT HAPPENS IN A SMEAR TEST?

The examination for cervical screening is similar to the self-help techniques described on p. 34. It involves a speculum and something like an ice-lolly stick. You will be asked to raise your skirt (knickers off) and lie down on the couch. The next step is to open the legs wide, and breathe slowly in and out while the doctor inserts the speculum. This may be a bit uncomfortable, but it shouldn't hurt. Some clinics offer mirrors so you can watch the procedure. Once the doctor has a clear view of the cervix, s/he will collect some of the local cells by rubbing the stick against the membrane. Whatever is gathered will be put on a slide, sealed and sent to a laboratory. It currently takes eight to ten weeks for a smear result. Some clinics offer an emergency service, but the lab fees may cost an extra £5. Normally, a smear is done free of charge — you only pay for the consultation if you go privately.

Some doctors will cover you up with a blanket. This may suit you or it may annoy you. If you want to watch the doctor in action, let her or him know. This is a great way to learn how some of the medical procedures work.

I TENSE UP WHEN I HAVE A VAGINAL EXAMINATION

This is perfectly reasonable and normal. Here are some tips which may help:
1. Bring along a friend. Ask them to hold your hand or chat to you while the smear is being taken.
2. Practise deep breathing techniques (see p. 45). These will help you through countless anxious situations. Although the speculum will not hurt you, the pressure of tight tummy muscles against the instrument may cause discomfort. If you concentrate on relaxing those muscles, you will feel more comfortable.

3. Tell the doctor or nurse about your worries before the examination. Ask to see the speculum and wooden spatula. They won't seem so frightening once you are familiar with them.

WHY IS A SMEAR TEST NECESSARY?

The smear provides an early warning system in cancer detection. The slightest change in cervical cell activity can be monitored and treated before cancer has a chance to develop. Cervical cancer is curable if found in good time.

WHAT ARE THESE CELL CHANGES?

Smear tests come back with a variety of results denoting cell changes. Sometimes the variations are to do with irritation or recent surgery — even a coil or having a baby can alter the cervical tissue. In some cases, the abnormality is a sign of pre-cancerous development, and in this case may need further treatment. Here is a summary of the most common smear results.

Atypical cells   This is a common reading and indicates that the cells gathered in the smear differ in some way from other cells on the cervix.

Cervical erosion   Sometimes the words cervical erosion and cervical eversion are used inter-changeably. This is when the inner cells begin to appear on the outside of the cervix. Health-care workers now realise this is not a dangerous condition in itself and doesn't necessarily need treatment. Sometimes, for severe erosion, the area is cauterised (the destruction of tissue by burning).

Inflammatory smear   This results from local irritation or infection present near the cervix when the smear was taken. This can be screened by taking swabs.

Scanty smear   This may happen if we are tense, or don't go for a smear at mid-cycle. The phrase means the health-care worker failed to collect enough cells for an accurate test result. This is common and means you will need the smear repeated.

In the case of atypical cells, and some inflammatory smears or cervical erosion, a repeat test may be requested within three to six months of the original screening. This is a precautionary measure and does not mean you have cancer. Because cervical cancer is being linked to semen and some sexually transmitted diseases (herpes, genital warts), barrier methods of contraception (condom, diaphragm) may offer some protection.

WHEN IS THE BEST TIME TO HAVE A SMEAR?

Cervical cells seem to be most 'typical' at mid-cycle. This is around the same time as ovulation in many of us and occurs half-way between two periods.

DOES A SMEAR TEST CHECK FOR VAGINAL CANCER?
No, but vaginal cancer is very rare. In the case of DES daughters (see p. 124) vaginal cancer screening is advisable. This would involve taking smear-like samples from several different areas of the vagina. If you are one of these women, you will have to specifically request this type of screening.

HOW LONG DOES IT TAKE FOR CERVICAL CANCER TO DEVELOP?
It may take as long as fifteen years. This is why early detection can save lives.

I BLEED MID-CYCLE. SHOULD I WAIT UNTIL AFTERWARDS TO HAVE MY SMEAR?
Probably. If you bleed at any stage outside your normal period — and on a regular basis — you should have the causes investigated. Some doctors prefer to see you when the bleeding stops since it may be difficult to get an accurate cell reading with a heavy discharge.

If you bleed after intercourse, you may have an infection, and this should be investigated.

HOW OFTEN SHOULD I BE SCREENED?
If you have herpes or genital warts, every year; otherwise every two years.

GYNAECOLOGICAL PROBLEMS

I HAVE BEEN REFERRED TO A SPECIALIST FOR AN EROSION. SHOULD I WORRY?
Erosion is not usually something to worry about, but it can be irritating. If more serious disease is suspected, a *colposcopy* (COL-PAW-SCO-PEE) may be performed. This is an examination with a vaginal telescope which searches for abnormality. If irregularities are noted in the cervix, a biopsy may be taken. This means some of the cervical tissue is removed and sent to a lab for screening.

WHAT IS A PROLAPSED WOMB?
This is a saggy uterus. It may be caused by weak pelvic floor muscles. Kegel exercises (p. 50) can reduce its instance in some women, or you may be fitted with a ring (like the outer ring of a diaphragm) to hold the womb

in place. Sometimes surgical repair and/or hysterectomy is performed to correct a prolapse. Read as much as you can about this before you give your consent for such treatment.

WHAT IS STRESS INCONTINENCE?
Incontinence is an inability to hold urine in the bladder. The result is we leak and wet ourselves if we laugh or cough. This may be the result of poor muscle control and can be alleviated by Kegel exercises (p. 50) or surgery.

WHAT ARE OVARIAN CYSTS?
These are fluid-filled sacs attached to the reproductive organs. They are rarely cancerous but take up space and can be painful. They are usually removed with surgery.

WHAT ARE FIBROIDS?
These are non-cancerous fibrous growths in the uterus which may be uncomfortable but are not dangerous.

WHAT IS ENDOMETRIOSIS?
This is a health condition (END-O-ME-TREE-OSIS) where the uterine lining (the endometrium) is found outside the uterus. It seems to be a very common complaint and can be very painful because bleeding occurs internally at the time of menstruation.

WHAT CAUSES IT?
It seems to be the result of endometrium somehow escaping through the fallopian tube tissue and resting in the pelvic area (although it can travel further in the body). These bits of endometrium then implant themselves and respond to the same hormone activity which causes menstruation. Because the tissue is endometrial, it bleeds during a period and, having no outlet, it irritates the organs it surrounds. This irritation is what causes pain. Sometimes scar tissue forms, organs become linked (*adhesions*) or cysts develop. The most common place for the endometrium to lodge is around the ovaries and uterus or fallopian tubes.

WHAT ARE THE SYMPTOMS?
The first symptom is pain, often associated with menstruation or ovulation. Or there may be considerable discomfort during intercourse, when passing wind, or during a bowel movement. Some of us notice the pain during internal examination, while others of us never seem to be rid of the agony.

Endometriosis may also show itself with symptoms of diarrhoea or constipation, heavy or irregular periods, ongoing symptoms of PMS, swollen abdomen, insomnia, low energy levels, fatigue, depression, bleeding from the bowel during a period and infertility.

CAN YOU DESCRIBE THE PAIN?

For many of us, the pain is sharp around menstruation or ovulation and a dull ache at other times. Cramping also occurs. You may feel it early in the morning, late at night and sometimes with accompanying nausea. Many women say it feels like appendicitis.

Many women who are diagnosed as irritable bowel sufferers later find that they have endometriosis (see p. 41).

HOW DO I FIND OUT IF I HAVE ENDOMETRIOSIS?

The first way is by looking at your symptoms combined with a pelvic internal examination. If endometriosis is likely, the doctor should refer you to a gynaecologist who will perform a *laparoscopy* under general anaesthetic. A laparoscope is a telescope which enters the tummy through an incision near the navel and pubic hair. It will be able to detect the disease.

HOW IS ENDOMETRIOSIS TREATED?

Since the pain of endometriosis is triggered by the same hormones which prompt menstruation, hormone therapy is often used to counterbalance the effects of some hormone activity. Since pregnancy and menopause seem to eliminate the disease, hormone therapy tries to duplicate these. Without ovulation and menstruation, endometrial areas shrivel up.

The most popular drugs used for treatment of endometriosis are Danazol (also used as the morning after pill for women who cannot take oestrogen) or Duphaston — a preparation used for severe PMS. Both drugs are very expensive but are now available through the medical card scheme. As with any other hormone therapy, there may be side-effects like nausea, irregular bleeding, depression and headaches.

In severe cases of endometriosis, surgery is suggested. Since the disease does disappear in menopause, the decision to opt for surgical hysterectomy needs to be carefully considered. In some cases, minor surgery is sufficient

Alternative help includes acupuncture, altering the diet to exclude fats and include high fibre (see p. 35), homeopathic remedies like Kali-phos 6 (also good for fatigue), oil of evening primrose, vitamin B6, vitamin C and dolomite.

Exercise should be gentle and soothing — swimming, cycling or yoga are good. Running can jar the tissue and cause pain.

WHAT IS PELVIC INFLAMMATORY DISEASE?

Pelvic inflammatory disease is a broad name used for any infection which affects the fallopian tubes, ovaries and/or uterus. In this order they are medically named *salpingitis, oopheritis* and *endometritis*. They are usually caused by sexually transmitted diseases and most commonly by *gonorrhoea* and *chlamydia*, but using the IUD (coil) can also trigger the disorders. PID is one of the biggest causes of infertility in women, yet it often remains undiagnosed.

WHAT ARE THE SYMPTOMS?

Many of the symptoms which signal a sexually transmitted disease may eventually, if untreated, lead to PID. Some women notice only a dull ache and/or discharge over a long period of time. Others find the pain so acute, they have to be rushed into hospital. This pain may come from the tummy or the right side. Other symptoms include chills, fever, back pain, urinary problems — burning or retention — leg pain, swollen abdomen, swollen glands near the legs, nausea or vomiting, rashes, fatigue, painful ovulation and/or menstruation, cramping and irregular bleeding.

IS IT DANGEROUS?

PID can be very dangerous, even life-threatening. *Peritonitis* (an inflammation of the abdominal lining) or abcesses are serious side-effects. Some ectopic pregnancies are caused by tubal damage following a PID, and infertility may result. Some PIDs affect a newborn's eyes, pharynx and lungs. There may even be an increased risk of miscarriage and stillbirth associated with some infections like chlamydia.

HOW IS PID TREATED?

Usually by high doses of antibiotics. Both partners will need to be treated. Often, the antibiotics are begun straight away, and you are reswabbed three weeks later. As antibiotics may cause thrush, you will need to alter your diet to prevent this or ask your doctor's advice.

HOW DO I KNOW IF I HAVE PID?

You will need to be completely screened by a doctor in an STD clinic or in the GPs surgery. Sometimes, you will be referred to a specialist and a scan may have to be performed (see p. 139). You should not delay if you suspect you have a PID. It constitutes a serious health risk.

DIETHYLSTILBESTROL (DES)

DES (diethylstilbestrol — DIE-ETH-ILL-STILL-BEST-ROL) is a synthetic hormone used in Ireland in the 1960s to prevent miscarriage.

More recently, it has been prescribed for menopausal symptoms. Research shows that a serious side-effect of DES is vaginal cancer in the daughters of users. There also seems to be a link between increased risk of breast cancer and the hormone. If you have ever taken DES, or if your mother took it at any stage during her pregnancy with you, you may be at risk of such cancers.

HOW CAN I BE SCREENED?
First of all, get a copy of your medical records from the doctor who treated either you or your mother. This may be difficult and you might need legal advice.

If you are in the risk category, you will need to have a special type of smear test done (see p. 120). If you are the daughter of a DES user, you must demand this service: it is not done routinely.

FOR MORE INFORMATION, CONTACT:

DES Action
Long Island Jewish Hospital,
New Hyde Park, New York,
11040 USA

WHAT IS A HYSTERECTOMY?
This is an operation to remove the uterus (womb). There are various degrees of hysterectomy and you should learn about each so you can ask the appropriate questions of your doctor. If you have any doubts about the necessity of a hysterectomy, get another opinion.

HOW IS IT DONE?
Hysterectomies are usually performed *abdominally*. This means an incision is made in the tummy above the pubic bone. Although not very common, a *vaginal hysterectomy* may be done if you have a prolapse of the uterus and other repair work needs to be done (see p. 126).

WHAT IS REMOVED DURING A HYSTERECTOMY?
There are four types of hysterectomy.
Total hysterectomy This is when *only the uterus* is removed, although we commonly assume that the ovaries are taken out in this procedure. If in doubt, ask your doctor.
Sub-total hysterectomy This is an older procedure and isn't as common today. This means part of the uterus is removed — the cervix is retained

along with the ovaries.

Hysterectomy and bilateral salpingo-oophorectomy (SAL-PIN-O-OOF-O-REK-TO-ME). This is when the ovaries and uterus are removed. In this case menopause symptoms can occur immediately because the hormones produced by the ovaries are suddenly withdrawn.

Radical hysterectomy When the fallopian tubes, uterus, ovaries, ligaments and lymph nodes are removed — often in cancer cases.

Sub-total hysterectomy (Uterus tipped to show line of surgical incision, ovary hidden. After surgery the cervix and the stump remain, requiring regular Pap tests.)

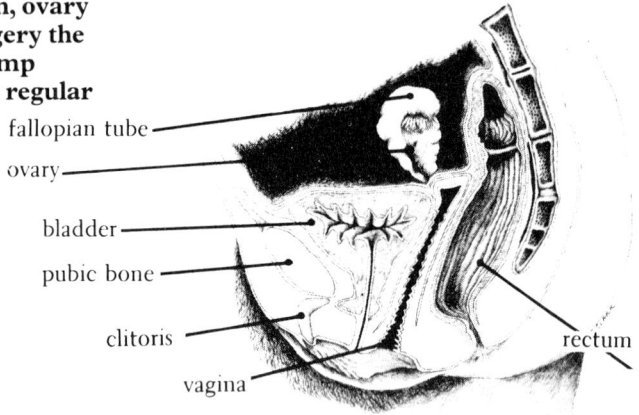

fallopian tube

ovary

bladder

pubic bone

17.

clitoris

vagina

rectum

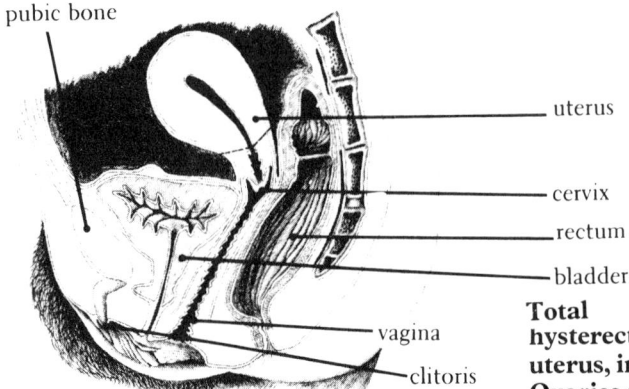

pubic bone

uterus

cervix

rectum

bladder

vagina

clitoris

Total hysterectomy (Removal of uterus, including cervix. Ovaries and fallopian tubes are attached to top of vagina.)

WHY ARE HYSTERECTOMIES PERFORMED?

Hysterectomies may be necessary in the case of severely diseased reproductive organs (cancer, unbearable endometriosis, severe infection, fibroids, prolapse) but are sometimes performed in Ireland to get around the ethical question of female sterilisation. Many women report their doctor saying to them 'Well, you've completed your family, what do you need this equipment for?' and are shocked by the doctor's lack of understanding.

Yet again, women are the pawns in a church/state game where our health and welfare are at risk. Free, safe and easily accessible sterilisation by laparoscopy (see p. 122, 199) and tubal ligation (see p. 178) is infinitely preferable to a hysterectomy where we suffer all the side-effects and dangers of major surgery.

HOW DO I PREPARE FOR THE OPERATION AND HOW WILL I FEEL AFTERWARDS?

After getting as much information as you can, go to the library and read books on the subject. In this way, you will be able to ask questions about your health.

Inform the doctor of any medication you are taking that may interfere with the anaesthetic and stop smoking at least a week before the operation.

Get plenty of rest and extra nutrition for the week or two leading up to the operation. Exercise if possible, so you will feel fresh and fit.

You will have to sign a consent form. Read it carefully and specify whether you give permission to remove other organs or not. Some women have awakened minus their appendix and have been outraged at the presumption the surgeon took with their bodies.

Afterwards, you will feel pain and nausea but these do pass and medication is usually given to alleviate some of the discomfort. You may be in hospital ten days and depending on the type of hysterectomy, your age and general health, you may feel incapacitated for six to eight weeks or more. You will be encouraged to move around as soon as possible since exercise promotes the healing process.

You may notice a bloody discharge for some days. If this becomes smelly or irritating, you may have an infection, so tell the doctor or a health-care worker.

It's best to avoid tight clothing or lifting and carrying until you are fit again.

WHEN WILL I BE ABLE TO RESUME SEXUAL INTERCOURSE?

Usually within six weeks of the operation, when the top of the vagina has healed. If in doubt, or you are still feeling discomfort, talk to a health-care worker. Some women notice that intercourse feels a little different without a uterus — but this is not unpleasant.

WILL I BE DEPRESSED?

There are many factors that contribute to mixed feelings after a hysterectomy. For some of us the freedom from contraceptive worries and pregnancy is liberating. For others menopausal symptoms leave us confused and feeling unwell.

Many women describe a period of grieving — they have associated their uterus with their sexuality and ability to bear children. Some women feel a hysterectomy affects their 'femaleness'. Friends and counsellors can help us to work through these worries and feelings. Remember, too, that any operation leaves us feeling under par and that the hormone activity which alters in some cases of hysterectomy may contribute to our feelings of sadness.

In the meantime, eat healthy foods and keep active. Talk to friends and other women who have similar experiences. The directory can put you in contact with self-help groups or set one up in your own area.

MY DOCTOR ADVISED ME TO AVOID SEXUAL RELATIONS AFTER A RECENT GYNAECOLOGICAL OPERATION. DOES THIS MEAN INTERCOURSE?

After a gynaecological procedure the doctor may say something like 'No sex for six weeks'. We may wonder if this means every aspect of sexual contact. It's best to ask the doctor if all sexual contact is excluded.

RECTAL EXAMINATION

If we have piles, or an itchy bottom, we may ask a health-care worker to examine our back passage. This is a rectal exam. The rectum is the tissue leading from the anus. Some rectal investigations are necessary in sexual assault cases and for screening sexually transmitted diseases or worms.

A rectal examination can be very unpleasant and make us feel like we need to pass a bowel movement. If you set out to have a rectal examination, it may help to empty the bowel first.

During the investigation, the doctor will dilate the opening of your back passage with a finger and may take a swab with a cotton bud. You will be asked to lie on your side for this, and the whole procedure shouldn't take more than a minute or two.

For self-help advice see p. 41.

11. FERTILITY

Fertility is the term we use to describe our ability to conceive a pregnancy. Many of us want to have children, but for various reasons are unable to get pregnant through sexual intercourse. There may be physical barriers like vaginismus, impotence, blocked fallopian tubes, a disability in one or both partners, or a low sperm count. Sometimes our sexual orientation rules out intercourse.

Until recently, little help was available for women who sought alternatives to 'natural' methods of conception. Both artificial insemination by partner (AIH) and by donor (AID), are now available in the Dublin Well Woman Centre. St James's Hospital is experimenting with *in vitro* (test-tube) fertilisation and British clinics are accepting Irish referrals.

Sexual difficulties like impotence (when erection and ejaculation are not possible) can be overcome with counselling. Hormone treatment may lead to pregnancy simply by stimulating lazy ovulation.

The ethics of such reproductive technology have caused problems for health-care workers and women alike. Some of us worry that money spent on test-tube procedures might be better used in investigating the causes and treatment of infertility. Others fear an abuse of embryo (two-to-eight-week-old pregnancy) research.

Then there is the over-emphasis on 'having a child of our own', when there are so many children waiting to be fostered. There's no denying that strong social pressures make us feel abnormal if we remain childless. Having the choice of fertility taken out of our control can be distressing enough, but being badgered by well-meaning friends can only increase our feelings of anxiety. Fifteen per cent of couples are infertile: this is no small statistic. Perhaps it's time we started re-examining the 'normality' of natural procreation.

HOW DO I KNOW IF I AM FERTILE?
There is no quick and easy test for this outside having sexual intercourse and waiting to see what happens. If you have regular periods, then it's likely you are ovulating. Once you have been seriously trying to conceive for a year or more without success, you can seek professional advice. Each

couple is different. Sometimes there is a medical reason for infertility, and sometimes no cause can be found.

If you are referred by a GP for fertility testing, you will probably be seeing a gynaecologist. There are several tests you may have to undergo. The first one is the simplest. Your partner will be required to produce a fresh semen sample in a sterilised container. This is usually achieved through masturbation. It will be checked for quantity and quality of sperm. If all is in order, the next step is to examine you. Some of the tests are unpleasant and may involve a general anaesthetic. Uterine mucus is tested for hostility to sperm, and a laparascope may be used to detect possible tubal blockages (see p. 123). The tests may take months, and still no medical grounds for infertility may be found.

WHAT CAUSES INFERTILITY?

The single biggest cause is tension. This may be the result of trying too hard, or from being overworked, worried or bored. A stressful, anxious environment is not ideal for the conception and development of a healthy foetus.

Sometimes there are the medical reasons already discussed. It may be difficult to conceive immediately after stopping a course of hormone pills (including the contraceptive pill), but time will sort this problem out. Smoking and drinking don't help either. In some cases, uterine infections have been cited as promoting temporary infertility. Once cleared, fertility resumes as normal. It is important to be screened for this possibility (see p. 191).

WHAT IS AID?

AID stands for artificial insemination by donor. This type of reproductive technology is used when the man is infertile but the woman is able to conceive. The sperm of a suitable, fertile and usually anonymous male is borrowed and inserted into the uterus during ovulation. The sperm has been kept frozen in small straws which are thawed prior to insemination. This type of procedure is usually done in a clinic. You will be in the same position on the couch as you would be for a smear test. A speculum is used so the sperm can be directed at the cervical opening. It is possible to rent a sperm bank (which looks like a gas cylinder and keeps the sperm frozen with liquid nitrogen). The clinic staff will teach you how to use it.

IS IT EXPENSIVE? IS THERE A WAITING LIST?

Yes. The initial counselling fee is about £25. A check-up will mean another £15. Inseminations by clinic staff costs £25 each. You would normally have two inseminations during ovulation. Renting a bank is £100 minimum, the straws about £15. At the moment no medical card scheme applies.

There is a waiting list of about six months from first enquiry to first insemination. The paperwork will be processed most quickly if all medical records are submitted as soon as possible. There is no point applying for AID if you haven't undergone fertility testing which states that your partner is infertile, or unless you are otherwise suitable (see below).

MY PARTNER IS FERTILE, BUT HAS A GENETIC DISEASE WE DON'T WANT TO PASS ON. ARE WE SUITABLE FOR AID?

Yes. So are couples where the man has had a vasectomy, but the woman is fertile, and lesbian couples.

WHAT IS THE SUCCESS RATE?

This varies. In Ireland there are at least twenty babies conceived through AID. The statistic is probably greater, but the parents don't wish to make the news public. If you live near the clinic, and travel to and from it is not upsetting, the success rate is greater than if you journey from Bantry once a month. AID is never suitable for women who are themselves infertile.

WHAT SORT OF SPECIAL TESTS DO I NEED FIRST?

The clinic will request documentation from the doctor who tested you for infertility. You don't have to tell the doctor why you need copies of these forms. That is your own business.

HOW CONFIDENTIAL IS THE SERVICE?

At the moment, in Ireland, confidentiality is guaranteed. However, British regulations may change in the near future to allow any offspring of AID to request and receive information about the donor. If this law is passed, the children of British donors will have the right to know key facts about their donor/father. It is up to you whether you tell the child s/he is the product of AID; it is important to bear in mind that the child will grow up and the choice of withholding such information may be taken out of your hands. What you say to your daughter or son at that time is worth considering.

WHERE DO THE DONORS COME FROM?

Donors for Irish insemination are found in Great Britain and usually have an Irish background.

HOW WILL I KNOW IF THE DONOR IS SUITABLE?

The staff at the clinic will match physical characteristics from donor and parents. The donors have all been screened for infections and genetic disorders (probably more than your current partner has been). There is no need to worry about the disease AIDS infecting the semen samples, as they are heat-treated especially to prevent this (see p. 193). However, as with any pregnancy, there is no guarantee against birth defects.

Some women worry in case the donor has some psychological or social illness. Will it be inherited by the offspring? Most research in this area concludes that it is the way children are reared, rather than their genetic code, which establishes personality traits.

WHAT IS AIH?

AIH stands for artificial insemination by husband/partner. This type of insemination is suitable for fertile couples who are unable to have sexual intercourse. Reasons for this include disability, impotence, vaginismus and emotional worries. Clinics offering AIH usually offer sexual counselling prior to advocating AIH if the situation warrants. This is because sexual intercourse is the most efficient way to conceive a pregnancy. It is also the cheapest. If intercourse is desirable, and can be managed without undue stress, the clinics feel this approach should be tried first. The final decision is yours.

The actual procedure for AIH is to gather sperm through masturbation, and put it into something called a rocket cap. This cap is then placed over the cervix. The sperm can then begin travelling to the uterus. A counsellor can give more details.

In the case of a disabled male partner who is unable to masturbate, it is sometimes possible to stimulate sperm production and ejaculation under an anaesthetic. The clinic will advise you here.

WHAT IS IN VITRO FERTILISATION?

This is also called test-tube fertilisation, and refers to the joining of sperm and egg *outside* the uterus. The woman usually has one of her eggs removed through laparoscopic surgery (see p. 123). Sperm is gathered through masturbation. In the lab, the two are fertilised and replaced in the uterus where they have a chance of implanting on the lining as normal.

Any tubal blockages are by-passed. Sometimes the eggs and sperm of different partners are used, but the technique is the same.

WHERE DO I GO FOR IN VITRO FERTILISATION?

While one Dublin hospital, St James's, has perfected the techniques, the ethical committee is reviewing the situation. This may change at the time of going to press. You can always be referred to Great Britain, but this of course is expensive and time-consuming.

12. PREGNANCY

The idea of pregnancy has probably crossed the minds of most women at one time or another. Sometimes we choose to become pregnant, and sometimes that decision is taken from us. In most parts of Ireland, inadequate access to safe and reliable contraception has limited many of our options. Even in an ideal situation, where pregnancy is planned, we can still experience feelings of confusion and fear. Is this the best time? Is this the right partner? Do I need a partner? Do I want another child so soon? Can I afford this? Will the delivery be safe? Will I be a good mother?

For many of us, having a partner alleviates some of these worries. But what about those of us who remain single? Are the same back-up services available? Will we be treated differently by doctors and hospital staff? What should we expect from the next nine months?

Regardless of whether or not we decide to continue with our pregnancy — partner or not — we may want some basic questions answered. There are both voluntary and professional bodies where details of our benefits and entitlements can be found. The directory and bibliography can put you into contact with further help in the area of pregnancy care, but first things first:

HOW DO I BECOME PREGNANT?
If you look back to the chapter on menstruation, you will see that an egg is released fourteen days before a menstrual cycle begins. This is called *ovulation*. It takes about three days for the egg, or ovum, to travel down the fallopian tube. If during this three days, we have sexual intercourse with a man, and he ejaculates semen from his penis into the vagina, then the sperm from that semen may fertilise the ovum.

HOW DOES THE PENIS GET INSIDE THE VAGINA?
When a man becomes sexually aroused his penis becomes hard and so can enter the vagina. There are many ways to let your partner's penis into your vagina. You can sit on top of him, or you can lie on your side or back, with your legs open. In any of these positions, the penis will fit into the vagina

(see illustration on p. 58).
If the man ejaculates near the opening of the vagina, or allows his penis into the vagina, there is a chance of pregnancy. Once the penis is hard a lubricating fluid, containing sperm, may be present, even without ejaculation.

You won't get pregnant if he comes on your leg, thigh, bottom, breasts or tummy unless semen is transferred in some way to the vagina, for instance if it gets on your hands.

ONCE THE EGG IS FERTILISED, WHAT HAPPENS?

The ovum, once fertilised, travels down the fallopian tube and into the uterus. Over the next fourteen days, the egg will implant itself on the uterine wall and become an embryo, then a foetus.

WHEN CAN I GET PREGNANT?

If you have sexual intercourse fourteen days prior to a period, you have a greater chance of conceiving a pregnancy, regardless of the length of your cycle. This is when ovulation takes place and an egg is released into the fallopian tubes. During ovulation, the uterine mucus alters to make fertilisation easier. Our regular discharge becomes slippery and wet, allowing sperm to travel with more ease.

If the penis ejaculates in the vagina, the sperm may travel through the cervix and into the uterus. From there, the sperm swims towards the fallopian tubes. If the sperm is unsuccessful, the unfertilised egg will come out with your next period.

Even though we are most fertile about fourteen days before a period, there is always a chance of early or later ovulation. It is even possible, although not common, for us to get pregnant if we have intercourse during menstruation. This is because sperm can live several days (up to seventy-two hours), and intercourse may stimulate premature ovulation.

IS IT COMMON FOR SO MUCH SEMEN TO COME OUT OF THE VAGINA AFTER INTERCOURSE?

After sexual intercourse, you may be surprised how much semen actually comes out of the vagina. Many of us notice quite a heavy discharge. This is normal.

WHAT HAPPENS ONCE THE EGG LODGES ON THE WALL OF THE WOMB?

Once the egg attaches itself to the uterine lining, it begins to grow quite rapidly. At the end of eight weeks, the foetus is quite developed, yet only about one inch in length. During this phase, uterine mucus begins to thicken, creating a stopper which seals off the cervical opening and provides a home for foetal growth.

At about ten to fourteen weeks, the foetus has acquired all its functioning parts, but still cannot survive on its own until it is nearly seven months old. As it develops, the uterine muscles expand to take the increased size. If the pregnancy continues, a baby is born at the end of nine months.

HOW DOES THE FOETUS GET NOURISHMENT IN THE WOMB?

When we are pregnant, we develop a tissue called the placenta. This is attached to the uterus by the *umbilical cord* (connected to the foetal belly button or *navel*). Oxygen and food are taken from our blood stream and filtered through the placenta to the foetus. Anything we eat, smoke or drink can affect the growing pregnancy.

WHY DO SOME WOMEN MISCARRY? IS IT PREVENTABLE?

Every miscarriage is different. Miscarriage happens when the foetus fails to continue developing and comes out in a heavy, sometimes crampy, period. There are many reasons for miscarriage: the foetus can be unhealthy, we may be unwell, the cervix may have been too loose to contain the pregnancy. Once a miscarriage starts, there is little we can do, outside rest, to prevent it. Some specialised techniques, like putting a stitch in the cervix, may help those of us who consistently miscarry. This procedure is done by a gynaecologist and is not always suitable for every woman.

HOW WILL I FEEL IN THE EARLY STAGES OF PREGNANCY?

You may feel nauseous or vomit in the mornings, or at any time of the day. You may feel like running to the loo more often, or you might recognise new vaginal discharges and increased irritation. Your breasts may tingle and swell or you may become constipated.

The best thing to do to avoid many of the digestive problems is to eat small, mildly flavoured, regular meals and get plenty of rest. A later chapter will discuss infection.

HOW WILL I KNOW WHEN THE BABY IS DUE?

Count nine months from the first day of your last period and then add seven days (one week). This is when the baby is due. So, if your last menstrual cycle began on 23 January, for example, count forward nine months to 23 October, add seven days, and your baby is due on 30 October.

WHERE DO I GO IF I AM UNHAPPY WITH THE PREGNANCY?

There are counselling centres in England and Ireland that can discuss an unplanned pregnancy with you. You have three options: continuing with the pregnancy and keeping the baby, continuing with the pregnancy and choosing adoption, fostering, or terminating the pregnancy. Counselling will help you come to terms with whatever decision you make. Ongoing support and, in some cases, financial assistance is available.

It is extremely important to seek help if you feel overwhelmed by the pressures of an unplanned pregnancy. Never let money or public opinion keep you from seeking assistance. You will not be turned away. Having said that, there are some agencies where sympathy is only offered if you plan to continue with the pregnancy. See the directory.

IF I CHOOSE TO CONTINUE WITH THE PREGNANCY, WHAT IS THE PROCEDURE FOR ARRANGING HOSPITALS ETC?

The first thing is to see your doctor (see Chapter 10) for a check-up and chat. You may also like to contact some of the agencies dealing with the maternity field and discuss the pregnancy with your friends. More and more GPs are looking after their clients during the nine months before delivery. Women feel more at home with a regular service outside the hospital environment. It's important to note that this sort of co-operative care is free to pregnant women.

Having gathered as much information as you can from all of these sources, you will be able to decide what hospital, what obstetrician (if going privately), and what method of childbirth you would like to use.

CAN I HAVE MY BABY AT HOME?

Yes, but the health authorities generally discourage us from having a baby at home, because it makes it easier for the professionals if we go to hospital. Second babies present fewer worries, so long as the first pregnancy presented no complications, it may be easier to arrange a home birth the second time around. It's best to arrange for a home birth well in advance, to ensure that everything goes smoothly administratively and personally.

Often when we think of pregnancy, we think of hospitals, queueing for ante-natal visits, intimidating equipment and the associated idea of illness that all this conjures up. It doesn't have to be like this, and birthing at home is an option that more and more women are taking up because it gives us some sense of control and relieves the anxiety of being away from home at this stressful time. It also means we can have a friend, not necessarily the father of the baby, at the birth.

But the health-care system doesn't make home births easy for us. Many women are told that home births are dangerous. In most cases, this is just not true. There are cases, of course, where complications arise and medical intervention becomes necessary; but home births would be much easier to choose if the government would spent some money to equip and staff emergency health-care teams (flying squads) to deal with problem home births. Once again, women are faced with medicine and health care that facilitate the authorities rather than the consumer.

If you are happy that you are unlikely to run into problems in labour and you can arrange a doctor to agree to do your ante-natal care and a midwife to attend the birth, one final thing you should consider is the question of pain relief. If you are a first-time mother you don't know how much of a problem this is going to be for you until labour actually starts. Even the best relaxation and breathing techniques can seem futile in the face of the pain of some labours, and you don't have the option of an epidural if you are at home. On the other hand, it is exhilarating to give birth to your baby at home, without drugs, and many women find the sheer comfort of being in familiar surroundings makes the pain more tolerable.

HOW DO I GO ABOUT ARRANGING A HOME BIRTH?

The first thing to do is to read as much as you can about natural methods of childbirth. In this way you can make an informed choice about how you want to deliver your baby. If you opt for a home birth, you need to contact the local Community Care Officer in your area Health Board. The Health Board is obliged to organise a doctor and midwife to assist you. In some rural areas, the Health Boards are uncooperative, but this does seem to be changing, and by making the demand, you are lobbying for an improvement in this area.

If you are finding things difficult, contact the Home Birth Centre (see directory). They have a list of sympathetic doctors and midwives. Sometimes if we organise this first, the Health Boards have little scope for argument. The Health Board should also be able to provide a list of health-care workers who provide ante-natal and back-up assistance.

Next, ring the GP and ask if s/he will offer the help and care you need. Don't waste your time making an appointment first only to find out when you arrive that s/he doesn't offer the service — ask them straight out on the telephone. This will save time and money. The doctor may feel more obliging if you arrange for the midwife first.

HOW DO I FIND A MIDWIFE?

Local GPs, health centres, Health Boards, family planning clinics, the Home Birth Centre, community information can help you to find a midwife, or you could even put an ad. in the newspaper.

WHAT IF I WANT TO GO PRIVATELY?

The VHI maintains that they will tailor your policy to meet your needs. Ring them and tell them of your plans. Or write a letter explaining your wishes well before you make a claim.

WHICH HOSPITALS ENCOURAGE NATURAL METHODS OF CHILDBIRTH?

Hospitals vary enormously in the methods they promote. Some discourage the use of *epidural* (a spinal injection which numbs us from the waist down), while others prefer us to lie on our backs throughout labour and delivery. Some hospitals have birthing chairs which many women feel makes delivery much easier. For a consumer guide to all these services contact the Association for the Improvement of Maternity Services in the directory.

WHAT ARE ANTE-NATAL VISITS? WHY ARE THEY NECESSARY?

Ante-natal (AN-TEE NAY-TAL) means before birth. Medical professionals feel we should have regular pre-birth check-ups to make sure both mother and foetus are healthy.

Many of us are unhappy with the way we are treated during ante-natal visits. In the larger maternity hospitals, waiting rooms are crowded, we may never see the same doctor twice, and the welfare of the foetus seems more important than the way we feel. It's essential to point out these shortcomings if you experience them. Only then will things change. If you are a single mother and do not want to see the social worker assigned to you make it clear to the hospital authorities. Until you do, single motherhood will continue to be viewed as a social problem, while very often it is assumed that married couples have no problems about the baby, just because they *are* married.

WHAT ARE ANTE-NATAL CLASSES?

These are classes which prepare us for childbirth. They can be started at any stage before the birth but should not be left too late. The classes deal with the actual delivery, how to breathe, breastfeeding, child development, health care, and relationship changes. The classes are designed to help us prepare for a new baby entering the home.

Most teachers assume that we plan to keep our baby. If we have chosen adoption, we may want to let the teacher know — or be prepared for the emphasis on mother, father, baby, all returning to the one house. We may like to talk over our feelings of fostering or adoption with someone at this stage.

WHAT IS A SCAN?

A *scan* is a radar reading of the foetus in the uterus. It is not painful and should not damage the foetus. The lab technician doing the scan, will ask you to arrive at the hospital with a full bladder. This raises the abdomen and affords a good view of the internal organs. Next, s/he will spread a clear lubricating oil on your tummy while you are lying down (blouse raised), and run what feels like a telephone receiver over the area protecting the foetus. When the technician locates the foetus, radar waves will produce an image on the television screen next to the couch. This gives the staff an idea of the size and the development of the foetus. The test is usually done when we are sixteen weeks pregnant. Scans are also used in place of x-rays today for investigating internal disorders like gall bladder disease or kidney stones.

WHAT IS AMNIOCENTESIS?

Amniocentesis (AM-NEE-O-SEN-TEE-SIS) is a test of the amniotic fluid. This is the liquid in the sac which surrounds the foetus. Some of the fluid is removed by injecting a needle into the tummy (a local anaesthetic makes the procedure only slightly uncomfortable) and extracting it. The sample is then sent to a laboratory for tests.

Amniocentesis is normally done between sixteen and eighteen weeks of pregnancy. Some of the results come within a few days and others take several weeks. The test will discover if the foetus has Down's syndrome (mongolism), spina bifida, or haemophilia. The test for Down's syndrome takes the longest and can also detect the sex of the child if we make the request.

There is a slight risk of miscarriage attached to amniocentesis. It is only recommended for women who have a history of any of the diseases listed, or who are over thirty-five years of age. It is not done routinely and is difficult to arrange in southern Ireland.

You can be referred to Belfast by your own doctor or one of the family planning clinics. The reason few hospitals provide amniocentesis in the south is that abortion is illegal. In the twenty-six counties, medical professionals seem to feel that if the foetus is seriously deformed, you must continue with the pregnancy, regardless of early detection of abnormality.

CAN YOU EXPLAIN THE DIFFERENCE BETWEEN A MIDWIFE, A GYNAECOLOGIST, AND AN OBSTETRICIAN?

An *obstetrician* is a doctor (consultant or specialist) who delivers babies. If we have our delivery in a hospital we are ultimately under the care of this type of health-care worker, although we may never see her/him.

A *midwife* is often the person who actually delivers our baby, with the supervision of an obstetrician. S/he is a trained nurse and can also attend at home births.

A *gynaecologist* is a doctor who specialises in caring for our sexual organs. If we are having problems with our uterus or vagina, we may be referred to a 'gynae' for expert advice though other health-care workers may be equally skilled at diagnosis. Since we are not ill during pregnancy, we don't see a gynaecologist before the birth, but some doctors combine the two roles of obstetrician and gynaecologist, and in fact the term gynaecologist is often used loosely to refer to an obstetrician.

The other main difference between obstetricians and gynaecologists, who are both doctors (consultants), and midwives is that consultants are unfortunately more than likely to be male and midwives to be female. If you choose to have a home birth attended by a midwife or by a midwife and a woman GP you can avoid involving men in your labour and delivery if this is important to you.

I HAVE BEEN CONFUSED AND MOODY SINCE I BECAME PREGNANT. IS THIS NORMAL?
Yes. Moods can fluctuate considerably during pregnancy. There are many understandable reasons for this. The first factor is hormonal changes. Other causes include changing finances, stress, anxiety, relationship worries, and being run down. Pregnancy is a big step; you needn't feel abnormal if it takes a bit of time to adjust to the idea.

Some tips which may help to deal with the moods include letting yourself feel blue — without feeling guilty; talking about your fears; excluding any physical reasons for anxiety by having a thorough check-up; eating and resting properly; and avoiding stressful situations which might tire you.

I AM THIRTY-EIGHT YEARS OLD. THIS IS MY FIRST PREGNANCY - WILL EVERYTHING BE ALL RIGHT?
Once you are over thirty-five, there are certain extra health risks involved in pregnancy. If you are healthy and don't smoke or take drugs, the chances of a healthy pregnancy are good. Having said that, it might be a good idea to discuss the risks with a genetic counsellor or a health-care worker before conceiving. This is especially true if there is any history of hereditary disease in either family.

A genetic counsellor is usually a doctor attached to one of the maternity hospitals. A GP (family doctor) or family planning clinic can refer you.

If you are already pregnant, you might like to consider amniocentesis.

IS IT SAFE TO HAVE SEX DURING PREGNANCY?

Unless you are told otherwise, sex is safe during the whole nine months of pregnancy. You may not always find intercourse comfortable, but there are other positions and methods of enjoying sexual contact. You may find lying on your side the most comfortable of all.

IS THERE ANY WAY TO STOP MORNING SICKNESS?

Not all of us are sick in the morning. Some women are nauseous all the time, especially in the first few months. This is the result of hormonal changes. You should try eating many small, bland meals rather than two or three large ones. If you live with other people, ask one of them to deliver tea and toast to the bedside *before* you get up; this can settle those irritating tummy juices which build up overnight.

If you live alone, invest in a flask. You can fill it with hot tea at night and keep a few biscuits by the bedside for the morning.

One very good method of relieving nausea is deep regular breathing in through the nose and out through the mouth. Avoid rich or spicy foods and simply stop cooking them for others — especially if the smell is off-putting. If your illness is so bad that you cannot keep anything down, you may need to seek a doctor's help. It's important not to take any anti-sickness medication (except natural remedies like peppermint tea and homeopathic preparations) without seeking a second opinion. Some drugs may lead to birth defects.

MY LEGS AND ANKLES ARE SWOLLEN

This is very common in pregnancy. It is sometimes called *oedema* (ee-dee-ma), and is the result of fluid retention. Oedema can be caused by hormonal changes. You should avoid caffeine, salty foods, and take vitamin B-6 in 50mg doses daily. Natural diuretics may help (celery, parsley). Oedema can be dangerous, and therefore should be monitored by a doctor.

It's important to give your legs a rest now and again. Remember that they are carrying an increased load. Propping them up on a stool will help. You should also sleep with a cushion under the foot of your mattress. This will help circulation and decrease the risk of varicose veins.

I AM CONSTIPATED

Many of us find regular bowel movements difficult during pregnancy. It's essential to eat a well balanced diet with plenty of fibre. Natural yoghurt eaten daily will help the body tick over nicely. It can be combined with raw bran flakes (a tablespoon each day). Regular exercise must be taken:

walking and swimming are perfect. You need to drink plenty of water, avoid caffeine, and too much cheese. A glass of warm water first thing in the morning will also set the digestive machinery into motion.

I HAVE TERRIBLE INDIGESTION

You need to be extra careful about diet during pregnancy. Hormones can play havoc with the digestive processes. You could cut down on food which contributes to these feelings — like curries, or onions and the like. Soda water or milk may help to calm the irritation. Keep away from any other medication unless it is homeopathic.

I HAVE TO PEE ALL THE TIME. IS THIS NORMAL?

Yes, it is normal and there isn't very much you can do about it. It is important to drink plenty of fluids during pregnancy but it may help to confine the intake to daylight hours. This will help to keep you out of the loo all night. The cause of increased urination has to do with hormonal changes and the pressure of the foetus on the bladder.

IT IS SORE AND BLOODY WHEN I GO TO THE TOILET. IS THIS DANGEROUS?

Fresh red blood and painful bowel movements are often caused by piles (haemorrhoids). These are caused by prolapsed (saggy) rectal (back passage) lining. They become sore and bleed if irritated by hard faeces (shit). To keep piles at bay, it is essential to include fibre in your diet and follow the same rules you would for constipation. Be sure to keep the anal area clean and dry to avoid infection and itching (p. 42).

I WAKE NEARLY EVERY NIGHT WITH LEG CRAMPS

As your body shifts its posture to adjust to the increased load of pregnancy, your legs may take the brunt of the strain. Stretching exercises may help. Once the cramp begins, push your heel *away* from the body, extending the calf muscle, and stretching the whole back of the leg. Deep massage may be of comfort too. High heels are a menace for creating this problem: because the calf muscle is held in such an awkward position all day, it naturally reacts when the body is relaxed.

WILL I GET VARICOSE VEINS?

Not every pregnant woman has varicose veins, and you don't have to be pregnant to get them, but pregnancy can be a cause. Varicose veins, where found in the legs or vulval region, are caused by pressure and bad circulation. You can help eliminate them by eating a high fibre diet, watching your weight, putting your feet up when possible, and by rocking back and forth on your feet if you are standing for any length of time. Regular sleep is important too. When you prepare for bed, put a large cushion under the mattress at the foot of the bed. This will help the blood in the feet to circulate more efficiently and reduce the risk of vein problems. Wear sensible shoes that exercise the legs.

I HAVE BEEN HAVING PROBLEMS SLEEPING AT NIGHT
This is a common complaint and there are several reasons for it. The foetus may have very different waking hours from yours, or you may have to get up in the night to go to the loo; there may be aches, pains and twinges that make it difficult to sleep. Your sleeping position may have to be altered during pregnancy and you may find it difficult to sleep on your back or side in the late stages. You may have financial or emotional worries about how you will cope with the new baby, and these may give you sleepless nights.

Here are some tips. Try to establish a routine which suggests sleep to the back of your mind. Try listening to soothing music or reading a light book. Bedtime herbal teas may help, but keep away from real tea or coffee as they contain stimulants. You might try a warm bath and massage, or some of the breathing techniques illustrated in chapter 4. If in the end you still can't sleep, get up and do something that will relax you by taking your mind off trying to sleep.

One other excellent tip is to fill the bath with cold water. Put on a heavy woollen jumper, but strip off from the waist down. Stand in the bath for three minutes, breathing slow, deep breaths. If you can bear it (and believe it or not, you don't feel that cold) sit in the bath for three minutes — jumper on. This will lower your body temperature and act as a sedative. Hop straight out of the bath, dry off, and put on warm night clothes before heading straight to bed. Sleep will come soon after.

MY TUMMY ITCHES LIKE MAD THESE DAYS. WHAT CAN I DO?
Wear loose clothes which don't chafe and natural fabrics which feel nice on the skin. Some women find that lotions or talcum powder help, while others hop into a warm bath. The itching is caused by hormonal changes and expanding skin tissue.

IS THERE ANY WAY TO AVOID STRETCH-MARKS?
If your skin is sensitive, it may be impossible to avoid stretch marks. They are usually the result of the skin expanding rapidly to take the growing foetus. Lotions and oils will moisturise the area but do little to stop the marks from appearing. Even thighs, breasts and bottoms can be affected by

stretch marks.

It's important not to put on too much weight in pregnancy. Excess weight puts stress on the heart, lungs and pelvic floor muscles (p. 51). Other suggestions include supplementing your diet with vitamins B-6 and E and the mineral zinc. These are meant to promote more elastic skin and can be found naturally in peanut butter.

I HAVE NOTICED A DISCHARGE FROM THE VAGINA. IS THIS NORMAL?
As long as there is no itch, bad smell or other symptoms of infection (see Chapter 14), the new discharge may simply be due to changing hormones. If it is bloody, or you suspect an infection, it's best to get the advice of a health-care worker.

I HAVE BEEN BLEEDING FOR THE LAST WEEK. I AM EIGHT WEEKS PREGNANT. IS THIS DANGEROUS?
If you bleed during any stage of pregnancy, it's best to get your doctor's advice. It may be a danger signal, but more often there is no need to worry.

HOW WILL I KNOW WHEN LABOUR STARTS? I'VE HEARD THERE IS A DISCHARGE
When labour begins, you may notice a pink, sticky discharge (the collection of mucous which provides a stopper in the cervix), or you may find that your 'waters have broken'. This means that the amniotic fluid breaks out of the uterus when contractions start. It will look like you've wet yourself quite heavily. However, many women find that the waters don't break until they are well into labour. Sometimes you will know labour is commencing with the start of regular contractions. If you attend ante-natal classes, many of these questions will be answered for you in more detail.

WHAT HAPPENS IN LABOUR?
There are several different stages to labour. They can all come on top of one another, very quickly, or appear in a more definable, drawn out pattern.

In the first and longest phase, *dilation* occurs (this means the cervix begins to expand; its opening enlarges). This is when the cervix widens. Some hospitals begin monitoring you at this stage. This may consist of machines and tubes to check for healthy foetal signs. Some women feel constrained by this equipment.

The second phase of labour involves giving birth. The contractions which have widened the cervix up to now will have dilated the opening to about 10 cm (about 4 inches wide) in a normal delivery — big enough for a baby's head to pass through. You will be asked to blow or push in

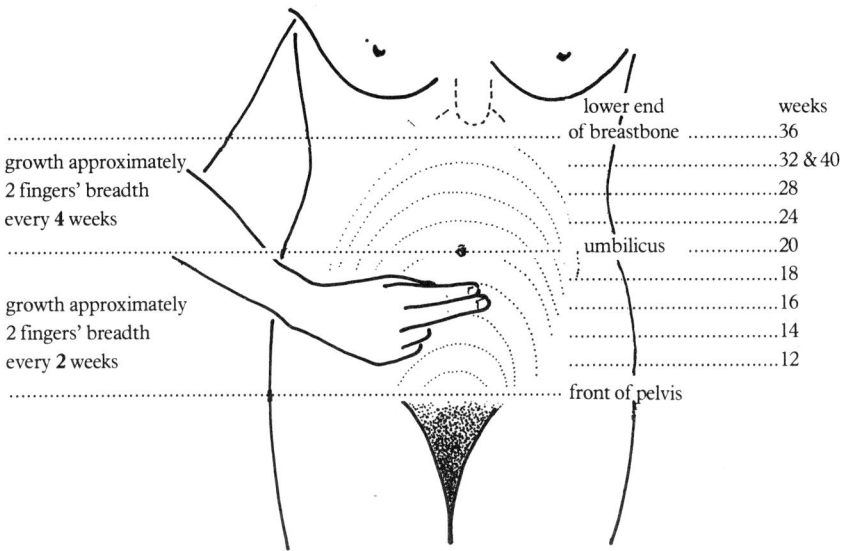

	weeks
lower end of breastbone	36
	32 & 40
	28
	24
umbilicus	20
	18
	16
	14
	12
front of pelvis	

growth approximately 2 fingers' breadth every **4** weeks

growth approximately 2 fingers' breadth every **2** weeks

18. Growth of uterus during pregnancy

alternating patterns to help ease the foetus out.

The third and final phase is the delivery of the *placenta* (afterbirth). This is another set of contractions which follow closely after the baby's birth.

Some women go through all these stages with no drugs or injections, in very little time. Other women can take twelve hours or much more. Some methods of delivery suit some women better than others. Talk to your ante-natal teacher, doctor or midwife: they may help you decide which is best for you.

DOES DELIVERY HURT?
Yes, delivery is painful and exhausting. This is why it's called labour. The degree of discomfort can depend on your own tolerance, the type of delivery technique you choose, and your general state of health and fitness.

I AM AFRAID OF PAIN AND THINKING ABOUT THE BIRTH SCARES ME
There is no doubt that childbirth can be and usually is an extremely painful experience. We all vary in the amount of pain our bodies can tolerate. For some of us the pain of childbirth is sharp, but not the agony it is for others. However, there is no need to suffer intense pain. Most hospitals offer, and you should demand, methods of pain relief. Unfortunately there is not much in the way of pain relief on offer to home-birth mothers.

The *pethidine* injection is a common method used in Irish hospitals, but it has fallen out of favour with many women, who find that it only makes them feel woozy and disorientated, and consequently even more out of control, without actually killing the pain. It has spoiled the birthing experience for many women. A good idea would be to try a *small* dose of this drug early on in labour and abandon it if you dislike its effects. There is also the danger that this drug may make the baby sleepy.

An alternative that many women prefer is gas-and-air. This may also make some women feel sick, dizzy or disorientated, but it has the advantage that you are in control of administering it yourself. You are given a mask, and you breathe the gas in as contractions reach their climax. This form of analgesic seems not to affect the baby.

But there is no doubt that an *epidural* is the most effective method of pain relief. This anaesthetic is injected into the spine and it numbs us from the waist down. Most women find it offers considerable or even complete pain relief. Of course there are disadvantages here too. Being hooked up to the epidural apparatus means we can't move about freely in labour (but then you may not be allowed to do this anyway) and because we very often can't feel the pushing sensation in the second stage of labour, a forceps delivery (which usually entails an episiotomy) may be necessary. On the other hand, the mother is awake, alert and relatively free from pain at the moment of birth. Women have been left paralysed after badly administered epidurals, but this is extremely rare. Minor side-effects include headaches.

If you prefer to avoid drugs in labour, you can learn relaxation and breathing techniques at ante-natal classes. The oxygen filtered through the lungs increases the blood supply to the muscles which helps to soothe them. There are many advantages to a drug-free labour, but there is no reason for any woman to feel guilty because she has opted to use other methods of pain relief. The natural childbirth movement has encouraged us to take control of our own labours, but there is the danger that we can be intimidated into denying ourselves pain relief 'for the sake of the baby'.

WILL I HAVE TO HAVE STITCHES?

Some women have stitches in the tissue between the vagina and anus (*perineum*--PARE-EE-NEE-UM) after delivering a baby. This is the result of the perineum tearing or being snipped by the doctor during the birth. If the doctor does this, it's called an *episiotomy* (EP-EE-ZEE-OT-O-MEE). This is a common procedure and makes the head of the baby come out more easily, preventing severe tearing, but it is painful and can lead to infection and discomfort when healing. You can ask your doctor not to do an episiotomy if you prefer. You then run the risk of tearing naturally, but some women feel a tear heals more easily than a cut. A few stitches are used to hold the opening together and these are removed after the area repairs itself.

If you give birth by caesarean section, where the tummy is opened above the pubic hairline, then you will have a row of stitches along the incision. This is major surgery and is done under general or epidural anaesthetic. Recovery can be painful. Doctors suggest this procedure increasingly in cases of breech birth (where the baby's bottom, legs or arms are coming first). If you have any doubts about suggested treatment, seek a second opinion.

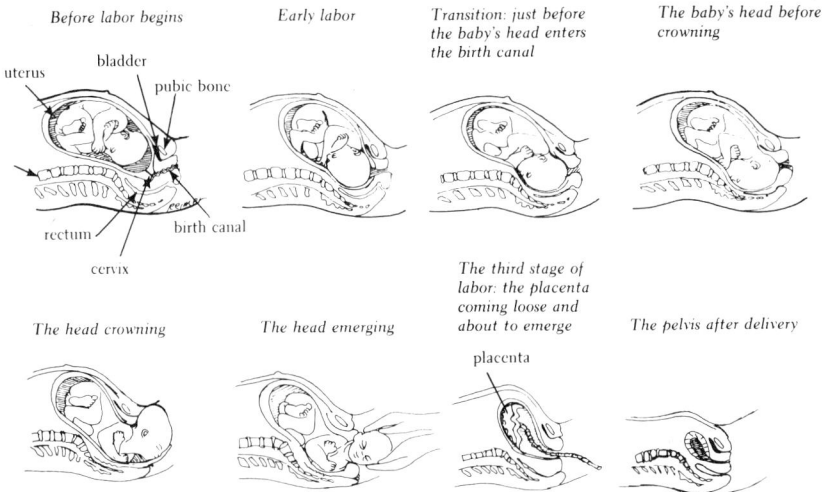

19. Pregnancy development

IS IT TRUE I COULD SHIT DURING LABOUR?

Some of us pass a bowel movement during delivery. It's not surprising when you consider how much pressure is bearing down on the intestines from the contractions and pushing. Some hospitals give an *enema* — something to clean out the bowels — before delivery, but many women find this procedure uncomfortable and embarrassing.

In the end, you will be concentrating so hard on the delivery, you won't notice any bowel movement, and the staff are well used to it. Don't let it worry you.

HOW LONG DOES IT TAKE TO RETURN TO NORMAL AFTER HAVING A BABY?

You will probably never feel exactly the same after having a baby. If you keep the baby, you may have up to a year of sleepless nights feeding and changing, which won't compare with your pre-baby schedule. Each of us responds differently to these changes. Immediately following the birth, you may notice some trace of vaginal irritation or infection that needs attention, and if you have had an episiotomy it may take months to heal completely. Or you may suffer from post-natal depression. Few of us get all the help we need from friends, relatives and health-care workers to cope with all the new stresses motherhood brings. It seems like society assumes as women we are born with these skills.

It's important to take things at your own pace — don't expect to be a supermum. Try and get some time to yourself, and encourage family and friends to share in the child-care duties. If you are having problems, talk it out with friends or a health-care worker before it gets on top of you.

IS IT NORMAL TO BE MOODY AFTER HAVING A BABY?

Within a few days of delivery, we all go through a 'blue' period due to hormonal changes. And there may be circumstantial reasons for sadness. We may be frightened and overwhelmed by new responsibilities, or we may feel lonely and confused. We may have to make decisions about the future of the baby, or secretly wish the whole thing had never happened. These feelings are perfectly normal. If they persist and distress you, talk to someone about it.

WHEN CAN I HAVE SEXUAL INTERCOURSE AGAIN?

Whenever you feel up to it. You should wait until any infections or injuries have healed. This usually takes a minimum of six weeks. If intercourse feels uncomfortable in the beginning, try some of the other forms of sexual contact.

Many of us are too tired to even contemplate sexual intimacy until well after our six-week check-up, but some partners are less than considerate with their demands. This will need to be worked out.

CAN I GET PREGNANT STRAIGHT AWAY AFTER HAVING A BABY?

Yes, you can get pregnant if you don't use contraception. This chance is somewhat reduced in breastfeeding women, but you are never 100 per cent safe. If you want to avoid pregnancy, there are a number of suitable contraceptive devices you consider (see Chapter 13). It's wise to give your body at least a year's rest before conceiving again. Contraception may or may not be discussed at your post-natal visit. Use the opportunity to ask all the necessary questions.

WHAT KIND OF CONTRACEPTION CAN I USE WHILE BREASTFEEDING?

Condoms, the cap, or the IUD can all be used, but any pills containing oestrogen should be avoided as they may injure the baby. The progestogen-only-pill (mini-pill) is currently used by breastfeeding mothers, but there is no long-term data on how this hormone may affect the child. Is the risk worth it?

20. Woman breast feeding child

IS BREASTFEEDING A GOOD IDEA?

It is meant to be the best form of nourishment for the baby. Only you can decide what is best for you. The advantages of breastfeeding are that it offers complete nutrition to the newborn; it's relatively easy to prepare (no bottles to heat in the middle of the night); it's cheaper than bottle-feeding; it can give some contraceptive cover; it helps to speed up uterine contractions and reduce the size of the tummy; and it's reported to be pleasant and sensual. It may also offer the baby some immunity to disease.

The disadvantages are that you are tied to feeding the baby at certain hours, unless you arrange for bottle supplements; it is difficult to share the feeding tasks, and leaky nipples can be both messy and sore.

Some women have trouble with breastfeeding because no-one has bothered to teach them how, or they lack confidence. Some women don't like the idea of suckling. For some babies, the breast can't fulfil all their demands. If you would like to breastfeed, but are having problems, talk to a friend or a health-care worker. There are many organisations in the directory which may be of assistance. The La Leche League is one.

WHAT DOES INDUCTION MEAN? MY DOCTOR SAYS I MUST BE INDUCED
Induction means to bring on labour sooner than it would occur naturally. There are various ways of doing this, the most common method being to put the woman on a special drip where tubes are hooked up to your arm. The doctor may feel worried about the foetus, or the risk of infection may increase once our waters break and contractions do not follow immediately. Some doctors simply like the baby to arrive on a specific date. Because induction is painful and can be dangerous (women have died as a result in only the last year), it's important you have a say in whether or not the procedure is performed. If there are no   apparent complications, and the baby simply isn't ready to come, induction may not be needed. Put your point of view across.

WHAT IS AN ECTOPIC PREGNANCY?
This is a pregnancy which develops outside the uterus. It happens when a

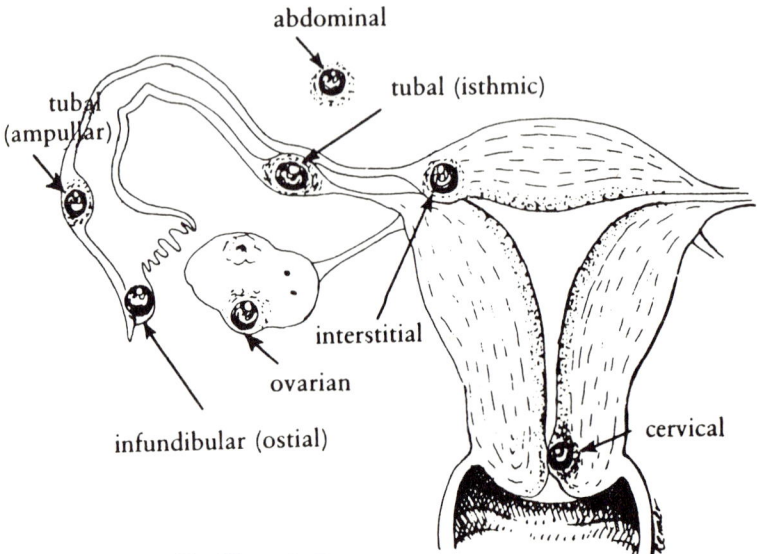

21. Ectopic Pregnancy

fertilised egg implants itself on some other organ — often the fallopian tubes. Since there is rarely enough space for a healthy pregnancy to develop outside the uterus, both the mother and foetus are in danger from rupture and infection. The surgical procedure used commonly in Ireland to deal with a tubal pregnancy, is to remove the tube with the foetus attached. In Irish law, this is not an abortion. Other medical techniques being devised will make it possible to remove the foetus, but leave the tube attached for future pregnancies. The current abortion legislation does not take this new technique into account, so in order to deal with an ectopic pregnancy legally, doctors may have to remove tube and all, even when it is not medically necessary.

WHAT ARE THE SYMPTOMS OF AN ECTOPIC PREGNANCY?
Initially, you may have all the normal signs of pregnancy: nausea, vomiting, tiredness, breast tenderness, and a missed period. As the pregnancy develops, the pressure on the tubes can cause cramping, stabbing pain (sometimes in the shoulder) and bleeding.

WHY IS A CAESAREAN SECTION SOMETIMES NECESSARY?
Natural delivery may be ruled out for a variety of reasons: some disabled women deliver a pregnancy in this way. Women who have viral infections like herpes may not want to deliver a baby through a diseased cervix. Some anatomical problems, like a small pelvis, or a cervix which won't dilate fully make caesarean section necessary.

WHAT CAUSES A MISCARRIAGE?
A miscarriage happens when the foetus comes out of the uterus before it is able to survive on its own. Most miscarriages occur in the first four months of pregnancy. The symptoms of impending miscarriage include heavy bleeding, cramping and clotting. Sometimes there is a feeling of faintness and a drop in body temperature. The second two side-effects are a sign that you should see a doctor.

Unfortunately, there is very little that can be done to save this type of pregnancy except rest. Miscarriage is the body's way of dealing with a pregnancy that isn't healthy enough to survive. In the case of repeated miscarriage, where the cause is directly related to cervical incontinence (a loose cervix), a stitch can be put in the cervix to help prevent further problems.

Since the Abortion referendum, women have complained that immediately after miscarrying in hospital, staff have presented them with the dead foetus to help the grieving process. This may be helpful in the case of still-birth, but it can cause undue stress for some women who have miscarried. If you wish to complain, do so to the hospital board by letter. Only in this way will the practice be changed.

I HAD A STILL-BORN BABY, AND I DON'T UNDERSTAND WHY

Unfortunately, health-care workers don't always know either. The best way to handle this type of situation is to make an appointment with your doctor and ask for an explanation. The ideal time is after the baby's post-mortem. This is a routine examination made on all still-born babies to find out why the baby died.

The birth of a still-born baby is distressing for women and their families. If you are finding it difficult coping with the situation, there are many organisations and individuals where you can turn for help. Talk about it to friends. Many women experience feelings of guilt and depression. This is normal, but you may need outside assistance to cope with it.

MY CHILD IS DISABLED. DID I DO SOMETHING WRONG?

There isn't always a clear reason pointing to a child's disability. Some handicaps have been linked to alcohol, drug and tobacco use. There are chemicals in the environment which may encourage disability in the undeveloped foetus.

If you plan to have another baby, you may like to avail of pre-conceptual genetic counselling. This will help you to decide if there is a great risk the disability is inherited (see amniocentesis, p. 139). A doctor can refer you for this.

There are as many joys as problems in bringing up a disabled child. You may like to contact one of the many voluntary organisations dealing with counselling and information on the subject.

I HAVE DECIDED TO GIVE MY CHILD UP FOR ADOPTION/ FOSTERING. WHAT IS THE PROCEDURE?

In Irish law, only single women can have their babies adopted. Just as many married women are unable to cope with an unwanted pregnancy, but may feel they have nowhere to turn for help. In this second case, fostering may be an option. There are many agencies dealing with this area. Some are listed in the directory. For more comprehensive details, see *New Families* by Charles Mollan and Laetitia Lefroy. (Dublin: Turoe Press, 1985).

There are also many personal support groups based around the country. If you want to spend the few months before giving birth away from your family, one of the agencies will be able to offer advice and accommodation.

13. FERTILITY CONTROL

If we decide to have sexual intercourse, we may want to avoid pregnancy. *Contraception* is the term used to cover any medication, method or device which prevents conception. Until 1985, contraception was available only to married couples in southern Ireland. New legislation has made it more accessible to women and men over eighteen years of age. Despite these new laws, doctors and chemists can refuse to prescribe or dispense contraceptive supplies on personal and moral grounds. Real fertility control is only available for those of us who know where to go and what to ask for.

For these reasons, it is important we pass any information we have on to other women who may not have the same access. In the directory section, I have listed the names and addresses of chemists who were willing to advertise their service. These are registered pharmacists who stock family planning supplies. There are many more stockists around the country, but they shunned publicity.

A list of doctors was harder to print. The Medical Council refused to allow a list of sympathetic doctors to be supplied within the pages of this book on 'ethical grounds'. The use of the word 'ethics' is curious here — for is it ethical to allow an unwanted pregnancy simply because a woman is denied access to contraception advice and information?

Do these ethics extend to the types of contraception we are offered? Is it ethical to test synthetic hormones on human guinea pigs? To spend research monies on costly remedies rather than preventive measures? To insert or inject contraceptives which promote disease? The answer, of course, is that the 'morality' of contraception is left up to those who are licensed to provide it. In Ireland, this falls to the hands of the doctors and, in some cases, the legislators. As usual, women's health is very low on the list of priorities.

HOW TO ARRANGE A DOCTOR WHO WILL OFFER CONTRACEPTIVE ADVICE

If we need the name of medical professionals in our area, there are several alternative sources of information. The health boards and health clinics keep lists. So do family planning clinics and community information offices. It is important to find a doctor who takes our concern for fertility control seriously. Once we have control over our fertility, we will be able to make real choices about the way we live.

There are many forms of contraceptive offering varying levels of protection. For some of us the 'percentage effectiveness' is a bit of a mystery. What exactly does 99.9 per cent safety mean? In the case of the Pill, this means that unless we make an error with it, or take some medication that interferes with the Pill's potency, we are virtually 100 per cent free of pregnancy risk. The effectiveness of any form of contraception can greatly depend on how motivated and confident we are. Some general worries should be alleviated within this chapter.

So how do we go about getting contraception? Making the first appointment can be embarrassing for some of us. It may be less embarrassing to go to a family planning clinic if there is one in your area than to go to your GP. Once we know a simple approach, it may seem easier. The most straightforward way to make an appointment is to simply ring or call into the doctor or clinic. If it helps, do so in privacy. All you need to say is 'I would like to make an appointment to discuss contraception. I have been thinking about the Pill, or cap or coil.'

When you ring, have a date and time in mind, a pencil and paper for writing any details down, and, if you are in a call box, enough change to keep from being cut off.

It's important to specify the type of contraception you require, even if you haven't completely made up your mind. The receptionist may have to arrange for a specific doctor to see you, or there may be health requirements which limit your choice. One example of this is the coil. The clinic will need to know if you are having a period, or if you have had any previous pregnancies. If you are not able to discuss this briefly on the telephone, an appointment may be made for a suitable form of contraception. Some clinics work by appointment and have special days for pills, other days for coils. Other centres work on a 'first come, first served' basis. To avoid wasting a trip, you should find this out before arrival.

Costs of services vary: visits/consultations are roughly £8 to £10 for a check-up or chat. Emergency services like the 'morning after pill' cost in the region of £15. This is because the doctor usually spends more time with an emergency client and will generally discuss the broad area of contraception in detail. Coils and caps usually require two visits, plus the price of the contraceptive device, so are more expensive: about £30. Condoms and spermicides can be bought over the counter or through the post for about £3 for twelve sheaths or pessaries.

Medical insurance companies do not reimburse you for contraceptive supplies but you can get them free on the medical card from the doctor, or at a reduced rate in some clinics. In northern Ireland these services are free.

WHAT WILL HAPPEN AT THE DOCTOR/FAMILY PLANNING CLINIC ON MY FIRST VISIT?

After you introduce yourself, you may be asked to answer written or verbal questions related to your health. This will cover things like childhood illnesses, current medication, surgical operations and genetic disease. If you prepare a list of this information, and other worries, in advance, you will feel confident and ready to meet the doctor. You can always take a friend along for moral support. You may be asked by the family planning clinic if you are married. Don't worry about this: they only want to know for their statistics. You don't have to answer if you don't want to.

The next step is a general chat with the nurse or doctor about all the contraceptive methods you have considered. Not every method may suit, or your doctor may not be skilled in the fitting of some, like the coil, and may refer you to someone else.

If you decide on the Pill, the cap (diaphragm), or the coil (IUD), you may be asked to undergo an internal examination, or breast check. Wearing a skirt and blouse will make things easier. You can simply lift the skirt, or unbutton the blouse, when the time comes. Many of the family planning clinics do not insist on an internal check-up at the first visit because they realise you may be shy or sexually inexperienced. It is important to let the doctor know if this is the case; some of the contraceptive methods, like the cap or coil, are uncomfortable to fit if you are unused to vaginal contact.

You may also be asked to produce a urine sample. This is not to test for pregnancy. It is a way to check your general state of health. If you want a pregnancy test, you must ask for this specifically.

Other routine tests which the doctor may suggest, or you can request, are for blood pressure, weight and cervical smear (see Chapter 10). Following the check-up, the doctor will either fit the cap or coil, or write a prescription for the contraceptive pill. Most of the family planning clinics keep these items in stock.

HOW REGULARLY DO I NEED A CONTRACEPTIVE CHECK-UP?

This really depends on the method you choose. A general check is always a good idea following the first three months of the Pill; most doctors insist on this. Afterwards, you need to be monitored for blood pressure and have a breast examination at six-monthly intervals.

If you opt for the cap, you may need a second visit within a week of the original fitting, to check the size is correct and comfortable.

Six weeks after a coil insertion, you should have a check-up to make sure everything is in place. The doctor will look for the string and make sure you feel happy with the IUD. This check-up is done two weeks after a period. After that, the coil can be checked every two years with a routine smear test.

THE CLINIC I ATTEND ASKED IF I WAS MARRIED. DO I HAVE TO BE?
No. The clinic asked for statistical purposes only. Once you are over eighteen, you can legally avail of contraception. If questions like this annoy you, leave the space blank.

HOW CONFIDENTIAL ARE FAMILY PLANNING CLINICS?
They adhere to the same ethical code as doctors, so records are completely confidential. Some women use a false name to be doubly sure. If you decide to do this, it's important to give correct information about age and general health. You won't receive proper medical care unless you do. No clinic will turn you away because of age, and they will never reveal information about you to outsiders without permission.

THE PILL

The expression 'the pill' is used in the rest of this book to cover the broad range of tablets known collectively as the *combined oral contraceptive pill*. The pill contains synthetic hormones in varying ratios. Depending on the brand, manufactured *oestrogens* are used in varying levels along with *progestogen*.

The pill works by sending hormonal messages to our sexual organs, telling them not to release an egg each month. Or they can alter the uterine lining so that sperm cannot travel easily to the fallopian tubes. Sometimes our body actually thinks we are pregnant. How the pill acts on the body depends very much on our individual make-up.

HOW SAFE IS THE PILL IN PROTECTING ME FROM PREGNANCY?
The pill is said to have a safety record of 99 per cent. This means that one out of every hundred women will get pregnant while taking the pill. The statistic doesn't necessarily mean that the one per cent of us who become pregnant are not protected by the pill. If you throw the pill up, have diarrhoea, take medication which lessens the effectiveness of the hormones, or forget to take the pills on time, your safety may be reduced. The pill can only cover you effectively if taken according to directions.

HOW WILL I KNOW THE RIGHT PILL FOR ME?

Basically there isn't a lot of difference between the pills. There are several different packaging designs which vary the dosage over the month. The basic pill form is the twenty-one-day pack where all the pills are identical. The second type of pill on the market, called the bi-phasic, has two different coloured pills. You are meant to take one colour in the first week and the remaining tablets over the next fourteen days. The third type of pill is the tri-phasic. This means that the packet contains three types of pill. There may be six of one colour followed by five of another, finishing with ten of a third colour. The bi-phasic and tri-phasic pills must be taken in the correct sequence.

The doctor can help you decide which pill will suit you best. Information which will guide her/him includes listing your age, menstrual pattern, any skin problems, other medication, and whether or not you smoke. You can always try another pill if the first one doesn't seem appropriate.

HOW DO I TAKE THE PILL?

You start the pill on the first or fifth day of a menstrual cycle. It is possible to begin a packet at either of these starting times, but its effectiveness may be altered. Once you commence, take a note of the starting day (Tuesday, for example). You will always begin a new packet on this day. Once you start the pill, continue taking one tablet each day for twenty-one days. It's necessary to take the pill at roughly the same time every day. After taking twenty-one tablets consecutively, break for seven tablet-free days. DO NOT RESTART THE TABLETS ON THE FIRST OR FIFTH DAY OF THIS BLEED. Instead, wait seven days and restart the pill on the following Tuesday, for example. This is twenty-eight days after first beginning the tablets. Once you begin the pill, you will always start on the same day with a new packet every month.

DO I GET A PERIOD DURING THE SEVEN DAYS?

Technically you don't have a period on the pill. You will have a bleed caused by withdrawing from the tablets. Because it is not a true period, it may look browner or lighter than normal. It may only last a couple of days.

I NOTICE MY PERIOD IN THE MIDDLE OF THE PACKET

If this happens, you are having 'break-through bleeding' (BTB). This may actually look like a period or more like a brown discharge. This is normal in the first month of taking the pill and can last for three weeks or more. It can happen if you forget to take a pill, or take it late; or you may notice BTB if you are taking another form of medication which interferes with the pill.

Ordinarily, the bleeding clears up with time and adjustment to the pill. If it continues more than six weeks, it may be a sign to change contraceptives.

There are varying opinions on how safe you are from pregnancy during BTB. If in doubt, ask a healthcare worker for advice. One simple and general guide is the 'fourteen-day rule'. This simply means waiting fourteen days after the bleeding stops before resuming full sexual intercourse. Also be careful not to have intercourse during the bleed except when it occurs in the seven-day break.

I TOOK THE PILL PROPERLY FOR A YEAR AND SUDDENLY GOT BTB FOR NO REASON

There is always a reason for break-through bleeding, but it is not always apparent. You may be run down, or under stress. The pill cannot always compensate for a drop in hormone levels. In some cases, you will need to change the pill, but it's best to see if the bleeding recurs first.

I GOT NO BLEED IN MY SEVEN-DAY BREAK. AM I PREGNANT?

If you have BTB while taking the Pill, you may not get a bleed during the break. The body can only discharge so much fluid. If you have been on the pill a long time, it could be a sign that you need a change, or that the pill is so effective, it covers you even during withdrawal. If you have unprotected intercourse during BTB, you will want a pregnancy test before recommencing the pill.

WHAT SHOULD I DO IF I FORGET TO TAKE A PILL OR TAKE ONE LATE?

If you forget to take the pill, or take one more than twelve hours late, it's best to avoid sexual intercourse following the fourteen-day rule. This means, don't have sex for fourteen pill-taking days (or use another form of contraception). If you notice break-through bleeding, wait until fourteen days after the bleeding stops before you resume sexual intercourse without added protection.

Some doctors advise taking two tablets together if you miss one night's tablet. Others feel this might risk stimulating ovulation. If you remember to take the pill within twelve hours, the manufacturer maintains you are safe. It's not wise to make a habit of this practice. If you forget more than two tablets, it's best to take a seven-day break and resume the pill. The fourteen-day rule applies.

I HAD SEX LAST NIGHT AND NOTICED BREAK-THROUGH BLEEDING WHEN I WOKE UP. AM I SAFE?

There is no hard and fast rule about this situation. Sperm can last several days, but so can hormone protection, even if there is BTB. It's best to seek medical opinion, since every case is different.

I TAKE MY PILL AT MIDNIGHT. LAST NIGHT I HAD SEX AT MIDNIGHT AND FORGOT TO TAKE MY PILL UNTIL MORNING. AM I SAFE?

The answer to the previous questions applies also in this case. You will most probably be protected, because you remembered to take your pill within twelve hours.

I THREW UP LAST NIGHT/HAD DIARRHOEA. AM I SAFE?

If you threw up the pill, then you are not safe. If your bout of diarrhoea lasted a day or so, so that your system did not absorb the pill, then you are not safe. If you were able to take another pill within twelve hours, then your protection resumed. If you throw up *more than three hours* after taking the pill, then the pill was absorbed, and there is no need to worry.

If in any doubt, follow the fourteen-day rule. Being ill probably won't make you feel sexy anyway.

HOW OFTEN SHOULD I HAVE A CHECK-UP WHEN I AM TAKING THE PILL?

Many women complain about the need for six-monthly check-ups while taking the pill. 'But, I feel fine,' is the usual comment. Because the pill is a prescription drug, it can only be given under doctor's supervision.

This is to monitor any unpleasant or dangerous side-effects which may result from taking hormones. Normally, the doctor will ask to see you after your first three months of taking the tablets. This is so s/he can take a smear test and check blood pressure. These are preventive measures and should give you the opportunity to discuss any other health worries that may have risen.

After the first check-up, the doctor will want to see you on a twice-yearly basis. If this is a problem, discuss it with your GP.

Medical card holders sometimes complain that their doctor insists on seeing them every month. Very often, no check-up is made and there is a long wait to be seen. Discuss this with your doctor. There is no reason s/he cannot prescribe a six-month supply of the pill. Some medical card doctors request a monthly review because it means a monthly fee from the Department of Health. If your doctor will not agree to less frequent consultations, and no other medical problem is being monitored during these visits, you have every right to seek another doctor within the medical card scheme.

WHAT SIDE-EFFECTS CAN I EXPECT?

You may have some or none, or they may disappear after the first month. Many of the more talked-about side-effects have been eliminated with the new low dose and tri-phasic pills. But some women still notice pre-menstrual syndrome. Others find their PMS disappears. It's possible to feel depressed, or you may note sore breasts and a weight gain. There is even a risk of increased vaginal irritations, like thrush. Vitamin B-6 can clear some of these symptoms and is always worth taking while on the pill. If any of these side-effects are not sorted out within eight weeks of starting the pill, you may want to discuss changing brands or discontinuing all together. It may be a question of how much you are willing to put up with for nearly 100 per cent protection.

WHAT IS THE DIFFERENCE BETWEEN LOW AND HIGH DOSE PILLS?

Years ago, in America, upwards of 80 micrograms, of the hormone *oestradiol* was given in the pill. In Ireland, 50mg was common. Nowadays, it is usual to take 30mg or less. With the tri-phasic pill, the strongest dose of hormones is given in the middle of the packet, when protection is most needed. During the rest of the cycle, you take a reduced level of the drug. If you are given 50mg today, there is probably a medical reason — like epilepsy or ill-adjustment to the lower doses. If you are aware of no reason, it might be wise to ask for a lower dose.

WHEN AM I SAFE TO HAVE SEX AFTER STARTING THE PILL?

If you start on day five of your cycle (see p. 157), you are safe to have sexual intercourse once you have completed fourteen pill-taking days without any show of bleeding or brown discharge. If you start the pill on day one of the cycle, you are safe straight away. However, women have complained that they bled the entire first month, and were worried about protection. It is doubtful that any pregnancy could implant on a uterine wall which was producing such a discharge, but if you are worried, follow the fourteen-day rule.

CAN THE PILL GIVE ME CANCER?

There has been a lot of research and just as much abuse of research about the link between some types of cancer and prolonged use of the pill. In the autumn of 1983, a British medical journal called *The Lancet* printed an article which related pill use to cervical cancer. Unfortunately, many of the research findings were out of date, so some confusion still remains. No research has completely ruled out the possibility of pill-related cancer, but it has pointed to pills which reduce the health risks. This is the reason for regular check-ups, and the increased use of low dose pills.

Information about breast cancer and the pill is different. The pill has been associated with the prevention of many breast diseases. In the case of cancer, hormones are thought to increase the rate of growth, but have not been proven to actually cause cancer. It's important to give yourself a monthly breast exam whether or not you take the Pill. (See p. 32).

The question of cervical cancer remains. Researchers are looking at the relationship between multiple partners and pill use. This may be the true cause of cervical cancer. There is a link between sexually transmitted disease and cervical cancer. In such cases, the Pill hormones may accelerate the growth of cancerous cells. If you have a cervical erosion or atypical cells, it's important to discuss continuing use of the pill with your doctor.

Ovarian cancer seems to be obsolete among women using the pill.

WHAT ARE THE OTHER DANGERS OF TAKING THE PILL?
Some women have developed a reaction to the pill known as 'deep vein thrombosis': this is when the hormone content of the tablets affects the blood circulation and may lead to clotting. Symptoms include a numbness or tingling, generally in the left arm or leg. Serious clotting could lead to a stroke; for this reason any suspicious symptoms should be checked with a healthcare worker.

IS THERE ANY AGE LIMIT FOR TAKING THE PILL?
Women should have a regular menstrual cycle for at least three-four years before starting the pill. Doctors are reluctant to prescribe the pill to women over thirty-five, especially if they are smokers or have varicose veins or high blood pressure, because of the increased risk of thrombosis.

WHEN SHOULD I TAKE A BREAK FROM THE PILL?
Doctors recommend taking a three-month break after three to five years of regular pill use. This means you should allow three normal periods to occur before you resume your tablets. You can restart the pill the same way you did initially. The reason you have a break on the pill is to make sure ovulation is normal.

HOW LONG DO THE HORMONES STAY IN THE BODY?
There is no easy answer to this. The general advice is that if you want to get pregnant, stay off the pill three months before trying to conceive. This should give your body enough time to discharge any hormone residue. In the case of contraception, the best rule to follow is, once off the pill, pregnancy is possible, so use another form of contraceptive protection.

Some women notice that their periods don't come back as normal when they stop taking the pill. It can often take three months for a regular pattern to establish itself. If you go longer without menstruating, it's wise to talk to your doctor. In some cases, fertility may be affected by prolonged use of the pill.

MY CHILD TOOK SEVERAL OF MY PILLS. IS THERE ANY DANGER?
A few tablets will not harm a child, although they may experience morning sickness. Always keep tablets away from children. Contraceptive pills are very appealing as 'sweetie' substitutes.

PROGESTOGEN ONLY PILL

The progestogen only pill (POP) (mini-pill) is an oral contraceptive method which contains no oestrogen and only a mild dose of progestogen. It is a tablet taken at the same time, every day (usually in the evening) which gives about 97 per cent protection from pregnancy. The POP is taken without any breaks, and allows most women to continue ovulating. It generally works by altering the uterine mucous, making it hostile to sperm, but in some cases, does prevent ovulation.

The advantage of the POP over the normal pill, is that it suits older women, smokers and some women with circulatory problems who would not be suitable for a higher dose pill.

WHY DO I NEED TO TAKE THE POP EVERY EVENING?
Because the progestogen only pill alters the mucous in the uterus, making it a spermicide, it is essential to take the pill daily for maximum protection. If you forget the pill for more than three hours, the spermicide action is reduced. The evening time factor is important if you have intercourse most regularly between 10 p.m. and 10 a.m. If you take the POP at tea-time, then you have maximum safety during these hours. If your schedule alters from this, you may want to change the time you take the pill.

WHAT IF I MISS IT OR TAKE IT LATE?
If you take the POP more than three hours late, then you are not safe. In general, the fourteen-day rule applies. (See p. 158). Some doctors suggest that four days is a sufficient time lapse for rebuilding hormone protection. This holds true as long as you take the pill as soon as you remember. This makes some sense, but has not yet been widely accepted.

If you forget more than one tablet, then the fourteen-day rule definitely applies.

MY DOCTOR ADVISED USING SPERMICIDES WITH THE POP. WHY?

Spermicides are thought to reduce the percentage risk of pregnancy in women taking the POP. They should be used with every act of intercourse until a regular cycle is established. After that, the pessary or cream can be used at ovulation for extra protection.

ARE THERE ANY SIDE-EFFECTS ASSOCIATED WITH THE POP?

The major side-effect is irregular bleeding. You may have periods more frequently in the beginning and it may take several months to establish a regular cycle. Some women notice less frequent periods, and this can cause worry. If regularity is important to you, the POP is not a good contraceptive choice.

Very often the odd bleeding pattern sorts itself out into a routine which is different from the one you had before taking the pill. If you stick with the tablets for six months, it may be worthwhile. If you have regular bleeds on the POP, it's a sign you are ovulating and not pregnant. If you have no bleed, the chances are that the POP is preventing ovulation — you are in fact better protected from the risk of pregnancy. Some women have regular pregnancy tests while taking the pill until they relax about its reliability.

Other side-effects include depression, and sore breasts, but many women who could never tolerate the normal pill are very happy on the POP.

WHEN DO I BLEED ON THE POP?

Since there is no regular pattern to bleeding on the POP, don't expect to bleed at the end of every packet. Each woman is different and you will establish your own cycle.

WHAT SORT OF WOMEN CAN TAKE THE POP?

If a woman is in good general health, then she can take the POP with a doctor's prescription. The same rules apply about twice yearly check-ups (see p. 155). The progestogen only pill is often sutiable for women between thirty-five and menopausal age. Some smokers and some women with weight, varicose vein or circulatory problems may also be candidates. Many women who suffer from PMS find that the POP relieves the symptoms.

IF I GET PREGNANT ON THE POP, IS THERE A RISK OF FOETAL DAMAGE?

Yes, as with any other drug, there is a risk of foetal damage.

THE POP SOUNDS GREAT. WHY DON'T MORE WOMEN TAKE IT?

Because it is relatively new, and underpublicised. As well as that, many women find the three per cent pregnancy risk off-putting. Despite the few shortcomings of the POP, many women are switching to it when they tire of other methods.

MORNING AFTER PILL

The 'morning after pill' is a form of oral contraception taken after *one* instance of unprotected sex. It is never taken on a regular daily basis, and should only be used once in any menstrual cycle. It is usually prescribed by a doctor in emergency situations — rape, or failed contraception, like a burst condom. It is not suitable to take during the fourteen days when you are adjusting to the regular pill. If you have unprotected sex during this period, you will have to discontinue taking the normal pill before the doctor will prescribe morning after treatment.

Also called the post-coital pill (PCP) — meaning after sex — the morning after pill is generally taken in a two-tablet dose and repeated twelve hours later.

HOW SOON AFTER SEX DO I HAVE TO TAKE THE PCP?

Both sets of tablets must be taken within seventy-two hours, and the sooner the better. This means you will need to see the doctor *before* sixty hours have elapsed in order to have both sets of tablets taken on time.

If you have intercourse on Friday midnight, you have until noon on Monday to start the course of hormones. Some family planning clinics are open seven days a week or your doctor may be willing to see you on Saturday or Sunday.

HOW DOES THE PCP WORK?

There are two ways the post-coital pill works. There is no way to tell how it will react with you. It can either postpone ovulation or prevent implantation of a fertilised egg on the uterine wall. In the first case, there is no egg to fertilise, and in the second instance, if the egg is fertilised, it will come out with the next period.

DO I NEED A MEDICAL EXAMINATION BEFORE TAKING THE PCP?

The doctor will usually check blood pressure and take a medical history before prescribing the morning after pill. Occasionally, a doctor will ask to make an internal examination, but this is not routine and you can certainly decline. The best procedure is to ring and find out what will be expected. After your check-up, the doctor will explain how to take the pills. S/he may also ask to see you when you get your next period. In many of the family planning clinics, you will be asked to sign a consent form. This will explain possible risks for any developing foetus. You will be given the PCP when you sign the form.

Some women send a friend in to collect the morning after pill. They feel too shy to go in themselves. No clinic will give the PCP unless they see you in person. There is no need to be shy. The staff are not interested in your sex life and only need to know when you had unprotected sex. If you write down the relevant details (time, cycle day, protection, if any), you will feel less nervous and the consultation will take less time. The doctor may also discuss future contraception with you.

WHAT ARE THE RISKS OF FOETAL DAMAGE IF THE MORNING AFTER PILL FAILS?

No one is exactly sure. Any drug taken in early pregnancy is potentially damaging. Even in a 'normal', drug-free pregnancy, there is a one in forty chance of abnormality.

HOW HIGH IS THE FAILURE RATE?

About three per cent of the women who take the PCP get pregnant. It is important to avoid sex *after* taking the 'morning after pill' because of the risk of increased fertility. Some statistics illustrate that actual pill failure is minimal. Yet more and more women are saying they got pregnant following the post-coital pill. The reason for this is plain. More Irish woman are learning about the PCP. They may have had many instances of unprotected sex in the month and decide to take the PCP when their period is overdue. They were in fact pregnant when they took the morning after pill, but too early for an accurate pregnancy test. Trying to avoid an unwanted pregnancy is understandable, but the morning after pill does not work for more than one sexual act, and should never be taken more than seventy-two hours after unprotected intercourse.

WHAT ARE THE SIDE-EFFECTS OF THE PCP?

Immediate effects include nausea (the doctor may prescribe anti-sickness tablets, or you can buy travel tablets), vomiting, headaches (not common), breast tenderness and feelings similar to those of pre-menstrual syndrome. All of these symptoms usually disappear within three days.

WHAT SHOULD I DO IF I THROW UP MY PILL?

If this happens within three hours of taking the tablets, you will need to repeat the whole procedure. If you get sick after three hours pass, the pills will already have been absorbed. This is probably what prompted the vomiting.

HOW CAN I AVOID GETTING SICK?

If you are prone to tummy upsets, try the anti-sickness tablets. Take one about a half an hour before the two morning after pills. Other tips include avoiding spicy foods, or food that makes you sick, and alcohol; keep your tummy full of bland items like tea and toast; and eat a light meal a half an hour before taking the PCP. If at all possible take the PCP at eleven at night and eleven in the morning. This will give you the opportunity to have breakfast or supper before taking the hormone tablets.

ARE THE ANTI-SICKNESS TABLETS DANGEROUS?

No, but they may make you sleepy, so it's wise not to operate any machinery, like a car, when you have taken them. Any drug can damage a developing foetus.

WHERE CAN I GET THE PCP AND IS IT EXPENSIVE?

The actual tablets are not expensive, and can be obtained through a doctor privately or in a family planning clinic. Many clinics charge about £15 for the consultation. This is because the clinic is very likely already heavily booked and the doctor is seeing you as an emergency. There is also more involved in a PCP consultation: many clients are distressed and want their future contraception needs discussed.

More rural doctors are prepared to prescribe the PCP than before. Some are willing, but unsure of the actual procedure. The larger family planning clinics will often have a list of doctors who provide this service. If your own doctor simply needs technical information, s/he can ring one of these clinics for details.

WHAT DO I DO IF I DISCOVER I AM PREGNANT AFTER TAKING THE PCP?

You will have to decide if you want to continue with the pregnancy. There is no test which can reassure you that the foetus will be perfect. You may like to see a pregnancy counsellor or talk over your options with a doctor. The decision is yours.

WILL TAKING THE PCP AFFECT MY ABILITY TO HAVE FUTURE CHILDREN?

There is no evidence to suggest this.

WILL THE PCP BRING ON A PERIOD?

Sometimes you bleed earlier than normal after taking the post-coital pill, but it's not always a true period. Equally, your period can be several weeks late or right on time. It really depends on what stage you take the PCP and how it reacts with your body chemistry. Worrying will only delay a period.

WILL I NOTICE A CHANGE IN MY PERIOD?

It may be lighter or heavier, and you may get two periods in close succession. This will sort itself out in a few weeks.

IS THE PCP AN ABORTIFACIENT?

It depends on when you think pregnancy occurs. For most of us, this happens when the fertilised egg implants on the uterine wall. If you share this belief, then the PCP is not an abortifacient (something which causes an abortion). If you feel pregnancy occurs when the sperm fertilises the egg, then the PCP can be considered an abortifacient. In this second case, there is no way to guarantee whether ovulation, and therefore fertilisation, was prevented by the PCP, or whether implantation was stopped.

AM I SAFE TO HAVE SEX AFTER TAKING THE PCP?

Because you may be extra fertile after taking the PCP, especially if ovulation is delayed, it is best to avoid intercourse until you find a suitable contraceptive method. Remember, the PCP can only be used once in a cycle.

INTRA-UTERINE DEVICE (IUD OR COIL)

The intra-uterine device (IUD) is a small piece of curled plastic with a string on the end. It is fitted into the uterus by dilating the cervix. Also called the coil, it gives about 97 per cent protection from pregnancy by creating an irritation in the uterus. Because the irritation may result in infection and tubal blockages, the coil is only advisable for women who have had a number of full-term pregnancies and are not worried about the fertility risk. Coils are now being linked with pelvic inflammatory disease (see p. 124) and subsequent infertility.

HOW DOES THE COIL WORK? HOW SAFE IS IT?

No-one is exactly sure how the coil will work for you. It may alter the uterine mucus, making it hostile to sperm, or it may irritate the womb lining.

The coil offers about the same protection as the progestogen-only (mini) pill: a three per cent failure rate. It seems to be safer after the first three months. By this time the irritation is built up sufficiently to provide maximum protection. Using spermicidal cream or pessaries will also lessen the risk of conception.

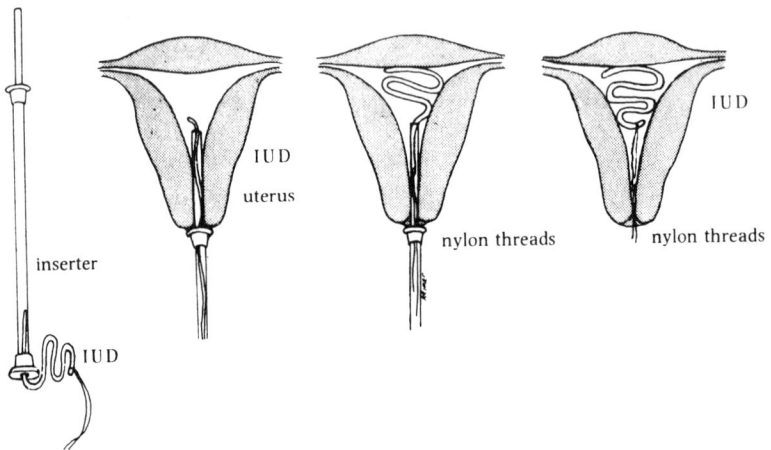

22. Insertion of IUD into the uterus

WHO IS SUITABLE FOR THE COIL?
Older women who have completed their families, women with light and relatively painless periods, and women who have no other gynaecological problems. The coil is suitable for women going through the menopause because it contains no hormones and gives the greatest amount of non-barrier protection outside the oral contraceptive methods.

The coil is unsuitable for women with recurring infections, or for those who come into regular contact with sexually transmitted diseases. It is also inadvisable for women who use injectable drugs without medical supervision. This is because of the increased infection risk from dirty needles.

HOW IS THE COIL PUT IN?

For a coil fitting, you will need to assume the same position you would for a smear test or infection screening, when a speculum is inserted (see p. 34). It is important to practise breathing techniques so that the tummy muscles are relaxed and the coil insertion is more comfortable. Once you are ready, the doctor will dilate the cervix with an instrument called a probe. This is a metal rod. Ask to see the IUD before it goes in. It too is attached to a long plastic probe which separates from the coil after insertion. The curly plastic bit at the end of the probe will remain inside your uterus and a string will hang outside the cervix. You will need to check the string after every menstrual period, to make sure the coil is still in place.

While fitting the coil, the doctor may sterilise the vulval area with iodine. This may show up in your knickers, so don't be alarmed. You will be given a sanitary towel and asked to come back in six weeks for a check-up.

WHEN IS THE BEST TIME TO HAVE A COIL INSERTED?

The ideal time to have a coil inserted is during a period. This assures the doctor that you are not pregnant and also means the cervix is wide enough for a comfortable fitting.

If the idea of having an IUD fitted during menstruation does not appeal to you, chat to the doctor. Some will try an insertion at other times if you agree to refrain from unprotected intercourse for a week beforehand and undertake a pregnancy test.

DOES IT HURT?

The coil can hurt when it is being inserted. There may be cramping for a few days afterwards. If this does not clear up, have the coil checked.

Occasionally, with an infection, the coil can cause pain or discomfort and this must be investigated. Low back pain around ovulation and painful periods are two other possible side-effects.

HOW LONG SHOULD THE COIL STAY IN?

The newer coils stay in for two to three years. This is because they contain copper and this wears out over time. Some of the older and larger coils, like the Lippes Loop, can stay in ten years. Any woman who has a coil, should have it checked when she is having her regular smear. Keep a note of the type you have.

WHAT IF I NOTICE THE STRING MISSING?

If the string goes missing, it doesn't necessarily mean the coil has come out. The string may have gone up into the uterus and a period can wash it back down. It is important, however, to have the IUD checked if this happens, as you may be at risk from pregnancy if the coil has been expelled. Sometimes the coil can shift its position in the uterus or perforate the walls and this should be investigated.

WHAT DO I DO IF THE COIL IS COMING OUT?
You may damage yourself if the coil is trapped at the cervix. See a doctor straight away to have it removed.

IF THE STRING IS MISSING, HOW IS THE COIL REMOVED?
The normal removal of the coil by the string is quick and painless: if the string is missing and the coil cannot be easily removed, you may be asked to have an anaesthetic so the IUD can be taken out with maximum comfort. This is rare.

WHERE DO I HAVE A COIL FITTED? IS IT EXPENSIVE?
Some GPs and most family planning clinics insert IUDs. Since it is a specialised skill, you may want to ring and find out when the appointments are scheduled. Do this before you expect your period.

The coil costs anywhere from £30 to £50, depending on who is doing it. This generally covers your six-week checkup too.

CAN MY PARTNER FEEL THE COIL?
No, but some say they feel the string. If this is a problem, the doctor may be able to shorten the string, but this can create problems when it's time to remove the coil.

I USED TO HAVE A DALKON SHIELD FITTED AND HAVE HEARD THIS MAY BE WHY I CAN'T GET PREGNANT
The Dalkon Shield IUD was taken off the market by its manufacturer A. H. Robbins in the 1970s, but by this time many women had suffered serious pelvic disorders affecting their fertility. In the United States and Britain, a lawsuit is pending,, but the closing date for claims is April, 1986. Still, if you had this type of coil fitted (check with your doctor or family planning clinic), you may be able to establish a claim. The address to write to is:

DALKON SHIELD,
PO BOX 444,
Richmond, Virginia,
USA 23203.

POST-COITAL IUD

The post-coital IUD (PCIUD), is a coil that is fitted within five to seven days after unprotected intercourse. Used post-coitally it seems to have a higher success rate than the PCP. For many women who learn too late about the 'morning-after pill', the PCIUD has provided contraceptive protection.

Only a few doctors and family planning clinics offer this service. The cost is about £35 to £40 which includes a pregnancy test and/or removal of the coil with a six-week check-up.

HOW DOES IT WORK?

The post-coital coil works the same way as the normal coil. It irritates the uterine lining making it difficult for a fertilised egg to implant on the lining.

IS IT MORE EFFECTIVE THAN THE MORNING AFTER PILL?

It can be, but it is difficult to insert in a woman who has never had a baby. An advantage is that you can retain it as future contraception.

I'VE NEVER HAD A FULL-TERM PREGNANCY. WILL THEY STILL FIT THE PCIUD?

The doctor will try to fit the coil, but will not force the issue if it is uncomfortable or difficult. The doctor will probably ask you to undertake having the coil removed once you get your next period.

CAN THEY PUT THE COIL IN ONCE MY PERIOD IS OVERDUE?

No. It has to be inserted within five to seven days after intercourse.

ARE ALL THE SIDE-EFFECTS AND PROCEDURES THE SAME AS WITH THE NORMAL COIL?

Yes.

I HAD UNPROTECTED INTERCOURSE ALL MONTH. WILL THE COIL BRING ON MY PERIOD?

The coil will not be fitted in these circumstances. The doctor will only insert it if the instance of unprotected sex took place in the week prior to your visit.

The coil can cause bleeding after insertion, but does not necessarily 'bring on' a period.

CAN I HAVE INTERCOURSE AFTER GETTING THE COIL?
Yes, but remember there is a three per cent failure rate and spermicides are a good idea.

DIAPHRAGM (CAP)

The cap or diaphragm is a *barrier* method of contraception. It provides a wall of protection between the cervix and any approaching sperm. It is 96 per cent effective when used with spermicidal cream or pessaries. This statistic can vary according to how confident we are in using the cap. Increasingly, research is showing that it is the spermicide which offers protection. The cap merely holds the cream in place.

To have a diaphragm fitted, it's necessary to make an appointment with a healthcare worker. During the consultation, the vagina is measured and we are taught how to use the cap. The fee for fitting and buying the cap and the cream and/or pessaries can come to as much as £35. Some doctors and all family planning clinics offer this service.

HOW DO I INSERT AND USE THE CAP?
Once the size of your cervix is matched to a cap, you will be shown how to insert the cap yourself. The nurse or doctor will measure you when you are lying on the couch. This involves an internal examination.

The cap is inserted by squeezing it into a tampon shape, and pushing it into the vagina with the fingers. This is made easy by the cream which you spread onto the diaphragm. Once the cap is inside the vagina, you will need to check that it covers the cervix and fits neatly behind the pubic bone. The nurse or doctor will show you what to look for. Some women squat to insert

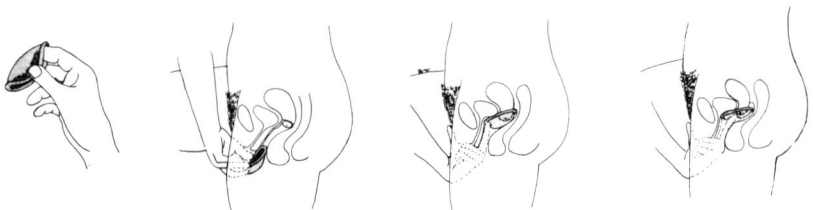

23. Inserting a diaphragm

the cap, and others do it lying down.

DO CAP SIZES VARY THAT MUCH?

Yes. Caps vary in size from about 60cm to 105cm. Women who have never had a baby will have a smaller vaginal vault (this is the area of space in the vagina).

Size 70 to 85 is average. Women who have been through a number of deliveries may wear a larger size.

Gaining or losing weight can affect the size of the cap. If you shift more than ten pounds or have a baby, it's best to have the diaphragm checked.

HOW DO I GET THE CAP OUT?

By reaching into the vagina with one of your fingers, pressing the outer ring against the pubic bone for resistance, and tugging the cap out gently.

HOW LONG BEFORE INTERCOURSE SHOULD IT BE PUT IN?

It can be put in right up to the last minute before sexual intercourse. With practice, it can be fitted while you are in bed, and you can teach your partner how to help. Keep a box of tissues handy. On the other hand, you can put the cap in up to two hours before intercourse. If you leave it any longer, you will need to replenish the spermicide cover with a pessary or fresh application of cream.

HOW LONG AFTER INTERCOURSE CAN I REMOVE THE CAP?

You must keep the cap in place at least six hours after sexual intercourse — some clinics advise eight hours. This means that in the six to eight hours after ejaculation, you must not touch the cap or shift its position. You should also avoid sitting in the bath as this can wash away the spermicide. A shower is fine.

WHAT DO I DO IF I HAVE INTERCOURSE AGAIN WITHIN THE EIGHT HOURS?

Before you have sexual intercourse again, use another application of spermicide. Put the pessary or cream on the *outside* of the cap. *Do not take the cap out.*

WHAT HAPPENS IF I WANT TO HAVE INTERCOURSE EXACTLY EIGHT HOURS AFTER I PUT THE CAP IN?

Once the eight hours have passed, you have two options: you can remove the cap and wash it, then reapply cream and insert it again; or you can use a pessary as you would for the situation above. You must wait another eight hours before removing the cap.

HOW LONG CAN THE CAP STAY IN?
The cap should be removed within twenty-four hours of insertion.

IS THE CAP MESSY?
Some women find the cap very messy, and other women don't mind. The creams can be awkward in the summer or on holidays when the heat melts them. Placing the packet in the fridge will help. Also the cream's perfume may be off-putting. Some products are tidier than others. The family planning clinics can advise you. There are some spermicides especially suitable for women with sensitive skin.

Some women talk of the advantages of the so-called 'mess'. The creams offer increased lubrication and make intercourse more pleasant, or you can use a spermicide jelly for extra lubrication. Other bonuses of the cap include the fact that you control its use, it is only used when you need it, and, if used efficiently, can offer as much as 98 per cent cover.

ARE THERE ANY SIDE-EFFECTS? CAN EVERYONE USE IT?
The only ill-effects of the cap are potential allergic reactions to the rubber and spermicides, or the risk of cystitis. If you are a chronic cystitis sufferer, the cap is not suitable, because it may put increased pressure on the urethra. Other than that, the only women who may be unable to use a cap are those with weak vaginal muscles.

DOES IT HURT?
No. You do not feel the cap inside you unless it is pressing against another organ. This sometimes happens if you forget to go to the loo. The cap may cause pressure on the bladder and create discomfort. If you notice pain at any other time, the cap is probably not a correct fit. Have this checked.

CAN YOU USE THE CAP WITHOUT SPERMICIDES?
It is possible, but your safety drops to about 80 per cent. The whole point of the cap is that it holds the spermicide in place, creating a barrier against sperm. If no spermicide is used, the sperm can sneak beneath the rim of the diaphragm and head straight for the fallopian tubes.

HOW LONG DOES A CAP LAST? SHOULD I HAVE IT CHECKED?
The life-span of a diaphragm varies according to use. If it is used every night for a year, it may begin to fray. If it is used twice a month, it can last several years.

It is important to wash the cap after each use in mild, soap-free water. Put it away in a dark place so that heat and light will not affect the rubber.

Make sure it is dry and in its original round shape first. If you allow your cap to lose its shape, the risk of pregnancy increases.

Make sure to check for holes before you use it. Hold the cap up to the light or fill it with water. If it leaks, you need a new diaphragm.

If you have a baby, you may need to have the size checked.

HOW LONG DOES A TUBE OF CREAM LAST?

It depends on how much you use. Some women put very little cream on the cap, while others completely cover it. You should use at least enough cream as would cover a tenpenny piece. The minimum amount of applications per tube is roughly eight to ten. The actual expiry date for spermicides is about five years after manufacture. A tube costs about £4.

CONDOMS, SPERMICIDES AND SPONGE

The condom (or sheath, rubber, johnny, French letter, durex) is a barrier form of contraception that fits over an erect penis. It is 96 per cent safe unless it bursts, and this happens anywhere from 5 per cent to 20 per cent of the time. It seems to be slightly porous and this contributes to its failure rate. The condom is made of thin rubber, shaped like a balloon, with a teat at the end. The open end of the condom is placed on the head of the penis, and rolled down to the bottom. The nipple end of the sheath must be left slightly loose, and empty of air. This will limit the chances of an accident, and leave room for the sperm to ejaculate — otherwise the force might burst the rubber. It's best to take off rings and be aware of long fingernails which might tear the condom.

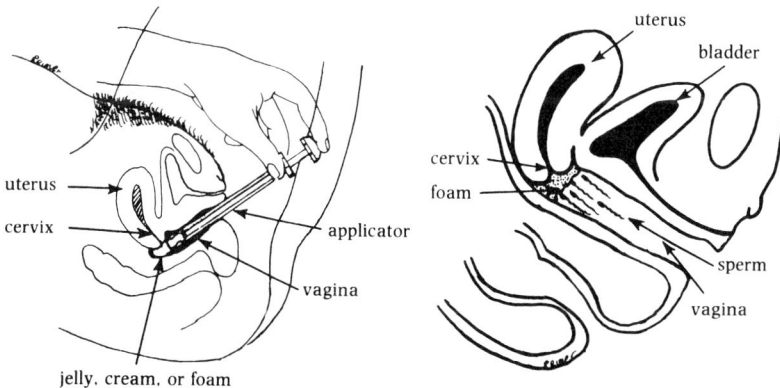

jelly. cream, or foam

24. Inserting foam, cream or jelly

Spermicides are often used with condoms to cut down on the risk of pregnancy in the case of a torn sheath. Cream or pessaries can be used, the latter being easier to insert. Condoms and pessaries cost between £3 and £4 a dozen. They can be purchased in family planning clinics and some pharmacies. Despite the fact that the sale of condoms has now been made legal to anyone over eighteen years of age, some chemists refuse to stock them. Other pharmacies, who do stock them, do not want the fact made public. The directory will be able to guide you to some of the outlets.

WHEN SHOULD A CONDOM BE PUT ON?
The sheath should be rolled onto the hard penis before any sexual contact takes place. It is not safe to have a bit of intercourse, withdraw, put the condom on, and then wait for ejaculation. Once the penis is erect, semen can escape, and pregnancy may result.

WHEN SHOULD THE CONDOM BE REMOVED?
As soon as sexual intercourse is over, the condom should be taken off. Make sure the penis is outside the vagina first! Some men stay hard for a while after ejaculation, and like to keep their penis inside, but there is a risk that the sheath will be pulled off by the vaginal muscles if he stays in too long. If any of the semen spills, there is a chance of conception.

ARE THERE ANY SIDE-EFFECTS ASSOCIATED WITH THE CONDOM?
Some women find the condoms irritating. This may be the result of a reaction to the lubrication, or because the actual rubber annoys the vulval tissues. There are allergy condoms available, and KY jelly may clear the lubrication problem without causing an allergic reaction.

THE CONDOM CAME OFF INSIDE ME. WHAT SHOULD I DO?
If you cannot remove it yourself, ask a friend or healthcare worker to oblige. This is a fairly common occurrence. The next step is to consider whether 'morning-after' contraception is needed. (See p. 164, 171).

I NOTICED A SLIGHT TEAR IN THE CONDOM THIS MORNING. I USE SPERMICIDES. AM I SAFE?
This is a tough one. If the spermicides provide enough protection on their own, then why do the manufacturers suggest using them only with another form of contraception, like the cap or condom? Yet they do offer some help. It's best to get a second opinion based on your particular circumstances.

HOW LONG DO CONDOMS LAST?

Condoms can only be used once, and then are thrown away. Always check for tears or holes before putting in the bin. The actual expiry date is about five years after manufacture.

CAN THEY PROTECT FROM INFECTIONS LIKE AIDS?

To a certain extent. In fact this is why they were first invented, but because they are marginally porous, they do not provide 100 per cent protection.

WHAT ARE SPERMICIDES?

Spermicides consist of various chemical formations designed to kill sperm added to creams, jellies, pessaries and foam. They must always be used in conjunction with another contraceptive method (except in some cases of menopause — see this section).

HOW ARE THEY USED?

This depends on the type of spermicide you choose. Creams can be applied to the sexual area by hand or applicator, or inserted into the vagina. Shop around for a brand that suits. The foam is usually squirted into the vagina, while the pessary can be inserted on the end of your finger, like a tampon.

Both the cream and jelly come in toothpaste tubes and are applied to the cap by squeezing the required amount onto the rubber surface. Or you can fill an applicator, insert this in the vagina, and inject the cream this way. All of the spermicides melt quickly and prove a little runny. Some women like to use light sanitary towels to protect their underpants, although spermicides don't stain.

DO ALL SPERMICIDES ACT THE SAME WAY?

All spermicides kill sperm. Some are more irritating than others, and some are not suitable for use with rubber products. The use of spermicides will vary according to your personal preference. Pessaries are easier to use with condoms, cream with a diaphragm.

ARE THERE ANY SIDE-EFFECTS?

Other than the allergic reactions some women get with spermicides, thrush-like symptoms have been noted. This may be the result of intercourse or a chemical reaction in the vagina. They will not harm your partner if taken orally, so if he can bear the taste, oral sex is fine. Some people don't like the highly perfumed smell of spermicides.

WHAT IS THE SPONGE?

This is a relatively new method of contraception which can be inserted into the vagina like a tampon. The sponge comes in one size only and does not have to be measured. It must be dipped in water before insertion to activate the spermicide. Once inside the vagina, it can be left for twenty-four hours. It is advisable to add an extra pessary for more than one act of intercourse. Unfortunately, the sponge has a 20 per cent failure rate and is not advisable for women who want foolproof contraception. As yet, it is not widely available, and it's expensive — about £5 for three. Distribution is random, so see suppliers in the directory.

ARE THERE ANY SIDE-EFFECTS?
The same side-effects as for the spermicides hold true here.

WHO IS SUITABLE FOR A SPONGE?
If you don't mind another pregnancy, the sponge may be suitable. It can also be used in place of other spermicides along with the condom or POP. Some breastfeeding women may feel the sponge gives them just the added protection they need, though it doesn't provide a hundred per cent protection. In some cases, menopausal women who have gone a year without a period may find the sponge just the cover they need.

STERILISATION
Sterilisation is a simple surgical procedure which puts an end to possible pregnancy. Both men and women can be sterilised. Male sterilisation is easier, and is called *vasectomy*. Female sterilisation can be done in two ways: the first is an older technique which involves major surgery and several days stay in hospital. The second, more popular type, is *tubal ligation* by *laparoscopy*. This second procedure only means an overnight stay in the clinic.

Vasectomy is done in many of the family planning clinics and some hospitals for about £100. It can be done through the medical card scheme. In the case of vasectomy, the operation takes only a few minutes and has relatively few side-effects (a few days of discomfort is common). Before unprotected intercourse can take place, your partner's semen will have to be tested for viable sperm. This is done about three months after the operation.

In most parts of Ireland, and for most women, sterilisation is inaccessible. Hospital boards of ethics in many cases refuse to allow female sterilisation for contraceptive purposes. This means that only middle-class women with money can avail of the procedure. The cost for tubal ligation in private Irish clinics ranges from £150 to £300. This is not redeemable on the VHI. Medical card holders can avail of sterilisation on an *ad hoc* basis in rural areas like Galway, Limerick and Portlaoise.

For many of us, having fertility control taken out of our hands and placed in those of an anonymous board of ethics is no longer tolerable. Many of us are taking action by lobbying hospital boards and the Department of Health. Our success depends on other women doing the same.

HOW IS FEMALE STERILISATION DONE?

There are two methods of sterilisation done in Ireland. One involves major surgery and about four or five days in hospital. The second type, called a *tubal ligation* by *laparoscopy* is very much simpler and only means an overnight stay for checking the tiny incisions.

Laparoscopy is a procedure where the tummy is opened only slightly at the navel and near the pubic bone. A gas is then pumped in through a tiny pipe, so that all the internal organs are easily seen (like blowing up a balloon). A sort of telescope is then inserted and the tubes are tied (tubal ligation) without major surgery. This is usually done under general or epidural anaesthetic.

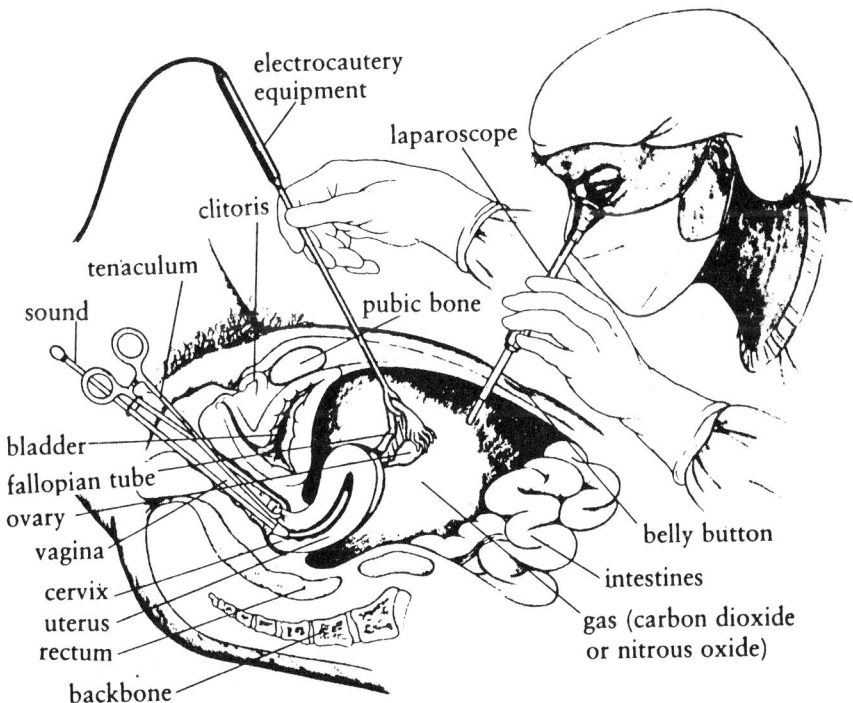

25. Side view of sterilisation (Tubal litigation) Laparoscopy

HOW LONG IS THE WAITING LIST?

In Cork, the waiting list is so long, they are no longer taking referrals. In the two Kildare clinics, you will have to wait two to three weeks. If you go to London, arrangements can be made within a few days.

The laparoscopic method leaves no scar and very little discomfort. The other method is major surgery, and you will need time to recover from the operation.

HOW DO I GO ABOUT GETTING STERILISATION?

The Royal Victoria Hospital in Cork, well known for providing sterilisation facilities, is no longer taking referrals because of the long waiting list. Private clinics (see Directory under sterilisation) can see you within a month or so of first contact. Many of the family planning clinics offer counselling and referral. There is usually a fee of £20 for this service in addition to the £150-£290 for the actual operation.

Once your appointment is made, you will simply arrive on the day, probably having eaten no food in the previous twelve hours, and wait your turn with the doctor. Some of the private clinics are very pleasant. If you are sterilised in hospital, the treatment will vary according to where you are.

Some GPs will refer for sterilisation, and in this case you will need a letter.

DOES IT HURT?

Because of the anaesthetic, you will feel nothing while the sterilisation is being carried out. There may be some discomfort afterwards, depending on the medical procedure. If you have a laparoscopy, bring loose clothing as the stitches at the waist may be irritated by a belt. If you have major surgery, it will take a few days to recover.

DO I HAVE TO TELL MY PARTNER?

This is a tricky one. Some women have no partner to tell and some doctors are willing to decide on each case individually. Other clinics insist on consent forms. A counsellor in one of the family planning clinics can advise you.

IS THERE ANY AGE LIMIT?

In the private Irish clinics, the brochure suggests you should be over 30. Birth certificates are not required. More emphasis is placed on the number of children you already have, and whether or not you have considered the finality of sterilisation.

If you are having any problems finding someone who will offer you

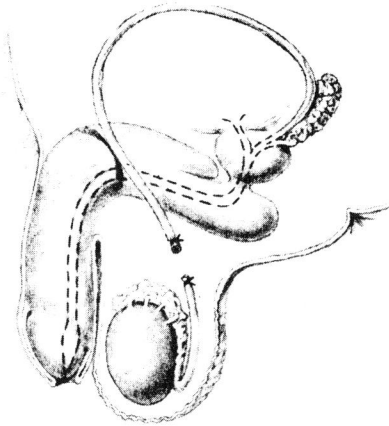

26. Male sterilisation (Litigation of the vas deferens) Vasectomy

sterilisation, chat to one of the counselling agencies who may have a solution.

DOES STERILISATION EVER FAIL?
No method of contraception is a hundred per cent foolproof, but sterilisation has the highest success rate of all. It is most unlikely to fail.

ARE THERE ANY SIDE-EFFECTS?
None, outside those associated with the operation, like soreness for a few days. Don't believe the scare stories about early menopause or pre-menstrual syndrome resulting from sterilisation. You will still ovulate as normal and still have regular periods. Instead of travelling to the uterus, the egg will be absorbed into the tissue surrounding the fallopian tubes.

IS A HYSTERECTOMY THE SAME AS STERILISATION?
No. A hysterectomy is major surgery to remove all or some of the female sexual organs (the ovaries and uterus). Sterilisation simply prevents one activity, the egg passing into the uterus. All the organs are left intact. It is true, however, that you cannot get pregnant after a hysterectomy

WHICH IS EASIER, THE VASECTOMY OR FEMALE STERILISATION?

Technically, the vasectomy is easier. It also only takes ten minutes in a doctor's surgery. No general anaesthetic is required.

Despite the relative ease of male sterilisation, some men are still frightened. They feel it may affect their sexuality, or ability to have an erection. After a vasectomy, ejaculation occurs as normal, but there is no sperm in the semen. Proper counselling will clear up any other worries.

The only major discomfort associated with the vasectomy is the injection of a local anaesthetic in the scrotum (balls). There may be aching afterwards, so men are advised not to lift heavy items for several days.

CAN STERILISATION BE DONE ON THE VHI?

The insurance company says no, but I have seen women get around this.

I HAVE HEARD IT IS REVERSIBLE.

Doctors are working on techniques to reverse sterilisation. So far, no method has met with great success. It would be unwise to have a sterilisation operation if you wanted more children.

NATURAL METHODS

'Natural methods' of contraception are very popular in Ireland, but they account for the majority of unplanned pregnancies. Some women query the use of the word 'natural', as these methods employ thermometers, calculators and various charts to detect fertility. Originally the term suggested that these methods were based on looking for natural signs, like high temperature, or vaginal discharges, to ascertain when ovulation took place. The key to natural family planning is to find out exactly when you ovulate, and to abstain from intercourse during this time.

Many of us adapt the natural methods to our own needs. We may feel sure we ovulate exactly mid-cycle every month. For those few days, we use condoms. During the rest of the month we may enjoy sexual intercourse relatively free from worry. This is only advisable if you know your body thoroughly. Without practice, there is a fairly high failure rate.

WHAT IS THE TEMPERATURE METHOD?

This is the technique used to detect fertility by thermometer. For a period of several months, you must take an early morning reading and jot it down in a little book. Eventually a pattern emerges. During ovulation, your temperature will rise, and this will signal you to avoid unprotected intercourse for the next few days. What you use for contraception until the pattern is established is up to yourself.

HOW DO I TAKE MY TEMPERATURE? WHERE CAN I BUY A THERMOMETER?

The most accurate reading is made by placing the thermometer in the rectum for three minutes. Some women prefer to use the mouth or vagina. Thermometers can be bought in chemists, family planning clinics and medical suppliers along with the charts. Remember to sterilise the thermometer after use.

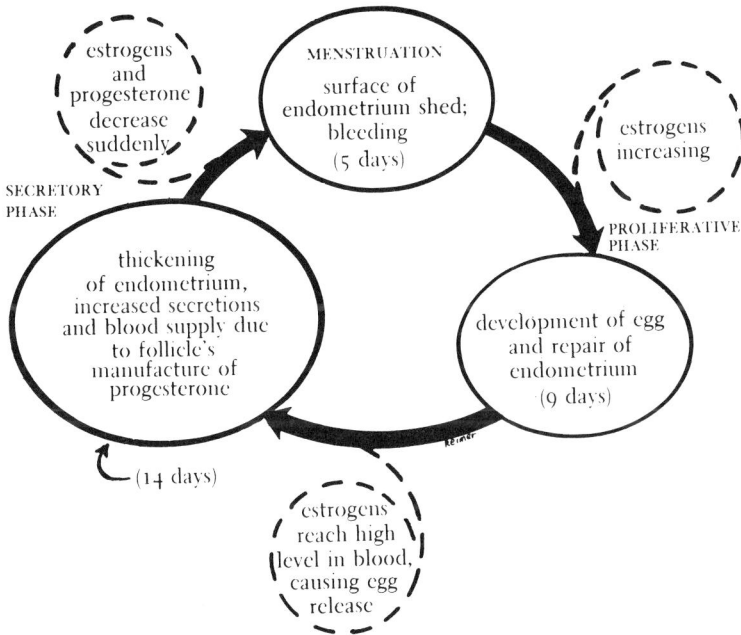

27. Menstrual cycle

WHAT IS THE BILLINGS METHOD?

This is a contraceptive practice based on checking for an ovulation discharge. It needs to be done on a daily basis. You will be looking for a change from the normal sticky discharge, to one that is wet and slippery. The increased lubrication during ovulation helps the sperm to travel more quickly to fertilisation. You must avoid unprotected sexual intercourse when this happens.

WHAT IS THE 'SAFE PERIOD'? IS IT SAFE AS CONTRACEPTION?

This is a common expression used by women who may practise no other form of contraception besides guessing when they are ovulating. To be frank, there is no 'safe period' of time when contraceptive protection is guaranteed. The very act of intercourse can trigger ovulation, even near the end of menses.

Most women who use this method, avoid intercourse mid-cycle without necessarily checking for signs of ovulation. This is extremely risky unless used in conjunction with a barrier form of contraception.

ARE THERE ANY SIDE-EFFECTS ASSOCIATED WITH 'NATURAL METHODS'?

There are no actual side-effects, but some people find abstention a strain. Many women do complain that they feel sexiest exactly when they are not meant to have intercourse — at ovulation. This does not mean you can't enjoy sexual contact. Some couples find this actually enhances their relationship. On the other hand, many women feel that they bear the brunt of contraceptive responsibility with natural methods. If it causes problems, there are other options available.

WHERE CAN I LEARN MORE ABOUT IT?

There are several family planning clinics, church-run courses, and independent counsellors in the various methods. See the directory.

WITHDRAWAL

The withdrawal method is another 'contraceptive' practice which has been responsible for many unplanned pregnancies. The term 'withdrawal' refers to the act of sexual intercourse where the man pulls the penis out of the vagina before ejaculation. The problem with this is that the man often 'comes' before he has had a chance to withdraw. As well as that, once the penis is erect, there may be sperm in the fluid which lubricates the penis, even before semen is ejaculated.

Some women complain that this method makes them tense worrying about the risk of pregnancy. They feel unable to relax enough to enjoy the sexual encounter. A lot of us feel this places the control of our fertility in the hands of our partner. But outside a possible pregnancy, there are no apparent physical side-effects.

ABSTINENCE

This means doing without sexual intercourse altogether. It doesn't mean that you need do without sexual contact. Try masturbation, fondling, kissing and many of the other forms of communication discussed in chapter 6.

DEPO-PROVERA

Depo-provera is an injectable hormone made with progestogen. Once it's introduced to the body, it remains for three months (minimum) and cannot be removed. Some women choose this form of contraception because they don't have to remember to take daily tablets or fit devices.

There are side-effects associated with the use of Depo-provera: weight gain, hair loss, depression, irregular and heavy bleeding. There have also been cancer scares connected to its use, but these have not been proved. As a result, it has been taken off the market in the United States. It is still available in African, European countries and Ireland.

WHY IS IT USED?

Some doctors think it is a good method, and there are women who agree. It has been offered to travelling women in the mistaken belief the travellers might not turn up for regular check-ups. This excuse is dubious, since Depo-provera must be re-injected at regular intervals anyway. If this is the reason we are offered injectable contraception, we must make it clear that the doctor's assumptions are incorrect.

In some cases of mental disability, Depo-provera is used for similar reasons. As with any other situation, this can only be decided on an individual basis.

DRUGS & CONTRACEPTION

Just a few words on this: different drugs can alter the effectiveness of some types of contraceptive methods, especially the hormone pills. It is always wise to seek a second opinion if in any doubt. Below is a list of medication which may interfere with its corresponding contraceptive:

The pill and pop   Anti-histamines, antibiotics, heroin, some anti-depressants and epilepsy drugs.

IUD/coil   Heroin (because of the risk of infection from a dirty needle).

*I AM A HEROIN USER. WHAT ARE MY CONTRACEPTIVE
CHOICES?*
Your choices are very limited. The pills are not effective and the coil may
prove dangerous. Other than the 'natural methods', you can use condoms,
the cap, or opt for sterilisation. It is important to have contraceptive cover
since the risk of foetal damage amongst pregnant heroin users is high.

*MY DOCTOR REFUSED TO HELP ME WHEN I TOLD
HER/HIM I WAS AN ADDICT*
Some doctors are frightened of heroin addicts and others simply don't
want to get involved. Many addicts need a lot of medical attention, and
most GPs haven't that much time to spare. There are many agencies where
help is available. See the directory.

I AM EPILEPTIC. CAN I TAKE THE PILL?
In most cases a low-dose pill is not suitable, but a high dose of the normal
pill may suit, since it won't be affected by your epilepsy medication. The
coil is not a good idea because of the risk of inducing a seizure during
insertion.

ABORTION

The word 'abortion' is a medical term used to refer to a termination of
pregnancy. Doctors sometimes employ the expression in the case of
miscarriage or where we undergo a D&C to remove a pregnancy from the
uterus. Abortion is not a contraceptive method because conception, and
therefore implantation of a fertilised ovum, has already taken place.

Abortion is illegal in Ireland. This has been the case since a law was
passed in 1861. In 1983, a constitutional amendment was held in southern
Ireland which granted equal rights to life to both mother and foetus. The
text of the amendment reads thus:

> *The State acknowledges the right to
> life of the unborn and, with due
> regard to the equal right of the
> mother, guarantees in its laws to
> respect, and as far as practicable, by
> its laws to defend and vindicate that
> right.*

Despite this legislation, at least 4,000 women go to Britain each year for termination of pregnancy. Access to information regarding *all* our pregnancy options — be it continuing with the pregnancy, fostering, adoption or abortion is essential. To a certain extent such information is available in Ireland (see directory). At the time of going to press, pregnancy counselling centres are still able to discuss all our choices, so we can make an informed decision. In some cases they are able to refer to Britain for further counselling.

WHERE IS ABORTION LEGAL?
In nearly every country in the world. The nearest location to Ireland is Britain, where abortion has been legal since the 1960s. To obtain a safe and legal British abortion, you must see two British doctors and a counsellor who will discuss your various options.

AT WHAT STAGE OF PREGNANCY ARE ABORTIONS PERFORMED?
Medically, the safest time to have a termination is between seven and ten weeks of pregnancy. In Great Britain, it is illegal after twenty-eight weeks. In practice, clinics will want you to be under twenty-four weeks.

WHAT HAPPENS IN AN ABORTION? ARE YOU CUT OPEN?
Most terminations are performed by D&C (dilation and curettage). You lie on a table and are given an anaesthetic. The doctor then inserts a speculum into the vagina to see the cervical opening. Once the os is dilated, the uterine lining is removed and any pregnancy comes out with the lining. You are not cut open.

In Britain, several procedures are used depending on the duration of the pregnancy. A D&C can be done up to about sixteen weeks in some clinics. After that, more elaborate methods are used, which may involved staying more than one night in hospital. In some cases, labour is actually induced.

DOES ABORTION HURT?

Since termination is performed under a general anaesthetic, you won't actually feel the D&C. Afterwards, you may experience menstrual cramping.

CAN I BE ARRESTED IF I HAVE AN ABORTION IN BRITAIN AND TELL MY IRISH DOCTOR?
No. However, some doctors won't want to help you following a termination. Most family planning clinics offer post operative care — especially those who also offer counselling. Maternity hospitals will see you

if you are worried and cannot contact a doctor. Some hospital staff are more understanding than others.

WILL ANYONE KNOW I HAD AN ABORTION?
Not unless you tell them. A doctor might suspect, but can never be certain.

WILL I BE ABLE TO GET PREGNANT AGAIN AFTERWARDS?
Yes, although there are exceptions to every rule. In fact, it is possible to become pregnant straight away, so it's wise to prepare a contraceptive method. The os (cervical opening) is unusually wide following an abortion, so sperm can travel more easily to the fallopian tubes.

HOW LONG AFTER ABORTION SHOULD I WAIT BEFORE I HAVE SEXUAL INTERCOURSE?
This is a matter of personal choice. It's best to avoid actual intercourse for a few weeks afterwards. You need to give your body time to heal, and will want to limit any infection risk. As far as contraception is concerned, the pill will make you safe fourteen days after starting it. British clinics will often give you a prescription to commence the day after the abortion.

HOW WILL I FEEL AFTER HAVING AN ABORTION?
This really depends on you. Some women are relieved, others are sad, some are a mixture of the two and others describe guilt feelings. With proper counselling, you *can* learn to make and accept whatever decision is necessary. We all live with difficult choices and our feelings about them can change with time. The counsellor will help you to examine all the options until you decide what is right for you. You may walk in the door knowing that a termination is your only alternative, and come our feeling that continuing with the pregnancy is the best decision — or vice versa. Remember, only you can choose, and you will have to live with that choice.

If for any reason you experience ongoing distress following an abortion, it's important to seek help from friends and/or a counsellor. Professional agencies have lists of sympathetic doctors and clergy who can review the situation with you.

IF I BECOME PREGNANT AGAIN, SHOULD I TELL MY OBSTETRICIAN ABOUT THE ABORTION?
It is always a good idea to give as much medical information to the doctor as possible. There are some blood groups, like rhesus negative, which need to be monitored in second and third pregnancies, so a previous pregnancy which ended in abortion has to be counted. Your physician will need to

know this. If you are worried about the whole hospital finding out, be sure to ask the doctor *not* to mark the abortion on your chart. Also let the obstetrician know if your present partner is privy to this information.

ARE THERE ANY COMPLICATIONS ASSOCIATED WITH ABORTION?

There is something called *retained products* which occurs in a small minority of cases. It means that not all the uterine lining was removed during the termination; there may be some foetal matter left inside the womb. You will probably experience heavy cramping and bleeding within a few days of the abortion and will need to see a doctor. Terminations performed before eight weeks of foetal development have a greater chance of this occurring.

It's extremely important to have a check-up roughly six weeks after the abortion.

Occasionally infections follow abortion, but these are easily cleared by antibiotics. Discomfort or feverishness are indicators of an infection.

WILL I BLEED LONG AFTERWARDS?

This varies with the individual. Some women bleed for a few days and others for a few weeks. As long as there is no clotting or cramping, everything should be as normal.

IS IT DANGEROUS TO HAVE MORE THAN ONE ABORTION?

No operation done under a general anaesthetic is entirely free from danger. If the cervix is dilated too often, you may have problems retaining a planned pregnancy later.

HOW MUCH DOES AN ABORTION COST?

The cost of a British abortion ranges from £120 sterling upwards. The price is not related to how good the doctor is. It's simply that private surgeons will charge more. Some clinics will try to help you with any financial burden, so don't hesitate to seek help. Remember to include the extra cost of counselling (about £20 per hour) and travel.

14. INFECTIOUS AND SEXUALLY TRANSMITTED DISEASES (STDs)

Sometimes we notice a change in vaginal secretions which irritate or itch. This can happen when bacteria gains a foothold in the sensitive vaginal tissue. Infections and irritations of the vulval area show themselves in a variety of ways. The first sign can be a discharge or unusual odour. There may be a burning sensation on urination. A first-time infection can provoke confusion and worry if we are not familiar with our bodies. Once we learn about normal secretions, and the easy treatment of unusual ones, we will be able to eliminate feelings of bewilderment and fear.

Below are listings of the most worrisome infections and syndromes which can be sexually transmitted. They are put in alphabetical order for easy reference. All, bar two or three, are commonly found in and around the vagina. For the most part they are curable by quick and easy means. But first, a few questions are answered about irritation in general.

WHY DOES THE VAGINA ATTRACT INFECTION?
The lining of the vaginal walls is more delicate than normal skin. It even has a special name, *mucous membrane,* and it is like the tissue in the mouth. Because of its soft texture irritation is made easier and the vaginal walls are less able to combat any virus, bacterium or fungus it may meet.

Some microbes, like thrush, are actually present all the time in our bodies, but certain conditions make them grow out of hand. These conditions include hormonal changes like puberty, menopause, pregnancy and taking the contraceptive pill. Physical irritants like tampons, spermicides, condoms and intercourse can contribute. Some illnesses and their treatment, like antibiotics and antihistamines can affect the body's resistance to disease. Even oral sex can alter the chemical balance of the vagina and bring on an itch.

WHAT DOES 'STD' MEAN? IS IT DIFFERENT FROM VD?

STD stands for 'sexually transmitted disease' and is a common expression used to categorise any infection picked up through sexual intercourse. In the past, many of the same irritations were dubbed VD (meaning venereal disease, having to do with "love" or sex). However, this term was often abused and gained a bad reputation. Many people felt there was a stigma attached to the old initials which prevented women from seeking help. With proper education, the situation is improving.

HOW DO I CONTRACT AN STD?

The most likely way to contract an STD is by having sexual intercourse. Your partner may already have the infection and pass it on to the warm, moist vaginal environment where bacteria thrive. You might also have an infection sleeping quietly in the vagina. An act of intercourse or use of tampons may awaken it by annoying the mucosa.

CAN I GET AN STD FROM A TOILET SEAT?

Technically, it is possible, if you sit exactly on the spot where another infected vulva sat. But how many of us actually touch this part of our body to a toilet seat? Normally, any virus or bacteria dies in the cold, bright environment of a loo. One exception is if you use the damp towel of an infected person immediately after they have dried themselves. For an infection to take place they will have to wipe their sexual parts and you must have done the same.

WHAT SHALL I DO IF I HAVE AN INFECTION? WHERE DO I GO AND HOW CONFIDENTIAL IS THE SERVICE?

If only we would begin thinking of all infections in the same light! I wonder how many of us are embarrassed to admit to a sore throat or swollen glands? A sexually transmitted disease is simply another type of infection affecting the sexual organs of the body. A doctor will be able to help you. They see countless other women for the same treatment every week. If you prefer to attend a special clinic there are some run privately (costing about £30 per consultation, upwards from £10 for treatment), and public clinics in the major hospitals. The directory will guide you. The public clinics run separate sessions for men and women. Both the service and the medication are free and completely confidential.

WHAT WILL HAPPEN AT THE INFECTION CLINIC?

The doctor will take a medical history, enquire into your sexual habits and take a series of swabs. In some cases, a blood sample may be required (see p. 111). Samples are taken from the vagina in three separate places (using a speculum and cotton buds), the anus, and sometimes the mouth. It is important to have a swab, because some apparent infections can mask more hidden ones. Not every form of medication suits all irritations.

WHAT ARE THE SYMPTOMS OF AN STD?
The symptoms vary according to the infection and not all discharges are a sign of diseases. Any strange secretion of unusual colour or smell should be investigated if it follows sexual intercourse.

It's always a good idea to see if a change in daily habits have prompted the new secretion. Are you washing the vulva with soap? This can encourage irritation quite suddenly and without warning. Are you wearing cotton underpants and avoiding tight trousers? If you leave no air to circulate, resident bacteria may grow unabated. Are you allergic to any new sanitary product or spermicide? Are you wiping your bottom front to back, so no bacteria from the anus infects the vagina? As long as you are certain the irritation is not sexually transmitted, these are simple self-help methods to avoid infection recurring. (See p. 199).

IF I HAVE AN INFECTION, SHOULD I TELL MY PARTNER?
If you have sexual contact with your partner or suspect s/he may have given you the infection, then it's best to tell. Some women who have multiple partners are worried about one partner's reaction. It's important to consider your own and your partner's health first. Talking the matter over with a friend, doctor or counsellor may help.

ACQUIRED IMMUNE DEFICIENCY SYNDROME (AIDS)

AIDS is not strictly an infection, but it is sexually transmitted. Until recently in Ireland, the syndrome hadn't been a concern to women. However, some women may be at risk as the disease widens its network of hosts. Those of us with sexual partners who need blood or plasma products may want reassurance. Bisexual women, artificial insemination clients, intravenous drug users, women whose partners are injectible drug users, and those of us working in the healthcare professions may want guidelines on how contagious the disease may be.

AIDS is a health condition. The AIDS virus attacks the body's immune system destroying its ability to fight disease. In severe cases this can mean serious illness and death.

HOW CAN I GET AIDS?
If you have sexual contact with an AIDS host, then it is possible to contract the virus. Even if you get the virus, you will not necessarily actually get AIDS. Saliva, semen and blood have all been linked to the transmission of AIDS, so you can acquire the syndrome through untreated blood transfusions, infected needles or artificial insemination. Fortunately, in Ireland, these services are being screened, and there should be no cause for alarm.

I THOUGHT ONLY HOMOSEXUALS GOT AIDS
In the United States, the majority of AIDS cases are among the male homosexual population, but in parts of Africa, where the disease originated, there is no such segregation. It is possible for any of us to contract the syndrome.

IS THERE A TEST FOR AIDS?
You cannot be tested officially for the virus in Ireland at the moment. Rumours abound that the blood transfusion board can detect AIDS. STD clinics can help. At present only a test called HTLV-3 can be done. This looks for antibodies in the blood associated with a virus connected with AIDS. A positive test result does not mean however, that you have AIDS.

WHAT SHOULD I DO IF MY PARTNER HAS AIDS?
Go along to your doctor or special clinic as soon as possible. They will be able to advise you.

WHAT IS THE TREATMENT?
At the moment, doctors can only treat the related illnesses, but not AIDS specifically. Rest, healthy eating and drug-free living can limit the chance of serious disease. It is also advisable to practice "safe sex". Concentrate on fondling, hugging and mutual masturbation. Avoid French kissing, intercourse (unless with condoms and spermicides); and using your partners toothbrush.

IS IT DANGEROUS?
AIDS can be fatal.

CHLAMYDIA TRACHOMATIS

Chlamydia (KLA-MID-EE-A), is a fancy latin name for a routine infection. It is the second most commonly found STD in women.

Unfortunately, chlamydia often exists symptom-free. Our male partner may notice first signs — a burning irritation when going to the loo. A doctor who does not swab may diagnose this symptom as NSU (non-specific urethritis). There seems to be a link between this infection and chlamydia but they are not always treated the same way.

DOES A WOMAN HAVE ANY SYMPTOMS?
Occasionally you will notice a grey or white thin discharge. This may be the result of other bacteria. Only about forty per cent of us will have symptoms.

IS IT DANGEROUS?
Chlamydia can affect the uterus and fallopian tubes. It has been known to contribute to pelvic inflammatory disease, a serious infection of the reproductive organs. Sometimes this leads to fertility problems (see p. 124). Fortunately, once the infection is cleared in a woman, fertility worries are often resolved. Men may not be so lucky.

WHAT IS THE TREATMENT?
Antibiotics are usually prescribed to treat chlamydia, and it's important to complete the entire course of tablets. It is important to avoid any sexual contact during this period. You and your partner will need to be rechecked a month later. Sometimes a second treatment is needed.

CYSTITIS

Cystitis is one of the most common and frightening infections when we know nothing about it. It is exacerbated by an inflammation of the tube leading into the bladder (urethra). The bladder is where urine is stored. Since the vagina and urethra are situated next to one another, it's sometimes difficult to know what is causing the irritation.

WHAT ARE THE SYMPTOMS?
A desire to go to the toilet, a burning sensation when you do, and very little passing of urine. Left untreated, cystitis can lead to back pain, tummy aches, fever and blood-stained urine.

WHAT CAUSES CYSTITIS?
Infection of the urethra can be encouraged by sexual intercourse, the use of tampons, condoms, spermicides, and perfumed body sprays. Some women notice an attack after using soap in the bath water and children can

get the infection if they wipe their bottom back to front.

HOW IS IT TREATED?
You can begin treating cystitis by drinking plenty of water. This will flush the infection out of the urethra. You will also need to discontinue any habit which leads to an attack. A serious infection may need antibiotic treatment.

Other self-help techniques
1. Have a glass of water after every trip to the loo.
2. Add a teaspoon of bicarbonate of soda to the drinking water; this will relieve the burning.
3. Urinate in a warm bath — this will be soothing.
4. Avoid using anything in the vagina that could put pressure on the urethra and bladder (tampons, the cap, intercourse).
5. To prevent further attacks, always drink plenty of water daily. Your bladder needs the activity to keep healthy. Go to the loo after sexual intercourse. Avoid using soaps and sprays that irritate the genital region. Keep away from spicy foods and caffeine during an attack. Use lubricating jelly if you feel dryness may be causing the irritation. If you have anal intercourse, be sure the penis is clean before allowing it near the vagina. Wash yourself only in plain water.

GARDNERELLA VAGINALIS

Gardnerella, like thrush, is not technically an STD. It has been associated with the use of tampons and often appears alongside other infections. A dry, irritated vagina, is the ideal home for gardnerella and symptoms are often noted before or after a period.

WHAT ARE THE SYMPTOMS?
An itch, a greyish discharge, and a fishy smell. But very often there are no symptoms. If irritation occurs near a period it may be easier to identify it.

HOW IS IT TREATED?
Gardnerella is treated with *metronidazole* (brand name: Flagyl), and sometimes antibiotics. Both partners need to be dosed twice a day for five days. Avoid alcohol during this time — it doesn't mix with the drugs and can lead to cramping. Sexual intercourse should be stopped temporarily.

IS IT DANGEROUS?
There is no evidence of long-term damage from gardnerella. Any infection

can alter the uterine mucus and make conception more difficult.

GENITAL WARTS

Condylomata acuminata is one of the pseudonyms for genital warts. They are sexually transmitted. Genital warts look like ordinary warts except that they grow around the vulva, buttocks, or thighs. You will need to be swabbed to see if any other infection is present.

WHAT IS THE TREATMENT?
Until recently, the standard remedy was to paint the warts with a liquid called *podophyllin*. Repeated use of this chemical is considered dangerous so doctors are now removing warts with a special machine. The technique involves freezing the warts: a local anaesthetic can be used.

ARE THEY DANGEROUS?
Genital warts have been linked with cervical cancer, so you will want to have a smear test done every year, even if the warts have disappeared.

GONORRHOEA

Gonorrhoea is one of the two major infections which fell under the old heading of VD. For this reason, it has frightened many women. In fact, gonorrhoea is an STD which is easily treatable.

WHAT ARE THE SYMPTOMS?
There may be no symptoms or you may notice a discharge. A male partner may complain of sores or pain on urination. You may see a yellow-green pus coming from the cervix and smell a mushroom-like odour. It can be found in conjunction with chlamydia.

HOW IS IT TREATED?
Antibiotics are given for gonorrhoea. A second test will need to be done after treatment. Be sure to complete any treatment.

IS IT DANGEROUS?
Gonorrhoea has been responsible for pelvic inflammatory disease, tubal problems and infertility. Secondary complications include arthritis and meningitis if left untreated.

HERPES

Herpes is a virus that has attracted a lot of media attention. There are two types of herpes.

Simplex one Usually presents as a cold sore on the mouth following a day in the sun, or after stressful activity. Shingles can be caused by herpes simplex one and can be found in all parts of the body. It is not usually an STD.

Simplex two This is a sexually transmitted virus which attacks with open sores, fever and 'flu-like symptoms. As yet, there is no cure, but attacks seem to lessen with time and good living habits.

WHAT ARE THE SYMPTOMS OF HERPES SIMPLEX TWO?
The first attack of simplex two may result in a crop of tiny blisters on the thigh, bottom or vulva. These can become ulcerated. Other symptoms are listed above.

HOW IS IT TREATED?

Since there is no cure for herpes, only symptoms can be treated. For some of us, urination is uncomfortable: peeing in a warm bath may help. Sudocrem may relieve the sores and bathing in warm salty water is helpful. Vitamin B-6 aids some sufferers. Since stress and fatigue seem to trigger off a herpes attack, it's essential to get plenty of rest and eat well.

IS IT DANGEROUS?
If you have herpes simplex two, it is important to have a yearly smear test. Atypical cells can be stimulated by the virus. It is also possible to transfer the virus to a baby during childbirth. This can be very serious to the baby's health. Be sure to tell your doctor or mid-wife if this is the case.

IS IT VERY CONTAGIOUS?
During an outbreak, and a few weeks after, herpes is highly contagious. If your regular sexual partner has herpes, it might be wise to use condoms on a regular basis.

PUBIC LICE (CRABS)

Pubic lice are also called crabs, and are tiny parasites which live on the surface of the skin. Crabs are usually picked up through sexual contact, but can be acquired by wearing the trousers of an infected person. Pubic lice like to attach themselves to the hairy areas around the vulva. They feed off the skin, like fleas. They are extremely itchy but quite harmless.

WHAT ARE THE SYMPTOMS?
Many of us see the lice before we realise there is an infestation. It can be alarming to note tiny movement in the knickers or frolicking specks among the pubic hair. Itching is a by-product.

HOW ARE THEY TREATED?
Your local chemist will stock an over the counter treatment called *Quellada*. Buy both the lotion and shampoo. Wash any affected area and apply the lotion. Repeat the whole routine ten days later. In the meantime, wash any clothes that may have come into contact with the lice and tell your partner (I'm sure s/he already knows).

SYPHILIS

Syphilis is an STD caused by something called *Teponema pallidum*. In older times, it was called the great pox, or VD. It is relatively uncommon in Ireland.

WHAT ARE THE SYMPTOMS?
The symptoms are the same for men and women. The first sign is a painless sore *(chancre)* which appears near or on the sexual organs. Since women's sexual parts are, for the most part, internal, the chancre may be unseen. The sore can also flare up near the anus. The second stage of the disease is an itchy rash all over the body. You may notice mouth sores, lumps and 'flu-like symptoms. If left untreated, syphilis lies dormant but can still be detected through a blood test. Years later, if still not cured, possible damage to the heart, lungs, eyes and nervous system can result. The disease can also be passed on to children, but this rarely happens nowadays because of ante-natal screening.

HOW IS IT TREATED?
After the blood test (see p. 191) comes back positive, antibiotic treatment will commence. This is very successful. Any sexual partner will need to be screened as well.

THRUSH

Thrush (or candida, monilia, yeast or fungal infection) is a common fungus present in all human beings. Vaginal irritation can lead to an over-production of the fungus with a resulting itchy, white, cottage-cheese-like discharge. Thrush may or may not be sexually transmitted and is more of a nuisance than a health risk.

WHAT CAUSES THRUSH?

Tampons, diabetes, the pill, pregnancy, spermicides, condoms, intercourse, cancer treatment, antibiotics, unbalanced diet, stress and oral sex, to name but a few causes.

Thrush will often clear itself following a period and many natural remedies will clear the symptoms.

WHAT IS THE TREATMENT?

A doctor will treat you with a drug called *Nystatin*. Before you try this, sample some of the self-help remedies.

1. Try to bath rather than shower, this will allow the bath water to rinse the vagina naturally.

2. Put a handful of salt in the bath or dilute a tablespoon in a basin and sit in the warm water.

3. Avoid using soaps, bubble-baths, oils and shampoo in the bath water: simple warm water is enough to cleanse the vulva. Wash the vulva morning and evening. Be sure to pat dry thoroughly.

4. Always wipe your bottom from front to back.

5. Watch your diet: sugar, wine and beer can encourage thrush.

6. Handwash underpants in soap rather than detergent. Rinse thoroughly afterwards.

7. Wear cotton underpants.

8. Never wear underpants at night while sleeping. Allow air to circulate around the vulva. Avoid nylon tights and trousers if possible. When possible use sanitary towels rather than tampons. Never use tampons twenty-four hours a day.

9. Avoid intercourse until the thrush has cleared: this allows the vagina to heal.

10. To soothe itching, apply natural Bulgarian yoghurt like a lotion or insert into the vagina.

MY DOCTOR SAID I HAD A THRUSH INFECTION AT MY BACKSIDE!

The fungus will grow happily in any warm environment. The mouth is another place of habitation. For more information on self-help, see p. 43.

IF MY THRUSH IS CAUSED BY SPERMICIDES OR THE PILL,
WILL I HAVE TO STOP USING THEM?
It may come to that. Some women find that when they alter contraceptive methods, or refrain from using tampons, their irritation clears immediately.

TRICHOMONIASIS VAGINALIS

Trichomoniasis (TRICK-A-MONE-EYE-ASS-ISS) or simply 'trich', is caused by a tiny parasite. It is generally sexually transmitted and can be found alongside other infections. It is commonly a heterosexual complaint. Smear tests can detect trichomoniasis and treatment will be needed to clear the symptoms in both partners.

WHAT ARE THE SYMPTOMS?
Classic trich appears with a greenish, frothy discharge. This is accompanied by an offensive fishy smell. Soreness, and discomfort during intercourse are side-effects.

HOW IS IT TREATED?
So far, no self-help remedies seem to completely eliminate the parasite. A clove of garlic wrapped in cheesecloth and put into the vagina is sometimes used. This should be dipped in vegetable oil before insertion and needs to be changed every twelve hours. Be sure to tie a string on the end for easy removal. Some woman have found that douching with herbal teas like slippery elm, bayberry, and golden seal, offers relief. (Be sure you let the liquid cool down first!)

IS IT DANGEROUS?
Because of the correlation between many of the STDs and infertility, a trich infection shouldn't be ignored. Unchecked, any irritation can spread to other organs.

15. ENTITLEMENTS

The government social services and Health Boards offer many of the services outlined in this book free of charge in southern Ireland. In the north, the National Health System (NHS) applies. For further details, a summary of services can be obtained from your local area Health Board or the Department of Social Services.

WHO IS ENTITLED TO A MEDICAL CARD?

The medical card scheme is based on the amount of money you earn in a given year. You are eligible if you fall into any of the following categories:
—If you are single and earn less than £66.50 per week before tax.
—If you are single and living with a relation and making less than £56.50 per week before tax.
—If you are married and as a couple earning less than £95.50 per week before tax.
—You are allowed an additional £10.50 for every dependent child (for example: if you are a single mother and earn less than £66.50, you are still eligible for a medical card if you earn £77.00 before tax — if you have two children, you are allowed £87.50 and so on).
—If you have dependent children over 16, you are allowed an extra £12.00 on your salary, before tax, to be still eligible for the medical card.

WHO IS ENTITLED TO THE HOSPITAL SERVICES CARD?

Anyone who earns less than £13,500 per year. Married women who are not in paid employment are assessed based on their husband's salary.

WHERE DO I APPLY FOR THESE CARDS?

Write or ring your local area Health Board for the appropriate forms to be sent out. Once you complete the paperwork and return the forms, you will probably wait six to eight weeks before you receive the card. In the case of the medical card scheme you will not be able to claim benefit until you receive the card. You will also be sent a list of medical card doctors.

WHAT DO THESE CARDS ENTITLE ME TO?

In the case of medical cards, you will be entitled to free services from your doctor (as long as s/he is participating in the scheme), free drugs and free hospital care.

Hospital services card holders are eligible for free in- and out-patient care in the public wards of public hospitals.

WHAT IS THE SPECIAL MATERNITY SCHEME?

This is available to any woman within either card scheme. This entitles you to six ante-natal visits with your GP (regardless of whether or not they are in the medical card scheme), and six post-natal visits entirely free of charge. You must apply to your area Health Board to avail of this scheme.

WHAT IS THE LONG-TERM ILLNESS SCHEME?

This is a provision which enables *any* person, regardless of income, who has a long-term illness, like diabetes, or muscular sclerosis, to avail of a number of free services, like drugs. Write to the Health Board in your area for further details.

WHAT ABOUT LONG-TERM DISABILITY?

Some are covered in a scheme run in conjunction with the rehabilitation board. Again, contact your Health Board and the Department of Social Welfare for your individual entitlements.

WHAT IS THE PRESCRIPTION REFUND SCHEME AND WHO QUALIFIES?

Anyone, regardless of salary, who spends over £28 in any month on drugs, is entitled to apply for a refund from the Health Board. To qualify, you will need to collect the appropriate receipt from your chemist.

WHAT ABOUT MEDICAL APPLIANCES, LIKE CRUTCHES, OR WHEELCHAIRS?

Whether or not you will be aided in the financial costs of these items depends on your individual income. For more details, contact your Health Board.

WHAT ABOUT DENTAL AND OPTICAL BENEFITS?

There is a long waiting list for persons availing of these benefits. First, you will need your medical card. Then you must apply separately for this scheme by contacting the Health Board in your area.

SUGGESTED READING LIST

The following is a list of books which may offer you more complete information on the topics discussed in *Woman To Woman*. Many are available in good bookshops throughout the 32 counties of Ireland. We suggest you also contact family planning and health organisations who may have a more complete and/or specialist list of books. The books listed vary in price from £2 to £6 plus postage.

Attic Press *Irish Women's Guidebook and Diary, 1987.*
Balaskas, Janice *Active Birth* London: Unwin, 1984.
Bartow, David *Sexually Transmitted Diseases: The Facts* London: OUP, 1981.
Beels, Christina *The Childbirth Book* London: Mayflower, 1980.
Birke, Lynda & Katy Gardner *Why Suffer? Periods & their Problems* London: Virago, 1984.
Boston Women's Health Collective *Our Bodies Ourselves* Harmondsworth: Penguin, 1978.
Brown, Paul and Carolyn Faulder *Treat Yourself to Sex* Harmondsworth: Penguin, 1977.
Brush, Michael *Understanding Pre-menstrual Tension* London: Pan, 1980.
Burkitt, Denis *Don't Forget Fibre in Your Diet* London: Martin Dunitz, 1982.
Burns, David *Feeling Good: The New Mood Therapy* New York: Signet Classics, 1980.
Butler, Pamela *Self Assertion for Women* London: Quartet Books, 1982.
Campling, Jo *Better Lives for Disabled Women* London: Virago, 1979.
Carpenter, Moira *Curing PMT, The Drug Free Way* London: Century Publishing, 1985.
Cartledge, Sue and Joanna Ryan (eds) *Sex and Love:* New Thoughts on Old Contradictions London: The Women's Press 1980.
Chamberlain, Mary *Old Wives Tales: Their Cures, Remedies and Spells* London: Virago, 1981.
Cherish *Singled Out: Singled Mothers in Ireland* Dublin: Cherish/Attic Press, 1983.
Clayton, Caroline *Thrush* London: The Sheldon Press, 1984.
Comberton, James *Drugs and Young People* Dublin: Ward River Press, 1984.
Conlon, Evelyn *Where Did I Come From* Dublin: Ard Buí/Women's Community Press, 1982.
Cooper, Wendy *No Change* London: Arrow, 1985.
Cousins, Jean *Make It Happy: What Sex is all About* Harmondsworth: Penguin, 1980.
Craft, Michael and Ann *Sex And The Mentally Handicapped: A Guide for Parents and Carers* London: RKP, 1982.
Craig, Marianne. *The Office Worker's Survival Handbook: A Guide to Fighting Health Hazards of the Office* London: BSSRS Publications, 1981.

Cullen, Mary & Terri Morrissey *Women & Health* Dublin: The Health Education Bureau, 1985.

Dally, Peter and Joan Gomez *Obesity and Anorexia Nervosa: A Question of Shape* London: Faber and Faber, 1982.

Dalton, Katherina *Depression after Childbirth* London: OUP, 1980.

Davidson, Nick & Jill Rakusen *Out of Our Hands: What Technology does to Pregnancy* London: Pan, 1982.

Davis, Adelle *Let's Eat Right to Keep Fit* London: Unwin, 1984.

Decker, Albert and Suzanne Loebl *We Want To Have A Baby* Harmondsworth: Penguin, 1980.

Delvin, David *The Book of Love* London: New English Library, 1985.

Dickson, Anne *A Woman in your own Right* London: Quartet, 1986.

Dublin Lesbian and Gay Collective *Our For Ourselves* Dublin: Women's Community Press, 1986.

Dublin Rape Crises Centre *Annual Reports Dublin:* Rape Crises Centre, 1985.

Ehrenreich, Barbara & Deirdre English *Witches, Midwives & Nurses* London: Writers & Readers Publishing Cooperative, 1973.

Eichenbaum, Luise & Susie Orbach *Understanding Women* London: Penguin, 1983.

Elkington, John *The Poisoned Womb* London: Viking Press, 1985.

Ernst, Sheila and Lucy Goodman *In Our Own Hands: A Book of Self Help Therapy* London: Women's Press, 1981.

Eva, Dave and Ron Oswald *Health and Safety At Work* London: Pan, 1981.

Faust, Beatrice *Women, Sex & Pornography* Harmondsworth: Penguin, 1980.

Ferryhough, Diane *Cystitis* London: Hamlyn, 1982.

Fisher, Richard *AIDS - Your Questions Answered* London: Gay Men's Press, 1984.

Franke, Linda Bird *The Ambivalence of Abortion* Harmondsworth: Penguin, 1979.

Gillebaud, John *The Pill* London: OUP, 1984.

Gillie, Oliver *How to Stop Smoking* London: Pan, 1979.

Greenblatt, M. D. *Alcoholism Problems in Women & Children* New York: Grune & Stratton, 1976.

Griffin, Susan *Pornography & Silence* London: The Women's Press, 1981.

Hamilton, Richard *The Herpes Book* London: Corgi, 1983.

Hauck, Paul *Depression: What Happens and how to Overcome it* London: The Sheldon Press, 1983.

Heiman, Julie & Leslie and Joseph LoPiccolo *Becoming Orgasmic* New Jersey: Prentice Hall, 1976.

Hemmings, Susan (ed) *Girls Are Powerful* London: Spare Rib, 1983.

Irish Transport and General Workers Union (ITGWU) *Safety In Industry* Dublin: ITGWU, 1981.

Jacobson, Bobbie *The Lady Killers: Why Smoking is a Feminist Issue* London: Pluto, 1981.

Johnson, Norman *Marital Violence* London: RKP, 1985.

Kilmartin, Angela *Understanding Cystitis: A Complete Guide to Self Help* London: Arrow Books, 1985.

Kitzinger, Sheila *Birth over Thirty* London: Sheldon Press, 1982.

Kitzinger, Sheila *The Experience of Breastfeeding* Harmondsworth: Penguin, 1984.

Kitzinger, Sheila *The Experience of Childbirth* Harmondsworth: Penguin, 1984.

Kitzinger, Sheila *Women's Experience of Sex* Harmondsworth: Penguin, 1985.

Kleinman, Ronald *Vasectomy* London: IPPF, 1976.

La Rouche, Janice & Regina Ryan *Strategies for Women at Work* London: Unwin, 1984.

Lanson, Lucienna *From Woman To Woman: Gynaecologists Answer Questions* Harmondsworth: Penguin, 1983.

Leach, Penelope *Baby & Child* Harmondsworth: Penguin, 1984.

Littleman, Richard *The Thirty Day Yoga Meditation Plan* London: Corgi, 1978.

Llewellyn-Jones, D *Everywoman: An Illustrated Guide From Menarch To Menopause* London: Faber and Faber, 1979.

London Rape Crisis Service *Sexual Violence* London: The Women's Press, 1984.

McCormack, Adriana *Coping with Your Handicapped Child* Edinburgh: WR Chambers, 1985.

McCutcheon, Ralph *Diets to Help Cystitis* Suffolk: The Chaucer Press, 1980.

MacLeod, Sheila *The Art of Starvation* London: Virago, 1981.

Maddeis, Jane *Stress & Relaxation* London: Martin Dunitz, 1984.

Marshal, John *Planning for a Family, An Atlas of Mucothermic Charts* London: Faber and Faber, 1979.

Meulenbelt, Anja *The Shame Is Over* London: Women's Press, 1983.

Mitchell, Juliet and Ann Oakley *The Rights and Wrongs Of Women* Harmondsworth: Penguin, 1976.

Mooney, Richard *Guide for The Disabled* Dublin: Ward River Press, 1980.

Moving Theatre *A Cure for what Ails You* Dublin: Moving Theatre/ Women's Community Press, 1986.

Nairne, Kathy and Gerrilyn Smith *Dealing With Depression* London: The Women's Press, 1980.

Norris, Stephanie & Emma Read *Out in the Open* London: Pan, 1985.

O'Donohoe, Noreen and Sue Richardson (eds) *Pure Murder: A Book About Drug Use* Dublin: Women's Community Press, 1984.

Oates, J. K. *Herpes, The Facts* Harmondsworth: Penguin 1983.

Orbach, Susie *Fat is a Feminist Issue* London: Hamlyn, 1983, also available with cassette tape.

Our Lives: Lesbian Mothers talk to Lesbian Mothers Manchester: Gay Centre.

Palmer, R. L. *Anorexia Nervosa* Harmondsworth: Penguin, 1984.

Pauncherot, Zandria *Choices in Contraception* London: Pan, 1974.

Pfeffer, Naomi & Anne Woolett *The Experience of Infertility* London: Virago, 1983.

Pickard, Barbara *Eating Well for a Healthy Pregnancy* London: Sheldon Press, 1984.

Pomeroy, Wardell B *Girls & Sex* Harmondsworth: Penguin, 1969.

Priest, Robert *Anxiety & Depression* London: Martin Dunitz, 1983.

Quinlan, Jane *The Billings Method* Cork: Family Life Centre, 1976.

Renvoize, Jean *Incest: A Family Pattern* London: RKP, 1982.

Rich, Adrienne *Of Woman Born: Motherhood As Experience and Institution* London: Virago, 1983.

Robinson, Nancy and Ian Swash *Mastectomy: A Patient's Guide To Coping With Breast Surgery* Northamptonshire: Thorson's, 1977.

Rose, F. C. and M. Gravel *Migraine: The Facts* Oxford: OUP, 1979.

Rynne, Andrew *Smoking Is Your Decision* Dublin: Ward River, 1979.

Scarf, Maggie *Unfinished Business: Pressure Points in the Lives of Women* London: Fontana, 1981.

Seaman, Barbara and Gideon *Women and the Crisis in Sex Hormones* London: Harvest Press, 1978.

Shorter, Edward *A Short History of Women's Bodies* Harmondsworth: Penguin, 1984.

Sloan, Liz and Ann Kizamer *Running a Sport for Women* London: The Women's Press, 1982.

Smith, Bryan *Joyce Smith's Running Book* London: Frederick Muller Ltd. 1983.

Steiner Scott, Liz (ed) *Personally Speaking: Women's Thoughts on Women's Issues* Dublin: Attic Press, 1985.

Stoppard, Miriam *Talking Sex* London: Pan, 1982.

Stanko, Elizabeth *Intimate Intrusions: Women's Experience of Male Violence* London: RKP, 1985.

Thompson, Ruth *Have you Started Yet?* London: Pan, 1980.

Trenchard, Lorraine & Hugh Warren *Something to Tell You* London: Gay Teenage Group, 1984).

Trenchard, Lorraine & Hugh Warren *Young Lesbians* London: Gay Teenage Group, 1984.

Ward, Elizabeth *Father Daughter Rape* London: The Women's Press, 1984.

Weideger, Paula *Female Cycles* London: The Women's Press, 1977.

Witkin-Lanoil, Georgia *Coping with Stress* London: Sheldon Press, 1984.

DIRECTORY

The directory is arranged in alphabetical order under the given name of an organisation. For example: The Irish Council on Alcoholism is found under **I** for Irish; The Association for the Improvement of Maternity Services is located under **A** for Association. Some major headings, like counsellors, and chemists, are listed under **C,** or their appropriate initial. The index at the back of *Woman to Woman* gives a cross reference so you will be able to find the appropriate organisation without having to know its name (for example: Reach to Recovery, a support agency for women undergoing breast surgery, can be traced by using key words like 'breast', 'mastectomy', and 'cancer'. Test-tube fertilisation will be located by looking for 'test-tube', 'in vitro', 'artificial insemination', etc.) Once the key word is found, you will notice a corresponding number **in heavy print.** Breast may have No. 375 alongside its listing which is the code number for Reach to Recovery. But it will also have other numbers which will also have other numbers which will put you in contact with breastfeeding support groups, cosmetic surgery and so on. The page numbers for listings which refer to text only are printed in light type.

1 **ABBEY FIELD (DUBLIN) SOCIETY**
111 Howth Road, Dublin 3
(01) 338948/893122

2 **ABILITY ENTERPRISES**
Ballindrine, Claremorris,
Co Mayo (094) 71629

3 **ACTION CANCER**
127 Marlborough Park South,
Belfast 9 (084) 661081

4 **ACTION ON SMOKING & HEALTH**
Ulster Cancer Foundation,
40 Eglantine Avenue, Belfast 9
(084) 663281

5 **ACTIVE RETIREMENT ASSOCIATION**
17 Rose Park, Kill Avenue,
Dun Laoghaire, Co Dublin
(01) 804969

6 **ACUPUNCTURISTS**
Bangor Oricular Therapy Centre
34 Gray's Hill, Bangor,
Co Down (084) 452870
Dr Livingstone
3 Winston Gardens, Belfast 9
(084) 658442
Chinese Acupuncture Clinic
Montrose Centre, Stillorgan,
Dublin 4 (01) 696811/696758
Dr Beth Anne Lee
Dundonald 89644
Kilkenny (051) 95258

See also telephone Golden Pages;
Association of Irish
Acupuncturists

7 **ADAM & EVE COUNSELLING CENTRE**
4 Merchant's Quay, Dublin 8
(01) 711910/711245/771128

8 **ADAPT**
Adapt House, Rosbrien,
Limerick (061) 42354/42950

9 **ADOPTION ADVICE CENTRE**
244/246 Harold's Cross Road,
Dublin 6 (01) 960042

10 **ADOPTION BOARD**
65 Merrion Square, Dublin 2
(01) 762004

11 **ADOPTIVE PARENTS ASSOCIATION**
17 Clyde Road, Dublin 4
(01) 682685

12 **AGE CONCERN**
128 Great Victoria Street,
Belfast 9 (084) 663281

13 **AGORAPHOBIA GROUP**
c/o Beacon House,
84 University Street, Belfast 7
(084) 228474

14 **AID FOR PARENTS UNDER STRESS**
Cathedral Street, Dublin 1
(01) 742066

15 **AIM GROUP/Centre for family law reform**
Dublin Branch & National
Headquarters, 64 Lower Mount
Street, Dublin 2
(01) 605478 10-12, M-F
Social Services Centre, Dundalk
(042) 32848

Social Services Centre, Henry Street, Limerick (061) 44111

Waterford Resource Centre, Barrack Street, Waterford (051) 74968

16 AL-ANON and AL-ATEEN
(for families of alcoholics), 64 Donegall Street, Belfast 1 (084) 243489

Basement Flat, 129 Patrick's Hill, Cork (021) 500481

12 Westmoreland Street, Dublin 2 (01) 774195

Ozanam House, St. Augustine Street, Galway (091) 67807

Social Services Centre, Limerick (061) 314111

17 ALCOHOLICS ANONYMOUS (AA)
General Service Office, 26 Essex Quay, Dublin 1 (01) 774809/714050

152 Lisburn Road, Belfast 9 (084) 681084

18 THE ALCOHOLIC REHABILITATION CENTRE
24 Dame Street, Dublin 2

65 Lucan Road, Chapelizod, Dublin

19 ALLY
c/o St Saviour's Priory, Upper Dorset Street, Dublin 1 (01) 740300

20 ALONE
3 Canal Terrace, Bluebell, Dublin 12 (01) 509614

21 ALONE PARENTS' ASSOCIATION
c/o 2 Tuckey Street, Cork (021) 964786 evenings

22 ALTERNATIVE/SELF HELP
Kate Boyle, Dublin (01) 984510

Sheila McCrann, c/o Letterpeak Post Office, Spiddal, Co Galway

Anne Hyland, c/o Anne's Kitchen, Annascaul, Co Kerry

Glynnis Carrie, Waterford (051) 82331

See also counselling, massage, homeopaths, aromatherapy

23 ALZHEIMER SOCIETY OF IRELAND
St John of God Hospital, Stillorgan, Co Dublin (01) 881781

24 AMETHYST
Anna Crivey Wood, Enniskerry, Co Wicklow (01) 863407

25 AMIE
c/o 13 Saleen Estate, Castlebar, Co Mayo

26 AN BORD ALTRANAIS (NURSING BOARD)
11 Fitzwilliam Place, Dublin 2 (01) 609788

27 ANA LIFFEY PROJECT
13 Lower Abbey Street, Dublin 1 (01) 740987 M-F 10-5

28 **ANOREXIA SELF-HELP
GROUP/BELFAST**
c/o Mental Health Association
(084) 710590

29 **ANOREXIC AID**
c/o Hinchogue Cottage,
Carrickmines, Co Dublin
c/o 6 Sullivan's Quay, Cork
(021) 24958 (Francoise Lettelier)

30 **ANXIETY/DEPRESSION
SUPPORT GROUPS**
Northern Ireland Mental Health
Association, Beacon House,
Belfast BT7 1HE

31 **AONTAS
NATIONAL ASSOCIATION
OF ADULT EDUCATION**
14 Lower Fitzwilliam Street,
Dublin 2 (01) 688692

32 **AOSTA
(ASSOCIATION OF
SERVICES TO THE AGED)**
19 Clover Lawn, Skehard Road,
Blackrock, Co Cork (021) 29217

33 **ARCH — RECREATION
FOR MENTALLY
HANDICAPPED**
8 Main Street, Dundrum,
Dublin

34 **AROMATHERAPISTS**
Anne Powers (01) 974596
(also chiropody, homeopathy,
shihatsu)

35 **ARTHRITIS CARE**
31 Newforge Lane,
Upper Malone Road, Belfast 9

36 **ARTHRITIS
FOUNDATION OF
IRELAND**
1 Sydney Parade Avenue,
Dublin 4 (01) 691737/697222

37 **THE ARTHROGRYPOSIS
ASSOCIATION OF
IRELAND**
19 Lower Beechwood Avenue,
Dublin 6 (01) 962914/945597

38 **ASSOCIATION OF
BREASTFEEDING
MOTHERS**
see Foresight

39 **ASSOCIATION OF
CROSSROADS CARE
ATTENDANT SCHEMES
LTD.**
94 Cotton Road, Rugby,
Warwickshire CV21 4LN,
England

40 **ASSOCIATION FOR THE
IMPROVEMENT OF
MATERNITY SERVICES
(AIMS)**
Carmel Fairmichael,
16 Ravensdale Park, Belfast 6
(084) 647106
Dee Neeson, 48 Wyvern,
Killiney, Co Dublin (01) 856947

41 **ASSOCIATION OF IRISH
ACUPUNCTURISTS**
9 Westcourt, Tralee, Co. Kerry
(066) 24694
(complete list of acupuncturists
countrywide)

42 **ASSOCIATION OF IRISH
WIDOWS**
12 Upr Ormond Quay, Dublin 1
(01) 770977

43 **ASSOCIATION OF
OPHTHALMIC
OPTICIANS**
10 Merrion Square, Dublin 2
(01) 682933

44 **ASSOCIATION FOR THE
PSYCHIATRIC STUDY OF
ADOLESCENTS**
St John of God's Hospital,
Stillorgan, Co Dublin
(01) 881781

45 **ASSOCIATION OF
PARENTS & FRIENDS OF
MENTALLY
HANDICAPPED
CHILDREN**
St Michael's House, Willowfield,
Goatstown, Co Dublin
(01) 987033

46 **ASSOCIATION FOR THE
RIGHTS OF THE
MENTALLY
HANDICAPPED (ARM)**
53 Avondale Lawn, Blackrock,
Co Dublin (01) 886523
(only for referral, group no
longer active)

47 **ASSOCIATION FOR THE
WELFARE OF CHILDREN
IN HOSPITAL**
(01) 895102
(01) 944241

48 **ASSOCIATION OF
SCIENTIFIC, TECHNICAL
AND MANAGERIAL
STAFFS**
38 Lower Leeson Street,
Dublin 2 (01) 762306

49 **ASSOCIATION OF
WIDOWS OF CIVIL
SERVANTS**
c/o M. Smith,
2 Cullenswood Gardens,
Ranelagh, Dublin 6

50 **ASTHMA SOCIETY OF
IRELAND**
24 Anglesea Street, Dublin 2
(01) 716551

51 **DUBLIN AUTOGENIC
TRAINING**
154 Meadowgrave, Dublin 16
(01) 989242

52 **BACH FLOWER &
HERBAL REMEDIES**
Dr E. Bach Centre,
Mount Vernon, Sotwell,
Wallingford, Oxford OX 10 OPZ,
England

53 **BARNARDO'S**
414 Antrim Road,
Belfast BT 15 5BA
(084) 775811/775812/3
62-66 Bedford Street,
Belfast BT2 7EH (084) 775811
244-246 Harold's Cross Road,
Dublin 6
(01) 977276/977313/965869

54 **BELFAST LAW CENTRE**
62-66 Bedford Street,
Belfast BT 2 EH

55 **BELFAST VOLUNTARY
WELFARE SERVICE**
Bryson House, Bedford Street
Belfast 2

56 **BEREAVED PARENTS' ASSOCIATION**
c/o Cystic Fibrosis Centre,
(01) 962433

57 **BETHLEHEM CONFERENCE**
Ozanam House,
53 Mountjoy Square, Dublin 1
(01) 747171

58 **BILLINGS CENTRE**
(01) 420825
(01) 786156

59 **BLIND CENTRE**
65 Eglantine Avenue, Belfast 9
(084) 664544

60 **BOARD OF EMPLOYMENT OF THE BLIND**
32 Ardee Road, Rathmines,
Dublin 6 (01) 976633

61 **THE BRABAZON TRUST (formerly Protestant Aid)**
74 Upper Leeson Street,
Dublin 4 (01) 603292/684298

62 **BREAST FEEDING SUPPORT GROUP**
Shantallow Health Centre,
Shantallow, Derry
(080504) 51350

63 **BRITISH DIABETIC ASSOCIATION**
32 Somerdale Park, Belfast 14
(084) 746899

64 **BRITISH DIETETIC ASSOCIATION**
Daimler House, Paradise Street,
Birmingham BI 2BJ, England

65 **BRITISH EPILEPSY ASSOCIATION**
Claremont Street Hospital,
Belfast 9 (084) 248414

66 **BRITISH PREGNANCY ADVISORY SERVICE (BPAS)**
11 Old Hall Street, Liverpool
(051)★ 227 3721
11/13 Charlotte Street,
London WIP HEF
(031)★ 637-8962
★These are the prefixes if ringing from southern Ireland
In Vitro Enquiries:
Sue Gregson,
BPAS Head Office,
Austy Manor, Woolton Waiven
Sally Hull,
West Midlands, England
(Henley Arden) 3225

67 **BRITISH RED CROSS**
87 University Street, Belfast 7
(084) 246200

68 **BRITISH UNITED PROVIDENCE ASSOCIATION (BUPA)**
No. 5 Templar Street,
Leeds LS2 7NZ (084) 224224
(Contact address for N. Ireland)

69 **BUTTERCUPS BEAUTY SALON**
Powerscourt Town House
Centre, Top Floor (26a),
Dublin 2 (01) 714866
(aromatherapy, reflexology, shiatsu)

70 **CAIRDE**
10 Fownes Street, Dublin 2
(01) 710895

71 **CAMPAIGN AGAINST SEXUAL EXPLOITATION (CASE)**
PO Box 1207, Dublin 4

72 **CAMPAIGN FOR THE RIGHTS OF LESBIANS & GAY MEN**
c/o the Dublin Resource Centre, 6 Crowe Street, Dublin 2

73 **CAMPHILL VILLAGE COMMUNITY**
Duffcarrig, Gorey, Co Wexford
(055) 25116

74 **CARA/FRIEND**
PO Box 44, Belfast 1
(084) 222023 M-W 7.30-10pm
16 Bishop Street, Derry
(080504) 262616 Thurs 7.30-10pm

75 **CARADAS (COMBINED ASSOCIATION FOR RESPONSIBLE ATTITUDES TO DRINKING & SOCIETY)**
Vintners Federation of Ireland,
52 Upper Mount Street,
Dublin 2 (01) 600500

76 **CARE FOR DUBLIN'S OLD FOLKS LIVING ALONE**
c/o 1 St Conleth's Road,
Walkinstown, Dublin 12

77 **CATHOLIC MARRIAGE ADVISORY COUNCIL**
All Hallow's College,
Drumcondra, Dublin 9

(01) 375649 (has a country-wide list of services)

78 **CATHOLIC PROTECTION AND RESCUE SOCIETY OF IRELAND**
30 South Anne Street, Dublin 2
(01) 779664

79 **CATHOLIC SOCIAL SERVICE CONFERENCE**
Red House, Clonliffe College, Dublin 3

80 **CENTRAL REMEDIAL CLINIC**
Vernon Avenue, Clontarf,
Dublin 3 (01) 332206

81 **CENTRE CARE (formerly Open Door)**
Pro-Cathedral, Dublin 1
(01) 745441 M-Sat 9am-7pm

82 **THE CENTRE FOR EDUCATION, COUNSELLING & PSYCHOTHERAPY**
2 Bridge View,
Sunday's Well Road, Cork
(021) 941910

83 **CHALLENGE**
Sion House, Sion Road,
Kilkenny (056) 21653

84 **CHALLENGE (Equality for women in the health/social welfare and income tax code)**
15 Clonard Drive, Dublin 14
(01) 986914

85 **CHEMISTS who provide contraceptive supplies**
Jim Kelly,
Broderick's Pharmacy,
Church Street, Athenry,
Co Galway 091-44012
P. V. Coleman,
Mardyke Street, Athlone,
Co Westmeath (0902) 72568
Austin Gleeson,
Pharmaceutical Chemist &
Dispensing Optician,
O'Connell Street, Birr,
Co Offaly (0509) 20063
Fitzgerald Pharmacy,
Spencer Street, Castlebar,
Co Mayo (094) 21252
John Heneghan Chemist,
Ellison Street, Castlebar
(094) 21908
White's Chemist,
Castlebellingham, Co Louth
(042) 72248
Super Drugstore Pharmacy Ltd.,
Laytown, Co Meath
(041) 27163/27461
Ferguson's Chemists Ltd.,
Pharmaceutical Chemist &
Dispensing Optician,
Hearing Aid Audiologist,
20 O'Connell Street, Limerick
and
Sarsfield Shopping Centre,
Sarsfield Street, Limerick
(061) 44917/44088

86 **CHERISH**
2 Lower Pembroke Street,
Dublin 2 (01) 682744

87 **CHESHIRE FOUNDATION IN IRELAND**
111 Monkstown Road,
Monkstown, Co Dublin
(01) 803404

88 **CHEST, HEART & STROKE ASSOCIATION**
c/o Riverview, Abercorn Road,
Derry (080504) 266111
28 Bedford Street,
Belfast BT2 7FJ

89 **CHILDLESSNESS GROUP NATIONAL ASSOCIATION OF THE CHILDLESS**
113 University Street, Belfast 7
(084) 225488

90 **CHILDMINDERS' UNION**
Glebe House, Midleton, Cork

91 **CHILDREN FIRST**
40 Ailesbury Lawn, Dublin 16

92 **CHILDRENS' LEUKEMIA RESEARCH PROJECT**
40 Clancy Avenue, Finglas,
Dublin 11 (01) 343986

93 **CHIROPRACTIC ASSOCIATION OF IRELAND**
126 Clontarf Road, Dublin 3
(01) 334026

94 **CITIZENS' ADVICE BUREAU**
6 Callender Street, Belfast 1
(084) 243196

95 **CLANE HOSPITAL & HEALTH CENTRE**
Clane, Co Meath
(045) 68305

96 **CLARE MOTHERS' ACTION GROUP**
5 Mill Bank, Rosslevan,
Ennis, Co Clare

97 **CLARENDON NIGHT
SHELTER**
63 Clarendon Street, Derry
(080504) 268581

98 **CLEFT LIP & PALATE
ASSOCIATION (CLP)**
31 New Park Road, Blackrock,
Co Dublin (01) 895480

99 **CO-COUNSELLING**
108 Larkfield Gardens,
Terenure, Dublin
(01) 966936

100 **THE COELIAC SOCIETY
OF IRELAND**
32 Clyde Road, Dublin 4

101 **COLLEGE OF SURGICAL
CHIROPODY (IRELAND)**
43 Paul Street, Cork
(021) 273200

102 **COMFORT FOR CANCER**
5 Summerhill Road, Sandycove,
Co Dublin (01) 806505

103 **COMMISSION ON SOCIAL
WELFARE**
8 Charlemont Street, Dublin 2
(01) 783355

104 **COMMITTEE ON SEXUAL
& PERSONAL
RELATIONSHIPS OF THE
DISABLED**
Brook House,
2-16 Torrington Place,
London WC1E 7HN
(see also SPOD)

105 **COMMUNITY
INFORMATION CENTRES
c/o NATIONAL SOCIAL**

SERVICES BOARD
71 Lr Leeson Street, Dublin 2
(01) 682422

106 **COMMUNITY LAW
CENTRE**
5 Churchfield Avenue, Cork
(021) 307969

107 **COMPLEMENTARY
MEDICINE
INFORMATION CENTRE**
Lacken, Blessington,
Co Wicklow (045) 65575

108 **CONFEDERATION OF
HEALTH SERVICE
EMPLOYEES**
27 Ulsterville Avenue,
Belfast 1 (084) 681675

109 **CONFERENCE GUILD OF
ST PHILIP NERI**
St Vincent De Paul,
Room 4, Ozanam House,
53 Mountjoy Square, Dublin 1
(01) 747171 M-Sat 7-9pm

110 **COOLEMINE INDUCTION
CENTRE**
19 Lord Edward Street,
Dublin 8 (01) 782300

111 **COOLEMINE
THERAPEUTIC
COMMUNITY**
Coolemine Lodge, Clonsilla,
Co Dublin (01) 214545/216564

112 **COOLOCK COMMUNITY
LAW CENTRE**
Northside Shopping Centre,
Coolock, Dublin 5
(01) 477804

113 **CONTACT YOUTH COUNSELLING SERVICE**
2a Ribble Street, Belfast 4
(084) 57848

114 **CORK CITIZENS' ADVICE BUREAU**
17a Drawbridge Street, Cork
(021) 25918

115 **CORK GAY COLLECTIVE**
24 Sullivan's Quay, Cork
(021) 295189

116 **CORK LESBIAN GROUP**
Women's Place, Quay Co-op,
24 Sullivan's Quay, Cork
(021) 967660

117 **CORK LESBIAN LINE**
(021) 967026 (Thurs 8-10pm)

118 **CORK POLIO & GENERAL AFTERCARE ASSOCIATION**
Bonnington, Montenotte,
Cork (021) 507131

119 **CORK UNEMPLOYED ACTION GROUP**
Carpenter's Hall,
Father Matthew Quay, Cork

120 **COSPÓIR — The National Sports Council**
Hawkins House, Dublin 2
(01) 714311

121 **COT DEATH SUPPORT GROUP**
Health Centre,
40 Carnmoney Road,
Glengormley (3151)

122 **COUNCIL FOR THE STATUS OF WOMEN**
64 Lr Mount Street, Dublin 2
(01) 607731

123 **COUNSELLING**
Maeve Byrne,
(01) 741550
Airplane phobia/relaxation
Eilish O'Donoghue,
(01) 960653
personal counselling
Joy O'Reilly,
Fivemilebourne, Co Sligo
(Leitrim) (071) 3887
Clinical Psychologist/Anxiety,
depression counselling,
Nicola Quinn,
19 Sandymount Avenue,
Dublin 4 (01) 602770
Co-counselling, psychosynthesis
Liz Sherry,
(01) 511038
assertiveness training
Patricia Walker,
(01) 983053 (mornings)
Career, relationship and
personal development

124 **COUPLE TO COUPLE LEAGUE**
19 Forest Edge, Stameen,
Drogheda, Co Louth

125 **CREATIVE COUNSELLING**
2 Springfield Park, Templeogue,
Dublin 16 (01) 884155/902620

126 **CREATIVE SELF-HEALING**
(01) 854807

127 **CRIMINAL INJURIES COMPENSATION TRIBUNAL**
12 Upper Pembroke Street,
Dublin 2

128 **CUANLEE**
Kyrl Street, Cork
(021) 509698

129 **CUAN MHUIRE**
Athy, Co Kildare
(0507) 31493

130 **CURA**
511 Ormeau Road, Belfast 7
(084) 644963
c/o Catholic Press &
Information Office,
169 Booterstown Avenue,
Blackrock, Co Dublin
(01) 710598
30 South Anne Street, Dublin 2
(01) 710598

Belfast: (0232) 644963 M-F 10-8
Cork: (021) 501444 M-Sat 10-10
Derry: (0504) 68467 M-F 9-5
Dublin: (01) 710598 M-Sat 10-8
Galway: (091) 7077 M-F 10-5:30
Kilkenny: (056) 22739
M-F 10-5:30
Limerick: (061) 318207 M-F 2-9
Sligo: (071) 3659 M-F 9-5:30
Waterford: (051) 76452
M-F 10-5:30
Dundalk: (042) 37533 M-F 12-4
Letterkenny: (074) 23037
M-F 11-2 & 7-9

131 **CYSTIC FIBROSIS
ASSOCIATION OF
IRELAND**
24 Lower Rathmines Road,
Dublin 6 (01) 962433/962186

132 **CYSTIC FIBROSIS
RESEARCH TRUST**
c/o Anchor Lodge, Cultra,
Co Down

133 **DADDY (DRINKING &
DRIVING DON'T YIELD)**
9 Castle Street, Cork
(021) 507328

134 **DALKON SHIELD
ASSOCIATION**
24 Patchwell Road,
London NW5 2JY, England
(031) 388-2388

135 **DARNDALE FAMILY
CENTRE**
80 Primrose Grove, Dublin 5
(01) 472219/472555

136 **DAYBREAK**
37 Montrose Drive, Beaumont,
Dublin 9 (01) 473859

137 **DAY CARE ASSOCIATION**
Women's Centre,
7-9 Artillery Street, Derry
(080504) 267672

138 **DENTAL BOARD**
57 Merrion Square, Dublin 2

139 **THE DENTAL HEALTH
FOUNDATION**
29 Kenilworth Square, Dublin 6
(01) 978921

140 **DEPARTMENT OF
HEALTH**
16 College Street, Belfast BT1
(084) 241771
Custom House, Dublin 1
,(01) 735777

141 **DEPARTMENT OF**
SOCIAL WELFARE
D'Olier House, Dublin 2
(01) 718222
2 George Street, Ballymena
46021
Brownlow Health Centre,
1 Legahorry Centre,
Craigavon BT65 5BE
Craigavon 44621
Waterside Health Centre,
Glengarriff Road, Glendermott,
Derry (08054) 45191
(retirement pensions, old age
pensions, blind pensions)
Phibsboro Tower
Dublin 7 (01) 309222
(widows, pensions)
Aras Mhic Diarmada
Dublin 1 (01) 786444
(disability benefit)
Townsend Street
Dublin 2 (01) 717171
(death grant, invalidity pensions)

142 **DEPRESSION GROUP**
Beacon House,
84 University Street, Belfast 7
(084) 228474

143 **DIABETIC RESEARCH**
FUND
c/o Adelaide Hospital, Dublin 8

144 **DIET EDUCATION**
PROGRAMME
Zero's Vegetarian Restaurant,
2 University Road, Belfast 7
(084) 233218

145 **THE DIORAMA**
14 Peto Place, London NW1 4DT

146 **THE DISABLED DRIVERS'**

ASSOCIATION OF
IRELAND & THE IRISH
ASSOCIATION OF
PHYSICALLY
HANDICAPPED PEOPLE
Ballindine, Co Mayo
(094) 71629

147 **DIVORCE ACTION**
GROUP
PO Box 1357, Dublin 6
(01) 606079/601046
4 Nassau Street, Dublin 2
19 Raleigh Row, Galway
(091) 62982

148 **DOCTOR ON CALL**
14 Rathgar Road, Dublin 6
(01) 976108

149 **THE DOWN'S SYNDROME**
ASSOCIATION OF
IRELAND
27 South William Street,
Dublin 2 (01) 793322
St. Jude's,
Carrick Road, Boyle,
Co Roscommon (079) 62511
Pinewood,
Point Road, Crosshaven,
Cork (021) 831571

150 **DROP IN CENTRES FOR**
DRUG USERS
Youth Development Project,
Donore Avenue, Dublin 8
Talbot Day Centre,
29 Upper Buckingham Street,
Dublin 1

151 **DUBLIN CENTRAL**
MISSION
Social Aid Centre,
7 Marlborough Place, Dublin 1
(01) 742123

152 **DUBLIN CENTRE OF COMPLEMENTARY MEDICINE**
Ashton, 6 Martello Terrace,
Sandycove, Co Dublin
(01) 858790/858684

153 **DUBLIN COMMITTEE FOR TRAVELLING PEOPLE**
12 Westmoreland Street,
Dublin 2 (01) 776761

154 **DUBLIN DENTAL HOSPITAL**
Lincoln Place, Dublin 2
(01) 682211

155 **DUBLIN PUBLIC HEALTH LABORATORY**
Eastern Health Board,
Old County Road, Crumlin,
Dublin 12 (01) 752921 Ext. 314

156 **DUBLIN RESOURCE CENTRE**
6 Crow Street, Dublin 2
(01) 771507

157 **DUBLIN WELL WOMAN CENTRE**
73 Lower Leeson Street,
Dublin 2 (01) 605229/605517
60 Eccles Street, Dublin 7
(01) 728051/381365

158 **DUNDALK CENTRE FOR COUNSELLING AND PERSONAL DEVELOPMENT**
Oakdene, Kincora Terrace,
Carrick Road, Dundalk
(042) 38333

159 **DYSLEXIA ASSOCIATION OF IRELAND**
37 Rathfarnham Park, Dublin 14
(01) 902214

160 **EKHART HOUSE**
5 Pembroke Park, Dublin 4
(01) 684687

161 **EMIGRANT WELFARE BUREAU**
35 Harcourt Street, Dublin 2
(01) 780866

162 **EMPLOYMENT EQUALITY AGENCY**
36 Upper Mount Street,
Dublin 2 (01) 605966/605257

163 **ENVIRONMENTAL HEALTH OFFICERS ASSOCIATION OF IRELAND**
9 Aston Quay, Dublin 2
(01) 772258

164 **EQUAL OPPORTUNITIES COMMISSION**
Chamber of Commerce,
22 Great Victoria Street,
Belfast 2 (084) 242752

165 **EUROPEAN ASSOCIATION OF PROGRAMMES IN HEALTH SERVICE STUDIES**
1 Carlton Villas,
Shelbourne Road, Dublin 4
(01) 689642

166 **EXTEND**
c/o League of Health,
Invergarry, Silchester Road,
Glenageary, Co Dublin
(01) 801564

167 **FAMILY AID**
PO Box 791, Dublin 1
(01) 961002

168 **FAMILY PLANNING
CLINICS (ring for
appointment)**
Family Planning Association,
113 University Street, Belfast 7
(01) 225488
Health Centre, Station Road,
Antrim (Antrim) 64931
Health Centre, Dobbin Lane,
Armagh (Armagh) 523165

51 Castle Street, Ballymena
(Ballymena) 2108

Health Centre, Newall Road,
Ballymoney (Ballymoney) 62

The Clinic, Windmill Hill,
Ballynahinch
(Ballynahinch) 562641

Bangor 468521/454184
Belfast:
Ballyowen, 129 Andersonstown
Road, Belfast BT11 (084) 610611
Braniel Health Clinic
(084) 791153
Cherryvalley (084) 799321
Cupar St Clinic (084) 221763
Dunluce Avenue (084) 240884
Holywood Arches Health Clinic
(084) 650188
Lincoln Avenue Clinic
(084) 748363
Mount Oriel Health Clinic
(084) 701845
Ormeau Health Clinic
(084) 220437
Shankill Health Centre
(084) 247181
Templemore Avenue Health
Clinic (084) 54321
Twinbrook, 25 Summerhill Road
(084) 612207

Whiterock Health Clinic
(084) 223153
(Rear Rochalls), Strand Road,
Bray (01) 860410
Health Centre, Taylor's Avenue,
Carrickfergus
(Carrickfergus) 64193
Augher Road, Clogher
(Clogher) 48628
Health Clinic, Castlerock Road,
Coleraine (Coleraine) 4831
Cookstown (Cookstown) 63280
4 Tuckey Street, Grand Parade
Cork (021) 860410
Altnagelvin Hospital, Derry
(080504) 45171
The Main Street, Castlewellan,
Downpatrick (Downpatrick) 3811
Pound Lane, Downpatrick
(Downpatrick) 3811
10 Merrion Square, Dublin 2
(01) 767852
IFPA, 15 Mountjoy Square,
Dublin 1 (01) 744133/740723
Cathal Brugha Street,
off O'Connell Street, Dublin 1
(01) 727363
Family Planning Services,
67 Pembroke Road, Dublin 4
(01) 681108/683714
59 Synge Street, Dublin 8
(01) 682420
(see also Dublin Well Woman
Clinic)
Dundonald (Dundonald) 2991
South Tyrone Hospital,
Dungannon (Dungannon) 22821
Thomas Street, Dungannon
(Dungannon) 23101
78a-79 Lower George's Street,
Dun Laoghaire (01) 850666
Enniskillen (Enniskillen) 247711
16 Merchant's Road, Galway
(091) 62992

40 Canmoney Road,
Glengormley
(Glengormley) 3151
Redburn Clinic, Holywood
(Holywood) 3697
Kilkeen Clinic,
Knockhree Avenue, Kilkeel
(Kilkeel) 62601
Health Centre,
Gloucester Avenue, Larne
(Larne) 75331
Limavady (Limavady) 63131
4 Upper Mallow Street,
Limerick (061) 312026
Linenhall Street, Lisburn
(Lisburn) 5181
Trimgate Street, Navan
(046) 21143
Monaghan Row, Newry
(Newry) 4186
Health Centre,
John Mitchell Place, Newry
(Newry) 4821
James Street Clinic,
Newtownards (Newtownards)
812661
Health Centre, Mountjoy Road,
Omagh (Omagh) 3521
16 Lower Georges Street,
Wexford (053) 24638

169 **FAMILY THERAPY
NETWORK**
8 Upper Hollybank Avenue,
Dublin 6 (01) 976705

170 **FEDERATION OF
SERVICES FOR
UNMARRIED PARENTS &
THEIR CHILDREN**
11 Clonskeagh Road, Dublin 6
(01) 698351

171 **FINANCIAL**

**INFORMATION
SERVICES CENTRE
(FISC)**
87/89 Pembroke Road, Dublin 4
(01) 680400

172 **FLATDWELLERS'
ASSOCIATION**
168 Rathgar Road (01) 710622

173 **FOCUS-POINT**
15 Eustace Street, Dublin 2
(01) 776421

174 **FORESIGHT/Pre-
conceptual care**
Woodhurst, Hydestile,
Godalming, Surrey GU 84AY,
England

175 **FOUNDATION FOR
PREVENTION OF
CHILDHOOD
HANDICAPS**
St James's Hospital, Dublin 8
(01) 537951

176 **FRIEDRIECH'S ATAXIA
SOCIETY OF IRELAND**
San Martino, Mart Lane,
Foxrock, Co Dublin
(01) 894788

177 **FRIENDS OF THE
ELDERLY**
7 Charlemont Street, Dublin 2
(01) 757818/755774/755500

178 **GALWAY WOMEN'S
HEALTH &
INFORMATION SERVICE**
Galway Social Services Centre,
Eglinton Street, Galway
(091) 63581

179 **GAMBLERS ANONYMOUS**
St Peter's Boys Club,
4 New Cabra Road, Phibsboro,
Dublin 7 (01) 775566

180 **GAM ANON**
Same details as above

181 **GAY COLLECTIVE**
Quay Co-op, 24 Sullivan's Quay,
Cork
PO Box 45, Eglinton Street,
Galway

182 **GAY HEALTH ACTION**
PO Box 97, Cork (021) 967026
Dublin (01) 710939
Mon.-Fri. 11.00-4.00pm

183 **GAY INFORMATION**
Cork (021) 967026

184 **GAY YOUTH GROUP**
(01) 710939

185 **GENERAL MEDICAL SERVICES PAYMENT BOARD**
Raven House, Finglas, Dublin 11
(01) 343644

186 **GINGERBREAD**
171 University Street, Belfast 7
(084) 231417
Derry (080504) 46014
12 Wicklow Street, Dublin 2
(01) 710291

187 **GROW**
11 Liberty Street, Cork
(021) 506520
58 Thomas Street, Dublin 8
(01) 715979 MWF 10-1

188 **THE HANLEY CENTRE**
The Mews, Eblana Avenue,
Dun Laoghaire, Co Dublin
(01) 809795/807269

189 **HEALTH BOARDS**
For Southern Ireland see
telephone directory under area
board. For example: Eastern
Health Board is under Eastern.
For Northern Ireland see
under Health and Personal
Services in telephone directory.

190 **HEALTH EDUCATION BUREAU**
34 Upper Mount Street, Dublin 2
(01) 766640

191 **HEALTH EDUCATION COUNCIL**
78 New Oxford Street,
London WC1A 1AH

192 **HEALTH & SAFETY AGENCY FOR NORTHERN IRELAND**
Canada House, North Street,
Belfast 1 (084) 243249

193 **HEALTH VISITORS ASSOCIATION**
Northern Ireland Centre,
Comber, Newtownards

194 **HEARTH**
14 Dyke Parade, Cork

195 **HELP AID AND RESCUE PERSONNEL (HARP)**
PO Box 1196, Dublin 16

196 **HELPING HANDS**
(01) 375483/307366

197 **HERBALISTS**
S. G. Donaldson,
22 North Street Arcade, Belfast 1
(084) 226967

Sean Boylan, Edenmore,
Dunboyne, Co Meath
(01) 255250
Naturally
6 Abbey Street, Bangor
(084) 452886

198 **HOME BIRTH CENTRE**
20 Vernon Grove, Rathgar,
Dublin 6 (01) 960750

199 **THE HOMEOPATHIC
ASSOCIATION OF
IRELAND**
c/o Jonathan Griffith
(045) 65575

200 **HOMEOPATHS —
FRAMAR PRIVATE
HEALTH ADVICE CENTRE**
595 Lisburn Road, Belfast 9
(084) 681018
Priscilla Jackson, 8 Rugby Villas,
Ranelagh, Dublin 6
(01) 377158
Irene Anne Power (01) 974596
Also see telephone Golden Pages

201 **HOMESTAY**
The Dell, Carrick Brennan Road,
Monkstown, Co Dublin
(01) 806833

202 **HOSTELS**
Ulida Housing Association
41 University Street, Belfast B7
(084) 243227
10 Paul Street, Cork
(021) 506316

Regina Coeli
Morning Star Avenue,
North Brunswick Street,
Dublin 7 (01) 723401
Shelter Referral
288 Merrion Road, Dublin 4
(01) 691686
Sunnyside, Barrack Street,
Dundalk (042) 35211
Triangle Women's Housing,
Girona Avenue, Portrush
(0265) 824309

203 **THE HOUSING CENTRE**
Room 906, Liberty Hall,
Dublin 1 (01) 725480

204 **HUME STREET
HOSPITAL**
Hume Street, Dublin 2
(01) 766935
(Special cancer screening clinic
for smear tests, psoriasis)

205 **HYSTERECTOMY
SUPPORT GROUP**
Darndale Family Centre,
80 Primrose Grove, Dublin 5
(01) 472219/472555
113 University Street, Belfast
(084) 225488

Also check your local health
board or women's group/family
planning clinics

206 **ILEOSTOMY
ASSOCIATION**
1 Woodfarm Avenue,
Palmerstown, Dublin 20
(01) 265355

207 **INCEST CRISIS LINE**
(01) 743796

208 **INCEST SURVIVORS**
Dublin Rape Crisis Centre,
2 Lower Pembroke Street,
Dublin 2 (01) 601470
(See also Sanctuary Trust)

209 **INFERTILITY SUPPORT GROUP**
c/o 15 Mountjoy Square,
Dublin 1

210 **INSURANCE INFORMATION SERVICES**
50 Northumberland Road,
Dublin 4 (01) 681162/777600

211 **IRIDOLOGY**
13 Martin Grove, Navan Road,
Dublin 7 (01) 383459/522722

212 **IRISH ALLERGY TREATMENT & RESEARCH ASSOCIATION**
PO Box 1067, Churchtown,
Dublin 14

213 **IRISH ASSOCIATION FOR THE BLIND**
8 North Great George's Street,
Dublin 1 (01) 742349

214 **IRISH ASSOCIATION FOR COUNSELLING**
The Mews, Eblana Avenue,
Dun Laoghaire, Co Dublin
(01) 801605

215 **IRISH ASSOCIATION OF HEALTH STORES**
5 Grosvenor Villas, Rathmines,
Dublin 6 (01) 832221/977607

216 **IRISH ASSOCIATION FOR NATURAL HEALTH**
Dun Mhuire, Greenfield Road,
Sutton, Co Dublin
(01) 323353

217 **IRISH ASSOCIATION OF NON-SMOKERS**
PO Box 1024, Sheriff Street,
Dublin 1

218 **IRISH ASSOCIATION OF SPEECH THERAPISTS**
PO Box 1344, Dublin 4
(01) 803142

219 **IRISH ASSOCIATION FOR SPINA BIFIDA & HYDROCEPHALUS**
Joseph Plunkett Tower,
Ballymun, Dublin
(01) 421222
Clondalkin (01) 593565

220 **IRISH ASSOCIATION FOR VICTIM SUPPORT**
(01) 733202

221 **IRISH CANCER SOCIETY**
5 Northumberland Road,
Dublin 4 (01) 681855

222 **IRISH CHILDBIRTH TRUST (CUIDIÚ)**
Glor na Blouse, Upper
Gloghree, Cork (021) 862243
64 Carysfort Downs, Blackrock,
Co Dublin (01) 888651
9 Cabinteely Crescent,
Dublin 18

223 **IRISH CHIROPODISTS ORGANISATIONS**
105a Cabra Road, Dublin 7
(01) 309708

41 Parkfield, New Ross,
Wexford (051) 22209

**224 IRISH COUNCIL ON
ALCOHOLISM**
19-20 Fleet Street, Dublin 2
(01) 774832/774649/774091

**225 IRISH COUNTRY-
WOMEN'S ASSOCIATION**
58 Merrion Road, Dublin 4
(01) 680453

226 IRISH DEAF SOCIETY
Deaf Community Centre,
31 Richmond Hill, Dublin 6

**227 IRISH DEAF SPORTS
ASSOCIATION**
31 Richmond Hill, Rathmines,
Dublin 6 (01) 972256

**228 IRISH DIABETIC
ASSOCIATION**
Ballyneety House,
56 St Lawrence Road, Clontarf
(01) 339577

**229 IRISH EPILEPSY
ASSOCIATION**
249 Crumlin Road, Dublin 12
(01) 516371/516500

**230 IRISH FOSTER CARE
ASSOCIATION**
60 Grangewood, Rathfarnham,
Dublin 16 (01) 944229

**231 THE IRISH FOUNDATION
FOR HUMAN
DEVELOPMENT**
Garden Hill, 1 St James's Street,
Dublin 8 (01) 528281

**232 IRISH GAY RIGHTS
MOVEMENT**

4 MacCurtain Street, Cork
(021) 505394
PO Box 739, Dublin 8
PO Box 131, Limerick
PO Box 36, Waterford

**233 IRISH GUIDE DOGS
ASSOCIATION**
Hill Farm, Model Farm Road,
Cork

**234 IRISH HAEMOPHILIA
SOCIETY**
(0404) 4464

**235 IRISH HEALTH CULTURE
ASSOCIATION**
66 Eccles Street, Dublin 7
(01) 304474/304686

**236 IRISH HEART
FOUNDATION**
4 Clyde Road, Dublin 4
(01) 685001

**237 IRISH HOLISTIC HEALTH
ASSOCIATION**
(01) 214038/966509/580145

**238 IRISH INFANT FORMULA
ACTION GROUP**
29 Kill Abbey, Blackrock,
Co Dublin (01) 894634/868452

**239 IRISH INSTITUTE FOR
THE ACHIEVEMENT OF
HUMAN POTENTIAL**
Kilnacourt House, Portarlington,
Co Laois (0502) 23139

**240 IRISH INSTITUTE FOR
BRAIN INJURED
CHILDREN**
(Same address and phone as
above)

241 **IRISH KIDNEY ASSOCIATION**
9 Eaton Square, Monkstown,
Co Dublin (01) 802551

242 **THE IRISH LUPUS SUPPORT GROUP**
40 Killester Park, Dublin 5
(01) 453317/318524

243 **IRISH MEDICAL ORGANISATION**
10 Lower Fitzwilliam Street,
Dublin 2 (01) 762087

244 **IRISH NURSES' ORGANISATION & NATIONAL COUNCIL OF NURSES IN IRELAND**
20 Lower Leeson Street,
Dublin 2
(01) 760137/760138/785905

245 **IRISH NUTRITION & DIETETIC ASSOCIATION**
c/o Dietetic Department,
St James's Hospital, Dublin 8
(01) 537941

246 **IRISH PHARMACEUTICAL UNION**
Ashleigh, 13 Main Street,
Dundrum (01) 987198/987699

247 **IRISH PSYCHOANALYTICAL ASSOCIATION**
2 Belgrave Terrace, Monkstown,
Co Dublin (01) 801869

248 **IRISH RED CROSS**
16 Merrion Square, Dublin 2
(01) 605441/605873

249 **IRISH SCHOOL OF**

ACUPRESSURE
Dun Mhuire, Greenfield Road,
Sutton, Dublin 13

250 **IRISH SOCIETY FOR AUTISTIC CHILDREN**
14 Lr O'Connell Street,
Dublin 1 (01) 744224

251 **IRISH SOCIETY FOR THE PREVENTION OF CRUELTY TO CHILDREN (ISPCC)**
20 Molesworth Street, Dublin 2
(01) 760423

252 **IRISH STILLBIRTH & NEONATAL DEATH SOCIETY**
8 Granite Terrace, Inchicore,
Dublin 8 (01) 752664

253 **IRISH SUDDEN INFANT DEATH ASSOCIATION**
34 Sycamore Road, Dundrum,
Dublin 16 (01) 983112/985179

254 **IRISH THORACIC SOCIETY**
St Vincent's Hospital,
Merrion Road, Dublin 4

255 **IRISH WHEELCHAIR ASSOCIATION**
Áras Chuchulain,
Blackheath Drive, Clontarf,
Dublin 3 (01) 338241

256 **IRISH WOMEN'S ABORTION SUPPORT GROUP**
1 Elgin Avenue, London W9 3PR
(031)* 289-1123, (031)* 603-8654
(emergencies, 24 hours)
*031 is the prefix when ringing
from southern Ireland. From

Northern Ireland or Britain,
01 is the London prefix.

**257 JEWISH ASSOCIATION
FOR FOSTERING,
ADOPTION &
INFERTILITY**
17 Fairlawns, Saval Park Road,
Dalkey, Co Dublin

**258 JOINT COMMITTEE ON
SMOKING & HEALTH**
4 Clyde Road, Dublin 4
(01) 685001

259 KEEP FIT ASSOCIATION
2 Morningside, Bangor,
Co Down

260 LA LECHE LEAGUE
Lucerne Parade, Belfast 9
(084) 668138
PO Box 1280, Raheny, Dublin 5
(01) 402304
Waterford (051) 55784

261 LAKE ISLE RELAXATION
c/o 1 Leeson Park, Dublin 6
(01) 885935

**262 L'ARCHE COMMUNITY
FOR MENTALLY
HANDICAPPED**
Moorfield House, Kilmoganny,
Kilkenny (056) 28251

263 THE LEAGUE OF HEALTH
Invergarry, Silchester Road,
Glenageary, Co Dublin
(01) 801564

264 LEGAL AID
Belfast: (084) 23511
Carlow: (0503) 31063
Clare: (065) 28178
Cork: (021) 500365

Mallow: (022) 21484
Donegal: (074) 22761
Dublin: (01) 741711/787295/712177
Galway: (091) 61650
Kerry: (066) 22351
Kilkenny: (056) 21685/21409
Leitrim: (078) 308
Limerick: (061) 314599
Louth: (041) 32908/36084
Mayo: (094) 22333
Sligo: (071) 61647
Tipperary: (052) 22267
Waterford: (051) 55814
Westmeath: (0902) 72174
Wexford: (0503) 23819

265 LESBIAN COLLECTIVE
Quay Co-op, 24 Sullivan's Quay,
Cork (021) 967660

266 LESBIAN LINE
Belfast (084) 222023
Cork (021) 967026
Derry (080504) 263120
Dublin (01) 710608 Thurs. 1-10pm

267 LIFE
Room 210, Bryson House,
28 Bedford Street,
Belfast 2 (084) 249414
91 Lower Baggot Street,
Dublin 2 (01) 767676

**268 LIFE WITHOUT WORK/
MENTAL HEALTH HELP**
Mental Health Association,
Dublin 4 (01) 695096

**269 LONDON IRISH WOMEN'S
CENTRE**
59 Church Street,
Stoke Newington, England

270 LUPUS SUPPORT GROUP
71 Lower Leeson Street,
Dublin 2

271 **MACROBIOTICS**
6 Parnell Road,
Harold's Cross Bridge,
Dublin 6 (01) 783943

272 **MARIE CURIE
MEMORIAL
FOUNDATION OF
IRELAND**
28 South Frederick Street,
Dublin 2 (01) 763533

273 **MARRIAGE
COUNSELLING SERVICE**
24 Grafton Street, Dublin 2
(01) 720341
Cork (021) 502906 10-5

274 **MARRIAGE & FAMILY
INSTITUTE**
5 Clare Street, Dublin 2
(01) 725034

275 **MARRIAGE GUIDANCE
COUNCIL**
76 Dublin Road, Belfast 2
(084) 223454

276 **MASSAGE**
Anne Dillon,
(midwife and massage therapist)
(01) 975155/803603
Jean M. Doorley,
(spinologist), Bray, Co Wicklow
(01) 868037
Brigid McLoughlin,
(spinologist), Cork City
(021) 509075
Britta Strong,
(Ki massage), Dublin
(01) 800179
Catherine Sutton,
(shihatsu), Dublin
(01) 966509
Seamus Keane,
(rolfer), Galway

(091) 24502
Risteard de Barra,
Limerick (Kilmallock) 46
Teresa Moloney,
Aherina, Kilmore, Limerick
(061) 73133
(See also aromatherapy,
alternative, therapeutic
reflexology)

277 **MASTECTOMY
ADVISORY SERVICE**
40 Eglantine Avenue, Belfast 9

278 **MASTECTOMY
ASSOCIATION OF
IRELAND**
14 Effra Road, Rathmines,
Dublin 6

279 **MEDIC ALERT**
High Grounds, Greystones,
Co Wicklow (01) 874117

280 **THE MEDICAL COUNCIL**
8 Lower Hatch Street, Dublin 2
(01) 602622

281 **MEDICAL WOMEN'S
FEDERATION**
5 Hampton Park, Belfast 7

282 **MEDICARE (Formerly
Fannins)**
15-16 Redmond's Hill,
(off Kevin Street), Dublin 2
(01) 782211 (Moira Burke)

283 **MEDICO-SOCIAL
RESEARCH BOARD**
73 Lower Baggot Street,
Dublin 2 (01) 761176/766076

284 **MEDI DISC**
St David's Castle, Naas,
Co Kildare (045) 79716

285 **THE MENDED HEARTS**
15 Coolemine Lawn,
Blanchardstown, Co Dublin
(01) 214105

286 **THE MENTAL HEALTH ASSOCIATION OF IRELAND**
2 Herbert Avenue,
Merrion Road, Dublin 4
(01) 695096/695375

287 **MENTRONICS SYSTEMS**
10 Hatter Street,
Bury St Edmunds,
Suffolk, England
(Bury St Edmunds) 70614

288 **METAMORPHIC TECHNIQUE**
8 Michael Street, Waterford
(051) 76181/86531

289 **MIGRAINE, NORTHERN IRELAND**
c/o Mrs Carson,
71 Ballylesson Road, Belfast 8

290 **MISCARRIAGE ASSOCIATION**
113 University Street, Belfast 7
(084) 225488

291 **MOOD DISORDER FELLOWSHIP**
37-38 Fenian Street, Dublin 2
(01) 681644

292 **MOUNTPLEASANT CLINIC**
31 Mountpleasant Square,
Ranelagh, Dublin 6 (01) 976413

293 **MULTIPLE SCLEROSIS**

SOCIETY
c/o M. Anderson,
23 Ardfoyle Terrace, Derry
2 Sandymount Green, Dublin 4
(01) 694599, (01) 696529
(Wed counselling)
Limerick (061) 314111
Sligo (071) 3089

294 **MULTIPLE SCLEROSIS SUPPORT/HOLISTIC,**
PO Box 772, Moseley,
Birmingham B13 0AD
(diet & self help therapy)

295 **MUSCULAR DYSTROPHY SOCIETY OF IRELAND**
23 Rockwood, Bray Road,
Stillorgan, Dublin (01) 888967

296 **NARCOTICS ANONYMOUS**
Dublin Central Mission Hall,
Abbey Street, Dublin 1
(01) 740691/903444

297 **NATIONAL ASSOCIATION FOR CEREBRAL PALSY**
Sandymount School & Clinic,
Sandymount Avenue, Dublin 4
(01) 695355/695608

298 **NATIONAL ASSOCIATION FOR THE DEAF**
25 Lower Leeson Street,
Dublin 2 (01) 763118/762597

299 **NATIONAL ASSOCIATION OF THE OVULATION METHOD OF IRELAND (NAOMI)**
79 Grand Parade, Cork
(021) 22213 M-F 9.30-1

300 **NATIONAL ASSOCIATION FOR THE MENTALLY HANDICAPPED**
5 Fitzwilliam Place, Dublin 2
(01) 766035

301 **NATIONAL ASSOCIATION OF TENANTS' ORGANISATIONS**
35 Meath Place, Dublin 8
(01) 758952 (after 6.30)

302 **NATIONAL ASSOCIATION FOR THE WELFARE OF CHILDREN IN HOSPITAL**
12 Carnamena Park,
Castlereagh, Belfast 6

303 **NATIONAL ASSOCIATION OF WIDOWS IN IRELAND**
12 Upper Ormond Quay,
Dublin 7 (01) 770977/770513

304 **NATIONAL BOARD FOR NURSING, MIDWIFERY & HEALTH VISITING**
RAC House, Chichester Street,
Belfast 1 (084) 238152

305 **NATIONAL BOARD FOR SCIENCE & TECHNOLOGY**
Shelbourne Road, Dublin 4
(01) 683311

306 **NATIONAL CAMPAIGN FOR THE HOMELESS**
PO Box 1459, Fenian Street,
Dublin 1 (01) 381555

307 **NATIONAL CHILDBIRTH TRUST**
5 Chartwell Park, Belfast 8
(084) 702017

(for southern Ireland see Irish Childbirth Trust)

308 **NATIONAL COUNCIL FOR THE AGED**
71 Lr Leeson Street, Dublin 2
(01) 682422

309 **NATIONAL COUNCIL FOR THE BLIND**
Armitage House,
10 Lower Hatch Street,
Dublin 2 (01) 761008/767159

310 **NATIONAL COUNCIL FOR CARERS & THEIR ELDERLY DEPENDANTS**
2 Annadale Avenue, Belfast 7
(084) 640011

311 **NATIONAL COUNCIL FOR TRAVELLING PEOPLE**
12 Westmoreland Street,
Dublin 2 (01) 776761

312 **NATIONAL DRUGS ADVISORY BOARD**
Charles Lucas House,
63 Adelaide Road, Dublin 2
(01) 764971

313 **NATIONAL DRUGS ADVISORY & TREATMENT CENTRE & DETOXIFICATION UNIT**
Jervis Street Hospital,
Jervis Street, Dublin 1
(01) 748412

314 **NATIONAL ECZEMA SOCIETY**
c/o Kilfenora, Gordon Avenue,
Foxrock, Dublin 18
(01) 893243

315 **NATIONAL FEDERATION**

**FOR COMMUNITY
ACTION ON DRUGS**
43 Arnold Grove, Glenageary,
Dun Laoghaire, Co Dublin
(01) 854051

316 **NATIONAL FEDERATION
OF PENSIONERS
& PENSIONERS
ASSOCIATION**
Davice Clinic, 14 Gardiner Place,
Dublin 1 (01) 726566 (2.30-4.30)

317 **NATIONAL LEAGUE OF
THE BLIND**
35 Gardiner Place, Dublin 1
(01) 742792/745827

318 **NATIONAL MATERNITY
HOSPITAL**
Holles Street, Dublin 2
(01) 608788
Menopause and cervical
disorder clinics

319 **NATIONAL
REHABILITATION
BOARD**
25 Clyde Road, Dublin 4
(01) 684181/609544

320 **NATIONAL
SCHIZOPHRENIA
FELLOWSHIP OF
NORTHERN IRELAND**
Bryson House, Bedford Street,
Belfast 7 (084) 248006

321 **NATIONAL SOCIAL
SERVICES BOARD**
71 Lower Leeson Street,
Dublin 2 (01) 682422

322 **NATIONAL SOCIETY FOR
THE PREVENTION OF
CRUELTY TO CHILDREN**

(NSPCC)
16-18 Rosemary Street, Belfast 1
(084) 240311

323 **NATURAL LIVING
CENTRE**
c/o Anne's Kitchen,
Annascaul, Co Kerry

324 **NATURE'S BEST**
1 Lambert's Road,
Tunbridge Wells, Dent,
England (Tunbridge Wells) 34143

325 **NATURE'S WAY**
Nature Cure Centres
ILAC Centre, Dublin 1
(01) 728391
Superquinn Shopping Centre,
Blackrock, Co Dublin
Church Square, Monaghan

326 **NATUROPATHS**
J. Hamilton,
129 University Street, Belfast 7
(084) 229079
John Garvey,
6 Roselawn Way, Castleknock,
Dublin 15 (01) 214038

327 **THE NO NAME CLUB**
Byrnes Grove, Ballyragget,
Kilkenny (056) 41127

328 **NORTHERN IRELAND
ABORTION CAMPAIGN**
18 Donegall Street, Belfast 1
(084) 243363

329 **NORTHERN IRELAND
ABORTION LAW REFORM
ASSOCIATION**
PO Box 161, Belfast BT9 6FT
(084) 243363

330 **NORTHERN IRELAND ASSOCIATION FOR CARE & RESETTLEMENT OF OFFENDERS**
22 Adelaide Street, Belfast 2
(084) 220157

331 **NORTHERN IRELAND ASSOCIATION FOR MENTAL HANDICAP**
84 University Street, Belfast 7
(084) 228474

332 **NORTHERN IRELAND ASSOCIATION FOR SPINA BIFIDA & HYDROCEPHALUS**
3 Townview Avenue North, Omagh (Omagh) 3018

333 **NORTHERN IRELAND CHEST, HEART & STROKE ASSOCIATION**
Bryson House, 28 Bedford Street, Belfast 2 (084) 220184

334 **NORTHERN IRELAND COUNCIL ON ALCOHOL**
40 Eglantine Avenue, Belfast 9
(084) 664434

335 **NORTHERN IRELAND COUNCIL FOR THE HANDICAPPED**
2 Annadale Avenue, Belfast 7
(084) 640011

336 **NORTHERN IRELAND HOME SAFETY COUNCIL**
117 Lisburn Road, Belfast 9
(084) 669453

337 **NORTHERN IRELAND PARAPLEGIA ASSOCIATION**

26 Bridge Road, Helen's Bay, Co Down (Down) 853310

338 **NORTHERN IRELAND POVERTY LOBBY**
17 Rugby Avenue, Belfast 7
(084) 244707

339 **NORTHERN IRELAND PRE-SCHOOL PLAYGROUPS ASSOCIATION**
11 Wellington Park, Belfast 9
(084) 668508

340 **NORTHERN IRELAND WOMEN'S AID FEDERATION**
14b University Street, Belfast BT7 1HP
(084) 249041/249358

341 **NORTHERN IRELAND WOMEN'S RIGHTS MOVEMENT**
18 Donegall Street, Belfast 1
(084) 243363

342 **NORTHLANDS ALCOHOLIC CENTRE**
68 Northland Road, Derry
(080504) 268886/263001

343 **OMAGH ADVICE CENTRE**
Bridge Street, Omagh
(0662) 3252

344 **OMBUDSMAN**
Office of the Ombudsman, 52 St Stephen's Green, Dublin 2
(01) 785222

345 **OPEN LINE COUNSELLING**
3 Belvedere Place, Dublin 1
(01) 787160/787664

346 **OPTICIANS' BOARD**
18 Fitzwilliam Square, Dublin 2
(01) 767416

347 **ORDER OF MALTA**
32 Clyde Road, Ballsbridge,
Dublin 4 (01) 685768

348 **OSTEOPATHS**
R. Boyd, 15 Farnham Road,
Bangor (084) 462626
D. Flanagan, Curracloe,
Drumcoo, Enniskillen
(Enniskillen) 24837
(see also telephone Golden
Pages)

349 **OUR LADY'S MANOR
GERIATRIC RESEARCH
COMMITTEE**
70 Upper Leeson Street,
Dublin 4 (01) 683591

350 **OUT AND ABOUT
ASSOCIATION**
St John's House, Seafield Road,
Clontarf, Dublin 3 (01) 338252

351 **OUTREACH ANOREXIA**
Beacon House, Belfast BT7 1HE
(084) 228474

352 **OVEREATERS
ANONYMOUS**
c/o Bryson House,
28 Bedford Street, Belfast 2
(084) 220184
Dublin (01) 694800
(meetings held countrywide)

353 **OVULATION METHOD
ADVISORY SERVICE**
618 Saintfield Road, Carryduff,
Belfast 8

354 **PARENTS' ADVICE
CENTRE**
Bryson House, 28 Bedford House,
Belfast 2 (084) 238800

355 **PARENTS' AID**
171 University Street, Belfast 7
(084) 234568

356 **PARENTS UNDER STRESS**
Centre Care (formerly Open Door)
Cathedral Street, Dublin 1
(01) 742066

357 **PARKINSON'S DISEASE
SOCIETY**
c/o Michael Kelly,
Chief Welfare Officer,
Community & Environment
Department, Dublin
Corporation,
68-71 Great Strand Street,
Dublin 1

358 **PATCH — PRISONERS
AID THROUGH
COMMUNITY EFFORT**
7 Upper Leeson Street, Dublin 4
(01) 602870

359 **PHENYLKETONURIA
(PKU)**
49 Drumleck Gardens, Derry
(080504) 59678

360 **PHYSICALLY
HANDICAPPED & ABLE
BODIED**
76 University Street, Belfast 7
(084) 225506

361 PLAYBOARD ASSOCIATION FOR CHILDREN'S PLAY & RECREATION
123-137 York Street, Belfast 15
(084) 242832

362 POISONS INFORMATION CENTRE
Jervis Street Hospital, Dublin 1
(01) 745588/723355

363 POLIO FELLOWSHIP OF IRELAND
7 Lr Hatch Street, Dublin 2
(01) 763245

364 POST-NATAL DEPRESSION SUPPORT GROUPS
113 University Street, Belfast 7
(084) 225488
Great James Street Health Centre, Great James Street, Derry (080504) 265177
Waterside Health Centre, Glendermott Road, Derry (080504) 45191
Dublin (01) 900972
Erne Health Centre, Enniskillen (Enniskillen) 24511
Kilkenny (056) 21685
(Also ring local health board and health clinic for groups in your area)

365 POSTURITE CHAIRS
38 South Richmond Street, Dublin 2 (01) 780252/780388
(Relief of back pain)

366 PRE-MENSTRUAL TENSION ADVISORY SERVICE
PO Box 268, Hove, East Surrey, England (Brighton) 771366
(See also Family Planning Clinics)

367 PRISONERS' AID THROUGH COMMUNITY HELP
76 Monkstown, Dun Laoghaire, Co Dublin (01) 809977

368 PRISONERS' RIGHTS ORGANISATION
35 Lower Buckingham Street, Dublin 1 (01) 725905

369 PROTESTANT ADOPTION SOCIETY & SINGLE PARENT COUNSELLING SERVICE
71 Brighton Road, Rathgar, Dublin 6 (01) 972659

370 THE PROTESTANT ORPHAN SOCIETY
28 Molesworth Street, Dublin 2
(01) 762168

371 THE PSYCHOLOGICAL SOCIETY OF IRELAND
(01) 902835

372 QUAY CO-OP
24 Sullivan's Quay, Cork
(021) 967660

373 RAPE CRISIS CENTRES
PO Box 46, Belfast BT27 AR
(084) 249696
Clonmel (058) 47218
PO Box 42, Brian Boru Street, Cork
27a McCurtain Street, Cork
(021) 968086
2 Lr Pembroke Street, Dublin 2

(01) 601470
15a Mary Street, Galway
(091) 64983
Letterkenny (074) 23067
4 Mallow Street, Limerick
(061) 311511
PO Box 57, Waterford
(051) 73362

374 **REACH TO RECOVERY**
c/o The Irish Cancer Society,
5 Northumberland Road,
Dublin 4 (01) 681855

375 **REBIRTHING**
Kali Victoire, 15 Oak Tree Road,
Stillorgan, Co Dublin
(01) 832423

376 **RECOVERY— THE
ASSOCIATION OF
NERVOUS & FORMER
MENTAL PATIENTS**
116 South Michigan Avenue,
Chicago, Illinois 60603 USA

28 Ballymany Park, Newbridge,
Co Kildare
90 Brian Road, Dublin 3
(01) 333031

377 **REDWOOD WOMEN'S
TRAINING CENTRE**
c/o Marika O'Connor,
The Sanctuary, Lanesville,
Monkstown, Co Dublin
(01) 809964

378 **REFLEXOLOGY**
Sheila Nugent,
14 Central Avenue, Cookstown

379 **REFUGES/SHELTERS**
Athlone: Auburn, Moate Road
Belfast: 143 University Street
(084) 662385/348

Bray: 75 Charnwood
Coleraine: (080265) 823195
Cork: Cuan Laoi, Kyrl Street
(021) 509800
Derry: (080504) 26596
Down: 39 Main Street, Bangor
(080247) 463608
Dublin: 47 Lower Rathmines
Road (01) 961002
Galway: Social Services Centre,
St Francis Street (091) 63581
Limerick: Adapt House,
Rosbrien (061) 42345
Newry: 14c Trevor Hill
(080693) 67174
Omagh: 36 Market Street
(080662) 47746
Portrush: 16 Lansdowne
Crescent (0265) 823195
Wexford: Killinick
(See also Rape Crisis Centres,
Family Aid & Samaritans)

380 **REHABILITATION
INSTITUTE**
Roslyn Park, Sandymount,
Dublin 4 (01) 698422

381 **RENT A CRECHE**
c/o Donegall Street, Belfast 1
(084) 237224

382 **RETIREMENT
PLANNING COUNCIL**
3 Lower Leeson Street,
Dublin 2 (01) 605925

383 **R.P. IRELAND —
FIGHTING BLINDNESS
(RETINITIS
PIGMENTOSA SOCIETY)**
67 Silchester Park, Glenageary,
Co. Dublin (01) 807631
(M-F 8-10pm only)

384 **ROYAL COLLEGE OF MIDWIVES**
Royal Maternity Hospital,
Grosvenor Road, Belfast 12

385 **ROYAL SOCIETY FOR MENTALLY HANDICAPPED CHILDREN**
4 Annadale Avenue, Belfast 9
(084) 691351

386 **ROYAL SOCIETY FOR THE PREVENTION OF ACCIDENTS**
117 Lisburn Road, Belfast 9
(084) 669 453

387 **ROYAL VICTORIA HOSPITAL**
Belfast (084) 340503
(Genetic counselling/
amniocentesis)

388 **RUTLAND CENTRE**
Knocklyon House,
Knocklyon Road, Templogue,
Dublin 16 (01) 946348/946761

389 **SACRED HEART HOSPITAL**
Ballinderry, Mullingar
(044) 41500
(Clinic for eating disorders,
obesity, anorexia, bulimia)

390 **ST ANN'S LIFE LINE**
St Ann's Church,
Dawson Street, Dublin 2
(01) 767727 M-F 12-3pm

391 **ST ANTHONY'S MEDICAL**

REHABILITATION CENTRE
Herbert Avenue, Merrion Road,
Dublin 4 (01) 693077/693541

392 **ST DYMPHNA'S**
North Circular Road, Dublin 7
(01) 302844
(Alcohol detoxification and
counselling)

393 **ST JAMES'S HOSPITAL**
James's Street, Dublin 8
(01) 537941
Fertility Clinic/In vitro
Fertilisation

394 **ST JOHN'S AMBULANCE**
9 Waring Street, Belfast 1
(084) 233144
29 Upr Leeson Street, Dublin 4
(01) 699077

395 **ST JOHN'S HOUSE**
Seafield Road, Clontarf,
Dublin 3 (01) 338252

396 **ST MICHAEL'S HOUSE**
Willowfield Park, Goatstown,
Dublin 14 (01) 987033

397 **ST VINCENT'S DAY CENTRE**
Henrietta Lane, Dublin 1
(01) 742018 9.12-4.30

398 **ST VINCENT'S HOSPITAL**
Elm Park, Merrion Road,
Dublin 4 (01) 692176
Special breast clinics/ anorexia,
bulimia

399 **SALVATION ARMY SOCIAL SERVICES**
13 Lower Abbey Street,

Dublin 1
(01) 740987 (day)
(01) 882137 (night)

400 SAMARITANS
66 South William Street, Dublin
1 (01) 778333
Antrim: (08494) 43555
Belfast: (084) 224635
Cork: (021) 21323
Derry: (080504) 63036
Down: (0849) 63036
Ennis: (065) 29777
Galway: (091) 61222
Limerick: (061) 42111
Newry: (080693) 66366
Omagh: (0662) 44944
Waterford: (051) 72114

401 THE SANCTUARY TRUST
22 Pimlico, Dublin 8
PO Box 1744 (01) 539040

**402 SAVE THE CHILDREN
FUND**
Wellington Park, Belfast 9

**403 SCHIZOPHRENIA
ASSOCIATION OF
IRELAND**
4 Fitzwilliam Place, Dublin 2
(01) 761988

404 SCHOOL OF T'AI CHI
68 Burleigh Court,
Burlington Road, Dublin 4
(administration only)
(01) 604665 (evenings)

**405 THE SCOLIOSIS SOCIETY
OF IRELAND**
6 Redsdale Road, Mt Merrion,
Co Dublin

406 SELF DEFENCE
Bangor (084) 456440
Irene McCavin,
Lifeline Centre,
MacCurtain Street, Cork
Carol Stephenson,
9 North Great George's Street,
Dublin 1 (01) 740268
Newtownards (080247) 816677
Kate Willyard,
Fire Dragon Kung Foo Club,
CYMS, Tralee

**407 SEPARATED PERSONS
ASSOCIATION**
67 Blessington Street, Dublin 1
(01) 381101 (Tues 11-4)

408 SEX AIDS
Stopes Sales
108 Whitfield Street, London W1
(mail orders)
(See also Dublin Well Woman
Centre)

**409 SEXUAL ASSAULT UNIT
— Rotunda Hospital**
Parnell Square
(top of O'Connell Street),
Dublin 1 (01) 748111
(ask for sexual assault unit)

**410 SEXUALLY
TRANSMITTED DISEASE
PUBLIC CLINICS (Special
clinics for STDs)**
Royal Victoria Hospital, Belfast
(084) 220159
Victoria Hospital, Cork
(021) 966844
Altnagelvin Hospital, Derry
(080504) 45171
Mater Hospital, Eccles Street,
Dublin 7 (01) 301937/301122

Cont.

Sir Patrick Dun's Hospital,
Grand Canal Street
(opposite Boland's Bakery),
Dublin 2 (01) 766942
Ardkeen Hospital,
Casualty Department, Waterford
(051) 73321
Private Clinics:
Dublin Well Woman Centre,
73 Lower Leeson Street,
Dublin 2 (01) 605229
Galway (091) 64000

411 **THE SICK & INDIGENT ROOMKEEPERS SOCIETY**
2 Palace Street, Dublin 2
(01) 752579

412 **SILVA MIND CONTROL**
Strand Road, Bray, Co Wicklow
(01) 828226

413 **THE SIMON COMMUNITY**
PO Box 1022,
Lower Sheriff Street, Dublin 1
(01) 711606

414 **SINGLE WOMEN'S ASSOCIATION**
38 Rosevale Court,
Brookwood Avenue, Dublin 5
(01) 311290

415 **SOCIAL WELFARE INFORMATION CENTRES (SOUTHERN IRELAND)**
(10) 726333 (maternity, pay related, occupational injuries)
(01) 300922 (deserted wives, assistance, widows, orphans)
For Northern Ireland see telephone directory under Health and Personnel Service, citizen's advice, community information.

416 **SOCIAL WORKERS IN MENTAL HANDICAP**
8 Upper Newcastle, Galway
(091) 21308

417 **THE SOCIETY OF CHIROPODISTS OF IRELAND**
5 Wicklow Street, Dublin 2

418 **SOCIETY OF REFLEXOLOGISTS OF IRELAND**
41 Parkfield, New Ross,
Co Wexford (051) 22209

419 **THE SOCIETY OF ST VINCENT DE PAUL**
Headquarters, 18 Nicholas Street,
Dublin 8 (01) 757053

420 **THE SOCIETY FOR SEXUALLY TRANSMITTED DISEASES IN IRELAND**
88 Ranelagh Road, Dublin 6
(correspondence only)

421 **THE SPASTICS SOCIETY**
12 Park Crescent,
London W1N 4EQ
(031) 636-5020

422 **SPOD RESOURCE GROUP**
(Sexual Problems of the Disabled)
PO Box 1000, Dublin 4
(01) 740723 Thurs. 2-4

423 **SPECTRUM**
70 Glasnevin Road, Dublin 11
(01) 343944

424 **SPORTS COUNCIL OF**

NORTHERN IRELAND
2a Upper Malone Road,
Belfast 9 (084) 661222

425 **STILLBIRTH GROUP**
Social Services Office,
Belfast City Hospital,
Lisburn Road, Belfast

426 **STILLBIRTH & NEO-
NATAL DEATH SOCIETY**
96 Stevenson Park, Tullyally,
Derry 47727
Dublin (01) 217717 /858905

427 **SUDDEN INFANT DEATH
SYNDROME SUPPORT
GROUP**
Mrs K. Glass, Rushall Road,
Derry (080504) 49195

428 **SUNBEAM HOUSE**
Vevay Road, Bray, Co Wicklow
(01) 868451

429 **TALBOT CENTRE**
29 Upper Buckingham Street,
Dublin 1 (01) 747492

430 **TALLAGHT WELFARE
SOCIETY**
1 Main Street, Tallaght,
Dublin 24 (01) 515911

431 **THERAPEUTIC
MASSAGE**
Maureen Hanse, 9 Malone Road,
Belfast 9

432 **THRESHOLD**
Capuchin Friary, Church Street,
Dublin 7 (01) 720769
52 Lower Rathmines Road,
Dublin 6 (01) 964634
8 Father Matthew Quay,
Cork (021) 21250

433 **TISSUE TYPING**
(01) 894342

434 **TRADE UNIONS**
See telephone directory under
specific union.

435 **TRANQUILLISER
SUPPORT GROUP**
Beacon House,
84 University Street, Belfast 7
(084) 228474
Tranx Release, PO Box 1378,
Sheriff Street, Dublin 1
St John's, Mountpleasant Clinic,
Mountpleasant Square, Dublin 6
(01) 965498

436 **TRANSCENDENTAL
MEDITATION**
20 Dartmouth Square, Dublin 6
(01) 606956
9 Parnell Square, Dublin 1
(01) 724287

437 **TRAVELLERS'
MOVEMENT
(MINCÉIR MISLI)**
90 Meath Street, Dublin 8
(01) 694766 Unit 1302

438 **TRUST**
Bride Road, Dublin 8
(01) 758372/972229, Unit 7913

439 **TWINS ASSOCIATION**
Tir na nÓg, 56 Willow Park,
Ennis, Co Clare

440 **ULSTER CANCER
FOUNDATION**
40 Eglantine Avenue, Belfast 9
(084) 663281

441 **ULSTER PREGNANCY ADVISORY SERVICE**
338 Lisburn Road, Belfast 9
(084) 667345

442 **UNION OF VOLUNTARY ORGANISATIONS FOR THE HANDICAPPED**
29 Eaton Square, Monkstown,
Co Dublin (01) 809251/803142

443 **VEGETARIAN SOCIETY**
3 Donegall Street, Belfast 1
(084) 240671

444 **VEGETARIAN SOCIETY OF IRELAND**
Blacklion Cottage, Greystones,
Co Wicklow
457 Collins Avenue, Whitehall,
Dublin 9

445 **VOLUNTARY HEALTH INSURANCE BOARD (VHI)**
VHI House, Lower Abbey Street,
Dublin 1 (01) 724499

446 **VOLUNTEER STROKE SCHEME**
54 Clanmahon Road,
Donnycarney, Dublin 5
(01) 314607/481059

447 **WEIGHT WATCHERS**
613 North Circular Road,
Dublin 1 (01) 787422/741552

448 **WELCARE**
Room 1214, 1st Floor,
Queen's Building,
Heathrow Airport, Hounslow,
England (031) 745 7495

449 **WELL WOMAN CENTRE**
113 University Street, Belfast 7

(084) 224914
(See also Dublin Well Woman)

450 **WESTERN CARE ASSOCIATION**
St Clare's, Station Road,
Castlebar, Co Mayo

451 **WHITETHORN CLINIC**
Celbridge, Co Kildare
(01) 271390

452 **WIDOWS' RIGHTS**
c/o Department of Women's
Affairs, Dáil Eireann, Dublin 2

453 **WHOLE HEALTH INSTITUTE**
4 Willow Mews, St Alban's Park,
Sandymount, Dublin 4
(01) 694544

454 **WOMEN'S ADVISORY COMMITTEE IRISH CONGRESS OF TRADES UNIONS**
1-9 Castle Arcade, Belfast 1
(084) 746576
WOMEN'S AID
See refuges

455 **WOMEN'S CENTRES**
18 Donegall Street, Belfast 1
(084) 243363
2 Bridge Street, Coleraine
(0265) 56573
24 Sullivan's Quay, Cork
(021) 967660
7-9 Artillery Street, Derry
(0504) 267672
16 Clanbrassil Street, Dundalk
(042) 32848

456 **WOMEN'S GROUPS**
See Irish Women's Diary &
Community Information

457 **WOMEN'S HEALTH FAIR GROUP**
59 Richmond Park, Belfast 9

458 **WOMEN'S HEALTH AND HISTORY PROJECT**
c/o NUPE, 523 Antrim Road, Belfast 1S (084) 776971

459 **WOMEN'S INFORMATION GROUP**
99 Ormeau Road, Belfast 7
(084) 238754

460 **WOMEN'S RIGHT TO CHOOSE GROUP**
Dublin Resource Centre, 6 Crowe Street, Dublin 1

461 **WOMEN'S SELF-HELP GROUP**
(051) 82331

462 **WOMEN TOWARDS RECOVERY**
(01) 551639

463 **WOMEN & CHILDREN'S DROP-IN CENTRE**
47-49 South Richmond Street, Dublin 6

464 **YOGA ASSOCIATION**
108 Lower Kimmage Road, Harold's Cross, Dublin 6

465 **YOUTH COUNSELLING SERVICE**
IFPA, 15 Mountjoy Square, Dublin 1
(01) 740723/744133/729574

466 **YOUTH INFORMATION CENTRE**
Sackville House (behind Clery's), Sackville Place, Dublin 1
(01) 786844

467 **YWCA**
50 Lower Camden Street, Dublin 2 (01) 752211

INDEX

How to use the Index

For easy access to information you should use the index to quickly identify the page numbers of the subject area you are interested in. Each subject dealt with is easily identified. If for example you look up Compulsive Eating you will be referred to Eating Disorders, and if you look up Breasts you will be cross-referenced to a number of sub-headings all related to the Breast. Common language is the key to the index, and almost any word you think of should refer you to the page number or organisation you are looking for.

The index gives a cross-reference under subject for the organisations listed, so you will be able to find the appropriate organisation without having to know its name. For example: Reach to Recovery, a support agency for women undergoing breast surgery, can be traced by using key words like 'breast', 'mastectomy', and 'cancer'. Once the key word is found you will notice a corresponding number **in heavy print.** Breast may have No. 374 alongside its listing which is the code number for Reach to Recovery in the directory. But it will also have other numbers which will put you in contact with breastfeeding support groups, cosmetic surgery and so on. The page numbers for listings which refer to text only are printed in light type.

PERSONALLY SPEAKING
Women's Thoughts on Women's Issues
edited by Liz Steiner-Scott

Personally Speaking is a time bomb, and it is the only kind of time bomb I can imagine ever having a creative and positive outcome. When it goes off in the minds of women, it will break through invisible walls of isolation, help women to recognise their own power and release a great deal of healthy energy ... It has already become my handbook ... I feel I am in the company of women who understand and with whom I empatise.
June Levine *Southside*.

'I found the majority of the essays provocative and persuasive ... accessible and clearly written. The book is guaranteed to spark off lots of lively (and heated) debate'.   *New Hibernia*.

'To be honest I thought it was just another woman's book until I burned the midnight oil reading many of the contributions ... However, this is different — 22 different women writers, of all ages, background and opinions have been skilfully gathered together between the covers of this new book and it is at once provocative, interesting, annoying and gives a marvellous picture of how Irish women feel about a variety of topics'.
Maureen Fox, *Cork Examiner*.

'At last we have the beginnings of a native feminist anthology'.
In Dublin.
ISBN 0 946211 108 £5.95pb   ISBN 0 946211 094 £12.95hb

RAPUNZEL'S REVENGE
Fairy Tales for Feminists

'*Rapunzel's Revenge* is a feminist re-writing of fairy tales which has Mary Maher revealing that Snow White organised the seven dwarfs into a trade union, Maeve Binchy exposing Cinderella's prince as a foot fetishist, and a truly gifted Joni Crone showing that feminist fairy tales can be written in fairy tale language. Wendy Shea's cartoon of Little Ms Muffet, saying to the spider 'C'mon, baby, frighten me to death' should be framed'.
In Dublin.

'Things will never be the same again down in the woods ... Maeve Binchy, Carolyn Swift, Mary Maher and several others give a sardonic feminist twist to the fairy tales we all grew up on.
Sunday Independent.

'*Rapunzel's Revenge*, a funny, sassy, heretical collection of fairytales ...'   *Irish Times*.

ISBN 0 946211 18 3 £3.50pb

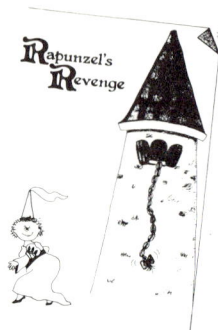

LIFTING THE LID
Handbook of Facts and Information on Ireland
Ursula Barry

All the scandals, hidden truths, secrets and other facts so often obliquely approached are now freely available in this exciting new title from Attic Press. *Lifting the Lid* is an easy to read handbook of facts and information on Ireland, with sections on crime, media, wealth, arts, law, work and unemployment. *Lifting the Lid* uncovers the hidden reality of living in Ireland, with special emphasis on the position of women in the labour force, under the law and within the welfare system.

If you have ever had difficulty finding out where to get information on making sense out of the maze of books, reports and government publications then *Lifting the Lid* is for you. This book provides a unique opportunity to explore the economic and political system in Ireland by bringing together much of the existing information, previously inaccessible because of its bureaucratic net, between two bright new covers, *Lifting the Lid* is guaranteed to keep you awake and thinking.

Lifting the Lid is illustrated throughout with cartoons and graphics which make the information simply to absorb and easy-to-use. It is an essential reference manual for students, community activists, trade unionists, tourist and all those interested in *Lifting the Lid* off the workings of Irish society. It also includes a comprehensive index and references.

ISBN 0 946211 25 6 £3.95pb   ISBN 0 946211 26 4 £10.00hb

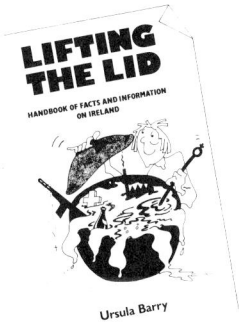

Ursula Barry

SINGLED OUT
Single Mothers in Ireland

Singled Out is a book written by women in Cherish, (an association of single parents), presenting realistic and practical information about single mothers in Ireland.

It provides food for thought on many issues including social attitudes past and present, employment and retraining, social welfare, housing and day care.

It is an essential source book for students, teachers, parents and social policy makers.

ISBN 0 946211 03 5 £1.95pb

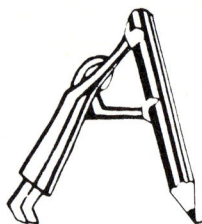

Attic Press

44 East Essex Street, Dublin 2, Ireland. (01)716367

Stock List and Order Form

Qty	ISBN	Title	Price
_____	019	*Missing Pieces Vol 1:* Women in Irish History	£ 2.00 pb
_____	031	*Singled Out:* Single Mothers in Ireland	£ 1.95 pb
_____	06X	*The Best of Nell:* A Collection of Writings Over Fourteen Years Nell McCafferty	£ 3.95 pb
_____	051	*The Best of Nell:*	£10.00 hb
_____	086	*Smashing Times:* A History of the Irish Women's Suffrage Movement 1889-1922 Rosemary Cullen Owens	£ 4.95 pb
_____	078	*Smashing Times:*	£10.00 hb
_____	205	*Irish Women's Guidebook and Diary 1986*	£ 2.95 pb
_____		Leather Slip-on Cover	£ 6.95
_____	183	Rapunzel's Revenge: Fairy Tales for Feminists	£ 3.50 pb
_____	175	*More Missing Pieces:* Her Story of Irish Women	£ 2.95 pb
_____	191	*Who Owns Ireland, Who Owns You!*	£ 3.95 pb
_____	140	*Did Your Granny Have a Hammer?:* A History of the Irish Suffrage Movement 1876-1922	£ 3.95 pack
_____	108	*Personally Speaking:* Women's Thoughts on Women's Issues edited by Liz Steiner-Scott	£ 5.95 pb
_____	094	*Personally Speaking*	£12.95 hb
_____	159	*Around The Banks of Pimlico,* Mairin Johnston	£ 5.95 pb
_____	167	*Around The Banks of Pimlico:*	£12.95 hb
_____	213	*A Woman To Blame: The Kerry Babies Case,* Nell McCafferty	£ 3.95 pb
_____	221	*A Woman To Blame:*	£10.00 hb
_____	23X	*Woman to Woman: A Health Care Guide and Directory,* Anne Roper	£ 4.95 pb
_____	248	*Woman to Woman*	£12.95 hb
_____	256	*Lifting the Lid:* Handbook of Facts and Information on Ireland, Ursula Barry	£ 3.95 pb
_____	264	*Lifting the Lid*	£10.00 hb
_____	272	*Feminist Fairytales 2*	£ 3.50 pb
_____	280	*Feminist Fairytales 2*	£ 9.50 hb

All prices are given in Irish Pounds and are subject to change without notice.

NAME.. Order Ref:..............

ADDRESS...Date ....